Education in the Commonwealth: The First Forty Years

From Oxford to Halifax and Beyond

Edited by

Lalage Bown

Council for Education in the Commonwealth

Commonwealth Secretariat

Designed by Wayzgoose
Printed by Formara Print Limited

Copies of this publication can be ordered from:
The Publications Manager
Communication and Public Affairs Division
Commonwealth Secretariat
Marlborough House
Pall Mall
London SW1Y 5HX
United Kingdom

Tel: +44 (0) 20 7747 6342
Fax: +44 (0) 20 7839 9081
E-mail: r.jones-parry@commonwealth.int

ISBN 0-85092-692-0

Price: £12.99

Contents

Acknowledgements

The various authors wish to express their gratitude for ready help given by the Librarians at the Commonwealth Secretariat and the Association of Commonwealth Universities.

Those from the Council for Education in the Commonwealth benefited substantially from several meetings with experts from the Secretariat and elsewhere, who read the chapters in draft and gave advice and information. They included: Gari Donn, Service Farrant, Ved Goel, Jonathan Jenkins, Henry Kaluba, Kees Maxey, Hilary Perraton and Cream Wright. Their interest and input are much appreciated.

Thanks are also owed to Val Povall and Liz Coley of Treble 'S' who processed the manuscripts and to Christabel Gurney, publisher's editor, and Rupert Jones-Parry, publisher on behalf of the Commonwealth Secretariat.

Foreword

The Commonwealth has a strong record and tradition of co-operation in education, encompassing articulation of values, exchange of ideas and direct learning from each other. This book is a reminder of that record and tradition and offers a refreshing kaleidoscope of Commonwealth educational action.

In their fourteenth triennial conference held in Canada in 2000, Commonwealth Ministers expressed the view that education:

> ... *contributes to a non-exploitative and non-violent society that will facilitate expansion of human capabilities and enhancement of competitiveness in a knowledge-based global economy. Education empowers the poor, safeguards the vulnerable, promotes economic growth and social justice, promotes the values of democracy, human rights, citizenship, good governance, tolerance and pluralism, and provides moral and spiritual guidance.*

These are far-reaching ideals, but Commonwealth members have committed themselves to them. The record illustrated in this book shows how over the years the Commonwealth as an organisation has on behalf of member countries worked steadily towards them.

We are grateful to those who have contributed to this publication and hope that readers will find it useful.

Don McKinnon
Commonwealth Secretary-General

Introduction

Education, we are reminded in this book, was the focus of collaborative Commonwealth endeavour even before the Commonwealth structures for co-operation
(which we now take for granted) came into being. Shared educational values, we
are also reminded in this book, form 'the glue which binds the Commonwealth
together'. Yet, in recent years, pressing economic and political challenges have led
member states rather to downplay their bonds of educational interest. That could
be unfortunate, since the Commonwealth has racked up useful successes in this
arena, in spite of limited resources, because of goodwill, joint understanding and
professional enthusiasm across boundaries.

This book is, in part, a record of those successes and achievements. The idea for
it grew in the run-up to the Halifax Conference of Commonwealth Education
Ministers (CCEM), since the year before it, 1999, was the 40th anniversary of the
first ever Commonwealth gathering to exchange ideas and develop programmes in
education. Dr Cream Wright and colleagues in the Secretariat proposed a history of
the first 40 years of Commonwealth education. The original plan was to have
covered a great many topics and to have included a volume of case studies, but the
project was temporarily aborted for budgetary reasons. It is to the credit of the
Commonwealth Secretariat that it is backing this, slightly more modest, study.

Five of the chapters here were written under the auspices of the Council for
Education in the Commonwealth (CEC), which has played a key role in keeping
the plan on track. Four authors wrote their chapters in close consultation with each
other and with an advisory group brought together by the CEC. A fifth chapter
reproduces a lecture given in the UK House of Lords for the CEC. The other two
chapters were contributed by a member of the Secretariat and the President of the
Commonwealth of Learning (COL).

The table of contents shows the scope of this book. The first part is a magisterial
survey by Dr Peter Williams of Commonwealth policies, activities and initiatives
since 1959, including a detailed description of official structures and arrangements. It is authoritative, coming from someone who was Director of the
Commonwealth Secretariat's Education Programme for a quarter of the period
surveyed here, and combines a broad sweep with much useful detail. The second

part sets the Commonwealth's education work in the world context of currents of thought about Education for All (EFA) and about gender in education. Sir John Daniel relates interest in EFA in the Commonwealth to the work of the UN in this field and particularly UNESCO as the leaders. Dr Jasbir Singh, who also worked for many years in the Commonwealth Secretariat, has shown how the Secretariat and education ministers gradually became sensitised to the needs for gender balance at all levels and across the education board.

Part Three moves to a particular set of issues relating to science, mathematics and technology in education. The topic has been prominent in most deliberations from 1959 onwards, in Commonwealth Education Conferences (CECs), CCEMs and specialist conferences. Dr Ved Goel clearly shows the importance of the latter in improving educational quality in the field and also the value of professional associations set up under the Commonwealth aegis in raising standards and morale. Dr Bonney Rust relates developments in Commonwealth policy-making to economic and demographic profiles in the various member countries in a way which gives full sense and life to his description of the different reports and meetings.

Part Four deals with higher education, which, as Peter Williams says in Chapter 1, especially lends itself to international activity and interchange. Dr Dhanarajan highlights one of the greatest innovations in the whole 40 years, which has dominated the fourth decade and beyond – the Commonwealth of Learning. Not surprisingly, other authors in this book refer to COL (in Chapters 1, 3, 4 and 5), since it is such an imaginative venture and points to a hopeful future, abreast of new methods and technology. The final chapter, by the editor, illustrates the strengths of Commonwealth links – in language and common scholarly patterns – but also the severe tensions which can be experienced in an international organism of such a diverse character as the Commonwealths. It concludes, however, that: 'It remains true that all members have something to learn from others and all have something to give'.

The aim overall has been to take stock of what has been done over 40 years in the name of Commonwealth education co-operation officially – that is through the mandates of successive conferences and through the initiative of the Common-wealth Secretariat. The book is written in the knowledge that there are very many less formal activities in education arising from the Commonwealth relationships – and that would be the subject for a different study. Here, we have tried to give a reasonably comprehensive picture of the successes of and setbacks to education work engendered by Commonwealth agencies. We have covered the 40 years between 1959 and 1999 in detail, but as the book finally goes to press in 2003, a number of the chapters take account of more recent events, such as the Halifax Conference in 2000, and of trends as they appear in 2003.

There has been close collaboration between some of the authors, through the initiative of the Council for Education in the Commonwealth, but each author's opinions are their own. This is a history of officially-sanctioned activity, but it is not an 'official history'; it has not in any way been vetted or limited by the Commonwealth Secretariat. This again is to their credit and lends strength to the underlying tone, in most of what is in this book, of admiration for the professionalism and motivation of Commonwealth education officials over the years.

Lalage Bown
Editor

List of Abbreviations

ACE	Aid to Commonwealth English
ACTS	Aid to Commonwealth Technology and Science
ACU	Association of Commonwealth Universities
ADEA	Association for the Development of Education in Africa
AFCLIST	African Forum for Children's Literacy in Science and Technology
AGEI	African Girls' Education Initiative
AION	Allama Iqbal Open University (Pakistan)
ASG	Assistant Secretary-General (Commonwealth Secretariat)
AUSAID	Australian Agency for International Development
CIDA	Canadian International Development Agency
C&G	City and Guilds (UK)
CGLI	City and Guilds of London Institute
CAETA	Commonwealth Association for the Education and Training of Adults
CAPA	Commonwealth Association of Polytechnics in Africa
CASME	Commonwealth Association for Science and Mathematics Educators
CASTME	Commonwealth Association for Science, Technology and Mathematics Educators
CCDSP	Canada Caribbean Distance Scholarship Programme
CCEM	Conference of Commonwealth Education Ministers
CCEAM	Commonwealth Council for Educational Administration and Management
CDC	Commonwealth Development Corporation
CEC	Commonwealth Education Conference (1959–1980)
CEC	Council for Education in the Commonwealth (present day)
CEDO	Centre for Educational Development Overseas
CELC	Commonwealth Education Liaison Committee
CELU	Commonwealth Education Liaison Unit
CEMC	Council of Education Ministers of Canada
CFTC	Commonwealth Fund for Technical Co-operation
CHEMS	Commonwealth Higher Education Management Scheme
CHESS	Commonwealth Higher Education Support Scheme
CHOGM	Commonwealth Heads of Government Meeting
CITEP	Commonwealth Industrial Training and Experience Programme
COL	Commonwealth of Learning
COMBINET	Commonwealth Business Network
CPII	Commonwealth Private Investment Initiative
CREDO	Centre for Curriculum Renewal and Educational Development Overseas

CREO	Center for Research on Education Outcomes
CSFP	Commonwealth Scholarship and Fellowship Programme
CUSAC	Commonwealth Universities Study Abroad Consortium
DAE	Donors to African Education
DfID	Department for International Development (UK)
EDD	Education Department (Commonwealth Secretariat)
EFA	Education for All
ELBS	English Language Book Scheme
ESDP	Entrepreneurial Skills Development Programme
FAO	Food and Agriculture Organisation (UN)
FAWE	Forum for African Women Educationalists
FEMSA	Female Education in Mathematics and Science in Africa
FTP	Fellowships Training Programme
GDP	Gross Domestic Product
GMS	Gender Management System
GTZ	German International Development Agency
GYAD	Gender and Youth Affairs Division (Commonwealth Secretariat)
HDI	Human Development Index
HIPC	Highly Indebted Poor Countries
HRD	Human Resource Development
HRDD	Human Resource Development Division (Commonwealth Secretariat)
HRDG	Human Resource Development Group
ICASE	International Council for Associations of Science Education
ICSU	International Council for Science
IGNOU	Indira Gandhi Open University
IIEP	International Institute for Educational Planning (UNESCO)
ILO	International Labour Organisation
IMF	International Monetary Fund
INSET	In-service Education of Teachers
INSTRAW	International Training & Research Institute for the Advancement of Women (UN)
LECT	League for the Exchange of Commonwealth Teachers
MINEDAF	Ministers of Education of Africa
NCERT	National Centre for Research and Technology (India)
NGO	Non-governmental Organisation
NZODA	New Zealand Overseas Development Administration
ODA	Overseas Development Administration (UK)
ODM	Overseas Development Ministry (UK)
OECD	Organisation for Economic Cooperation and Development
p.a.	per annum (yearly)
RECSAM	Regional Centre for Education in Science and Mathematics (Malaysia)

RSA	Royal Society of Arts
SAARC	South Asian Association for Regional Co-operation
SEPU	Science Education Policy Unit (Kenya)
SG	Secretary-General (Commonwealth Secretariat)
SIDA	Swedish International Development Agency
SMT	Science, Mathematics and Technology
SPEU	Strategic Planning and Evaluation Unit
STME	Science Technology and Mathematics Education
TMS	Teacher Management and Support
TVE	Technical and Vocational Education
UNDAF	United Nations Development Assistance Framework
UNESCO	United Nations Educational Scientific and Cultural Organisation
UPE	Universal Primary Education
USAID	United States Agency for International Development
USP	University of the South Pacific
UWI	University of the West Indies
UWIDITE	University of the West Indies Distance Teaching Experiment
WAMM	Meeting of Ministers Responsible for Women's Affairs
WCOTP	World Congress of Organisations of the Teaching Profession (now called Education International)

Part One
The History

Chapter 1

From Oxford to Halifax: Forty Years of Commonwealth Co-operation in Education

Peter Williams

1 From Halifax to Halifax

Halifax 2000 marked the fourteenth in the series of Commonwealth conferences in education, a series that began in the 1950s with the first Commonwealth Education Conference in Oxford in 1959. Although, from today's vantage point, it may seem as if that first conference took place in another age altogether, there are fascinating parallels between the fourteenth and the first conference in the series. Some of these parallels are curious oddities, others perhaps of greater potential significance.

Among the coincidences is, first, that the 1959 Conference in Oxford was presided over by the Earl of Halifax, a former British Foreign Secretary and at that time Chancellor of the University of Oxford. To natives of Nova Scotia or of Yorkshire, like the author, it gives special satisfaction to present the history of Commonwealth education co-operation in terms of 'The Road from Halifax to Halifax'!

Second, it is interesting to reflect that of the 14 conferences so far held, all but two have taken place in or just outside the host nation's capital city; the two exceptions are the first conference in Oxford and the fourteenth in Halifax. This contrasts with the Heads of Government Meetings where the last five have taken place in Limassol, Auckland, Edinburgh, Durban and Brisbane. Although the one about to occur (at the time of publication) will be in Abuja, in a Commonwealth where many of the larger countries (Australia, Canada, India, Malaysia, Nigeria, Pakistan, South Africa and even the United Kingdom) are multi-jurisdictional in their arrangements for administering education, it seems safe to bet that Oxford and Halifax will prove to be trend-setters rather than anomalies.

It is tempting to speculate whether there may be a sense in which the above two coincidences betoken some turn of the circle of Commonwealth educational co-operation back to decentralisation and participation after many years of 'statist' dominance. For the first Oxford Conference was as much a conference of academics and professionals as one of governments, so that it was in a sense symbolic, as well as an act of politeness, that Lord Halifax as Chancellor of the University was chosen to preside. Over the ensuing period, for reasons to be touched on, the Conferences became ever more 'governmental' in character, a process formally recognised when the title-switch for the series from the (eighth) Commonwealth Education Conference (Sri Lanka, 1980) to the (ninth) Conference of Commonwealth Education Ministers was made in Cyprus in 1984.

More recently, however, there has been an international change of mood in considering the relationship of government to society; new thinking that was reflected in the choice of 'The Changing Role of the State in Education' as the theme for 12CCEM in Islamabad in 1994. The role of players other than central government – of local and provincial governments, of the private sector, of voluntary and non-governmental organisations, of professional bodies – has had increasing recognition. This was given expression at 13CCEM in Gaborone, Botswana, in 1997 when a symposium parallel to the ministers' conference took place. That experience was deemed sufficiently useful to be repeated in 2000 in Halifax, enabling ministers to interact with partners and to infuse their conference deliberations with insights drawn from non-governmental colleagues meeting in the wings of their conference.

In another important sense the Halifax Conference marked a return to the beginnings of Commonwealth co-operation in education, beginnings that were to be found in Canada, rather than Britain. For in actuality it was not on the banks of the Thames in 1959 that the present era of Commonwealth education co-operation was first conceived: it was beside the St Laurence in 1958. The Oxford Conference was called in response to a decision of Commonwealth trade and economic ministers at their conference in Montreal in September 1958, convened by Canadian Prime Minister John Diefenbaker. It was in Montreal, not Oxford, that the idea of a scheme for Commonwealth scholarships and fellowships was conceived, with the United Kingdom agreeing to be responsible for half the total and Canada for a quarter.

This illustrates two important continuities running through from the 1950s to the present day. First is the pivotal leadership role that Canada has played in developing Commonwealth education co-operation. That is where it began. Canada hosted a further (the third) Commonwealth Education Conference in Ottawa in 1964. It has been a major supporter of the Commonwealth Scholarship and Fellowship Plan (CSFP), being after Britain the most generous provider of these awards; and it was the Canadian offer in Nicosia in 1984 to double its contribution to the plan that signalled a major enlargement of CSFP. Canada hosted the Heads of Government Meeting in 1987 when the creation of the Commonwealth of Learning was mooted, and the governments of Canada and of the Province of

British Columbia have throughout been financial mainstays of that organisation, itself based in Vancouver, whose remit is the promotion of Commonwealth co-operation in distance education. Canada also, incidentally, provided the Commonwealth with its first Secretary-General, Arnold Smith, and has been, with the UK, the principal funder of the Commonwealth Fund for Technical Co-operation (CFTC).

Second is the continuity of concern with the relationship between education and the economy. Ministers in Montreal in 1958 saw education and training as key motors of development. The context of their Montreal decisions was the growing interest in the economics of education, and increasing recognition that educational expenditure was an investment in economic growth and that high-level manpower was one of the keys to economic and social development. Concern with this relationship between education and development has continued, but in the last decades of the twentieth century a new dimension was added to the debate about education and the economy. This is the awareness that in some senses educational services are commodities that can be bought and sold, which takes one into the debates about privatisation, tuition fees for domestic and international students, and the marketing of education goods and services.

2 Four Decades of Change

In spite of the many connections and continuities between Oxford and Halifax, the context of this account of educational co-operation in the Commonwealth is a world undergoing evolution and change. This is true of the international community, of the Commonwealth itself, of international co-operation, and of education systems.

a. The Changing World

Since the late 1950s, the international political and economic scene has changed dramatically. Scores of countries, including a number of very small and barely viable new states, that were still under colonial rule in 1960, have attained independence from Britain and other European powers. The break-up of federations, such as those of the Soviet Union and Yugoslavia, has helped to increase the number of independent countries. Within the world community there have been important shifts of power. While the United States has become if anything more dominant, there has also been a dramatic rise in wealth and power of Japan, Germany and China; the development of the European Union and the strengthened economies of Italy, Spain and several northern European countries; an enormous accretion of wealth to oil-producing countries, especially in the Middle East; and the economic 'miracle' achieved by the countries of south-east Asia. For Commonwealth developing countries their external relations and commercial links, once dominated by the former colonial powers, have been greatly diversified, and they now have a much wider choice of economic and trade partners. The big new players in the world economic league have not in the main been Commonwealth countries, so that in terms of global economic and political power, the Commonwealth now pulls relatively less weight than in 1959.

While unprecedented prosperity has been experienced by many countries, where income per head has risen sharply as they have moved through the 'demographic transition', other countries have faced economic hardship. Growing indebtedness, adverse movement in their terms of trade and deterioration in the value of their currencies have left some developing countries in dire economic straits; in the face of rapid population growth they have endured periods of declining income per head. In a global perspective, income inequalities between countries have widened. It is as yet unclear whether the communications revolution, which has over the 40 years in question 'shrunk' the world by means of improved transport links and revolutionary developments of telecommunications by radio, television, telephone, fax, internet and e-mail, will narrow or further widen this gap.

Meanwhile the balance of national economies has shifted in significant ways. One trend has been from primary (agriculture) to secondary (manufacturing) production and, especially in the more developed economies, from manufacturing to the 'tertiary' service sector of communications and media, marketing and advertising, financial services, leisure and tourism. In consequence, the quality of human resources has become ever more important to profitable production. A second shift has been economic decentralisation, away from the state 'command and control' economy to a market economy where prices, incentives and privatisation are the watchwords. One set of complementary changes flowing from the changing role of the state has been the economic squeeze on the generally labour-intensive but non- revenue-producing public sector. Reluctance on the part of democratically elected politicians to increase the burden of taxation has meant that greater economic prosperity in society as a whole has been accompanied by severe financial constraints in the public sector. These in turn have been reflected in diminished resources put at the disposal of international organisations.

b. The Changing Commonwealth

These global trends have their reflection in individual Commonwealth countries and in the Commonwealth as a collective entity. Membership has grown from ten members in 1959 to 54 (ignoring temporary suspensions) today. Many of the newer members are very small countries; about half the Commonwealth countries have populations of one million or fewer. One consequence of increased membership is that Commonwealth meetings have lost some, though certainly not all, of the informality that used to be considered one of their main advantages compared with the United Nations and its agencies. To have 20 countries round the table is one thing; to have 54 is quite another.

Economically, the Commonwealth has certainly become more diversified. Britain is no longer the dominant player. The economies of Canada and Australia have grown considerably, while India has developed a major scientific and techno-logical capability despite its average income per head still being low. Some of the newer economies such as Brunei Darussalam, Singapore and Hong Kong (only part of the Commonwealth until 1997) have overtaken Britain in income per head. But these last are not very populous countries and a problem for the modern Commonwealth is imbalance in its composition; it is under-represented among the industrialised countries of Europe, the oil-producers of the Middle East, and the larger economies of east Asia: and over-represented among populous low-income countries.

In organisational terms the Commonwealth has changed greatly, having created and developed an institutional machinery of its own in the shape of a Secretariat, a Fund for Technical Co-operation, and the Commonwealth Foundation. Patterns of regular consultation in Heads of Government Meetings, ministerial conferences, expert groups and working parties have evolved and affect the education sector as much as others.

c. Changing Patterns of Co-operation

Over the 40-year period many changes have shaped the environment in which co-operation takes place, applying not just to the education sector. One may note:

- The emergence of major multilateral players like the World Bank, other develop-ment banks and EU/EDF, and of new bilateral donors like Germany, Japan, and the Nordic countries;

- The increasing significance of non-governmental and charitable organisations in co-operation activities, especially in emergency relief;

- The many intermediary commercial contractors specialising in management and delivery of assistance that have occupied the 'space' between donors and users of assistance. Some are located in the private commercial sector, some are consultancy arms of public institutions and others are not-for-profit NGOs;

- The increasing gap in prices and costs between industrialised and developing countries, making it less and less cost-effective to move developing country nationals for study and training in developed countries, or citizens of industrial-ised countries to serve as long-term teachers in developing countries. This has put a premium on: (a) using developing country resources and locations in co-operation programmes; (b) developing South–South co-operation; and (c) exploring the potential of short-term exchanges of personnel, of short- and split-site courses, and of interaction at a distance using modern communication technologies;

- There has been more interest in institutional development and emphasis on capacity-building and on long-term sustainability of assisted projects.

d. Changing Education

Finally, education systems have changed significantly. Most obviously, they have greatly expanded as a result of population growth (in some countries the population is three or four times as big as in 1959), of higher enrolment ratios, and of system-development and diversification to include more specialist and tertiary provision. Many Commonwealth countries have achieved universal basic education, even though achievement of Education for All is still far away in parts of sub-Saharan Africa and south Asia; and the number of new colleges and universities has multiplied manifold. Education systems which were once basically elitist have been democratised. In all but the smallest states they can no longer be centrally managed by small cadres of civil servants personally well known to one another. Systems and bureaucracies have taken over and education management has assumed much greater importance. The focus today is largely on pursuing organisational efficiency, on setting objectives and monitoring their achievement, and on keeping costs under control.

Education, being labour-intensive, has been particularly vulnerable to economic crises. This has impacted on teacher salary levels, producing an adverse knock-on effect on teacher motivation and the quality of education. In many countries the maintenance of school buildings has been neglected, books and materials have been in short supply, and the supervision and advisory services have been run down. In several systems of public education, tuition fees have been introduced or reintroduced, increasing the disposition of those wealthy enough to patronise private schools or out-of-school private tutoring.

The development of new communication technologies for transmission of knowledge and information, and for use in interactive learning, has offered the potential for revolutionising the way education takes place. The possibility of more independent study, and for the transformation of the teacher's role to that of learning facilitator, implies major change for education systems in future. They promise both to make schools different kinds of institution, and in selected instances to obviate the need for institutional attendance in order to learn. They also open up possibilities for engaging in international study while remaining at a home base. As indicated below, the Commonwealth has been among the first to recognise this potential.

3 Official Co-operation: Milestones on the Road, 1959–2000

The focus of this chapter is on the co-operative programmes in education overseen by Commonwealth Education Ministers' Conferences. It largely omits description and analysis of direct assistance for education and training to individual member countries through the Commonwealth Fund for Technical Co-operation. For readers' convenience, the story of official co-operation within the education ministers' purview will first be presented chronologically, in four somewhat arbitrarily drawn periods, designated in terms of the education conferences they covered (a list of conferences with dates is given at Appendix 1). The logic of the chosen demarcation boundaries will be explained, though their arbitrariness will be apparent. The four periods selected are

- 1959–1964, Oxford to Ottawa (1CEC to 3CEC)

- 1965–1980, Lagos to Colombo (4CEC to 8CEC)

- 1981–1994, Nicosia to Islamabad (9CCEM to 12CCEM)

- 1995–2000, Gaborone to Halifax (13CCEM and 14CCEM).

a. Oxford, New Delhi and Ottawa 1959–64

Notwithstanding the important antecedent conference in Montreal, the Oxford gathering laid the foundations for what followed and is the logical starting point. The first conference established the Commonwealth Education Liaison Unit (CELU) which organised, with host countries, the second and third conferences in New Delhi (1962) and Ottawa (1964). In 1965 the Commonwealth Secretariat was formed and a new phase began. It was in this first phase that many of the more populous dependencies in Africa attained their independence. By the time of Ottawa in 1964, some 20 countries were represented at the conference as Commonwealth members.

Reverting to the first conference, in the light of subsequent changes over the past 40 years, certain salient characteristics of Oxford seem noteworthy:

- Only ten independent Commonwealth countries were eligible to attend. These were the United Kingdom as host, Australia, Canada, Ceylon, Ghana, India, the Federation of Malaya, New Zealand, Pakistan and South Africa. As a self-governing dependency, the Federation of Rhodesia and Nyasaland also sent a delegation in its own right. Most of Africa, the West Indies and South Pacific countries, Malta and Cyprus had not yet attained independence.

- This was a Commonwealth Education Conference at which delegations included a large number of educational professionals in addition to ministers and civil servants. Its professional character was underlined by the fact that, under the presidency of the Earl of Halifax, the conference was chaired by Sir Philip Morris, Vice-Chancellor of Bristol University.

- The meeting focused entirely on Commonwealth co-operation in education, most notably working out the details of the Commonwealth Scholarship and Fellowship Plan. There was no other substantive theme, such as the ministerial conferences have today.

- The conference was serviced by the British Ministry of Education, as it then was. The Oxford Conference saw the need to establish ongoing consultative machinery, the Commonwealth Education Liaison Committee; and a small secretariat, the Commonwealth Education Liaison Unit, precursor of the Education Department of the Commonwealth Secretariat.

The discussions in Oxford were focused largely on the forms and mechanics of co-operation in education between member countries. In particular, the conference put flesh on the proposals for the Commonwealth Scholarship and Fellowship Plan to which over a thousand awards were promised. Of four committees which met during the conference, one dealt with the CSFP and one with technical education; and two others dealt with teacher training and with the supply of teachers, under-lining the concern at that time with staffing the expanding secondary and tertiary education systems of newly independent countries. Among the special concerns raised was the need for training staff to teach English as a second language, the sub-ject of the first in a series of specialist conferences, held at Makerere, Uganda in 1962.

b. Lagos to Colombo 1965–1980

The second period begins in 1965 with the creation of the Commonwealth Secretariat and the incorporation within it, as the Education Division, of the Commonwealth Education Liaison Unit in 1966. The period ends with the eighth Commonwealth Education Conference in Colombo, the last of the 'old-style' con-ferences, but also the first at which Commonwealth student mobility was an issue of fierce controversy. With the independence of Zimbabwe in 1980, the decolonisa-tion process was almost complete, and the Commonwealth now had approaching 40 full members (South Africa and Pakistan being temporarily out of member-ship), of whom 32 attended the Colombo Conference. The period was charac-terised by the holding of many specialist conferences, as well as the five CECs in Lagos (1968), Canberra (1971), Kingston, Jamaica (1974), Accra (1977) and Colombo (1980). In these years the Secretariat was active in the areas of technical and vocational education, teacher education, science and mathematics education, books and learning materials, and non-formal education (NFE).

The incorporation of the CELU into the Commonwealth Secretariat as its Education Division meant that Commonwealth educational co-operation formed part of a broader pattern of Commonwealth collaboration and had to fit into a wider set of priorities and administrative arrangements determined by the Commonwealth Secretary-General. In this period Arnold Smith of Canada was the first Secretary-General from 1965 to 1975, when he was succeeded by Shridath (Sonny) Ramphal of Guyana. Further major developments of the official machin-ery for Commonwealth co-operation took place with the creation of the Commonwealth Foundation in 1966 and of the Commonwealth Fund for Technical Co-operation in 1971.

c. Nicosia to Islamabad 1981–1994

The third period is inaugurated by the establishment of the Consultative Group, and later the Standing Committee, on Student Mobility. The latter met seven times between 1981 and 1992. It also marked certain radical changes in the form and length of the Conferences, now re-designated CCEMs, and in the organisation of the Commonwealth Secretariat, where a Human Resource Development Group was formed, incorporating education. Major developments in this period were the expansion of the CSFP, particularly from 1984 (the year of 9CCEM in Nicosia), the creation of the Commonwealth of Learning in 1987 (10CCEM in Nairobi) and 1988; and a marked strengthening of the infrastructure of Commonwealth higher education co-operation around the time of 11CCEM (Barbados, 1990). This was also the period in which programmes of support for education in small states, for teacher management and support in Africa, and for the advancement of women and girls took root. The Commonwealth report on human development strategies, *Foundation for the Future*, appeared in 1993. The period ended with the re-entry of South Africa to the Commonwealth in 1994, in time for 12CCEM in Islamabad in the same year. Emeka Anyaoku succeeded Sir Shridath Ramphal as Commonwealth Secretary-General in 1990.

d. Gaborone and Halifax 1995–2000

The period 1993–1995 marked something of a watershed, quite apart from South Africa's re-entry. In Islamabad, the Standing Committee on Student Mobility and Higher Education Co-operation was finally stood down. In the Secretariat, the Education Programme was merged with Health in a new Human Resource Development Division at the end of 1993, and there were major personnel changes in education in both the Secretariat and the Commonwealth of Learning. 13CCEM (Gaborone, 1997) saw a major innovation in the holding of parallel events to the ministerial conference in the form of a non-official 'civil society' Symposium and Trade Fair/ Exhibition. This was repeated in Halifax at 14CCEM in November 2000 and the idea is to be developed in Edinburgh (15CCEM), with a parallel symposium and a major exercise in youth exchange as well. A Commission on Commonwealth Studies reported in 1996 and its report was debated at Gaborone and in Heads of Government meetings. In April 2000, Don McKinnon of New Zealand became the fourth Secretary-General and a further reorganisation in the Secretariat has placed education in a new Social Transformation Programmes Department.

4 Evolution of the Ministerial Conferences

Direction is given to the business of official Commonwealth education co-operation by the ministerial conferences, held at intervals of roughly three years. As Section 3 has shown, these have been held at different venues throughout the Commonwealth, with two in Europe (Oxford and Nicosia), three in Asia (New

Delhi, Colombo and Islamabad), four in Africa (Lagos, Accra, Nairobi and Gaborone), two in the Caribbean (Kingston and Bridgetown), two in Canada (Ottawa and Halifax) and one in Australia (Canberra).

Country delegations have grown from ten at Oxford in 1959 to over 40 at the last three conferences, with over 80% of Commonwealth countries represented. In Barbados 40 countries were represented with 31 ministerial heads of delegation, in Islamabad 44 delegations and 35 ministers, and in Gaborone 42 and 30. Dependencies have attended as part of the delegation of the metropolitan country and the British delegation at the first few conferences was greatly inflated by inclusion of representatives from soon-to-be-independent African and Caribbean territories.

With a few exceptions, delegations have been headed by the Minister of Education except when, for example, general elections are being held at the time of the conference. Australia however, has only rarely sent the Minister of Education and has usually had a non-political head of delegation. Britain used to send her senior Minister/Secretary of State but more recently has sent a junior minister. Canada, a federation in which responsibility for education lies with the provinces, normally asks the current ministerial Chairperson of the Council of Education Ministers, Canada (CEMC) to lead its delegation. The delegations of these industrialised countries may also include ministerial or official representation from the development co-operation department of government, where budgetary responsibility for funding of Commonwealth co-operative programmes may lie. Some countries have divided the responsibility for education into two, with separate ministries dealing with higher education and with school education; such countries sometimes send both ministers, though only one can be designated 'head of delegation'.

In the initial stages of Commonwealth co-operation the national delegations included many members who were not ministers or civil servants, such as vice-chancellors, teachers' representatives or other education specialists. Over the course of time, however, the conferences and the delegations have taken on a more governmental character, a change that was formally signalled by the change of designation of the conferences in 1984.

Bodies invited to send official observers include selected intergovernmental organisations (UNESCO, World Bank, etc.), relevant international NGOs such as Education International (formerly WCOTP), and pan-Commonwealth associations active in education, of which by far the most important is the Association of Commonwealth Universities. Observers are present throughout, but in the plenary ministerial sessions are only permitted to intervene in the debate by special invitation of the Chair.

The pattern of conference organisation that developed early on was to hold a pre-conference meeting of officials for up to a week, among other things to review the work of the Secretariat in carrying out the mandates of the previous conference and to preview the agenda of the upcoming conference before ministers met. The whole process of the successive gatherings could take ten days or two weeks and was eventually found to be too cumbersome. 'Predigestion' of the agenda by officials, although facilitating well-informed professional discussion, tended to take the 'edge' off ministerial debates. For the 1984 conference in Cyprus, therefore, it was decided to cut down the preparatory official meeting to half a day and to limit the conference duration to three or four days. The meetings were henceforward known as Conferences of Commonwealth Education Ministers instead of Commonwealth Education Conferences.

The actual agendas of the conferences are agreed through a process of prior consultation between the Commonwealth Secretariat in London, the host government and other governments. The formal mechanism for approval of the proposed conference arrangements and for agreeing the agenda is the Commonwealth Education Liaison Committee (CELC) whose members are representatives of high commissions in London. A once-powerful body, the CELC's influence has diminished virtually to zero, for three reasons. The establishment of the Commonwealth Secretariat with its own system of accountability to Commonwealth governments meant that a separate governance structure for Commonwealth education co-operation became redundant. Second, the decision in the mid-1980s that the CELC should be chaired by a Commonwealth Secretariat official, instead of by an independent professional of stature, greatly reduced the autonomy of the CELC. Third, Commonwealth governments have often failed to appoint senior high-calibre personnel as their education attachés in London, so that the professional knowledge required to make the CELC more than a mere post-box has often been lacking in its membership.

In earlier times, before the Commonwealth Secretariat was formed, the CELC was a powerful body that oversaw the work of the Commonwealth Education Liaison Unit and was itself a decision-making body. It was chaired successively by Sir Philip Morris, Chairman of the Oxford Conference, Sir Allen Brown from Australia, and then by two long-serving chairmen, Professor Lionel Elvin, Director of the University of London Institute of Education from 1965 to 1974, followed by Sir Roy Marshall for a further ten years to 1984. Thereafter, the Chair has been taken by an Assistant/Deputy Secretary-General in the Commonwealth Secretariat.

The business of the conferences has generally been of two main kinds. From the beginning, there has been attention to Commonwealth co-operation, and in the early days delegations from the more developed countries often came to the conferences with new proposals for extending such co-operation. Thus the three aims of 3CEC in Ottawa in 1964 were: (1) to review progress in co-operation recommended by the two previous CECs; (2) to recommend improvements in existing forms of co-operation; and (3) to consider specific proposals for educational co-operation in other fields. Continuing up to the present day, a major part of the business therefore involves review of existing collaborative programmes like the Commonwealth Scholarship and Fellowship Plan, and more recently also the Commonwealth of Learning. Working Groups or sub-committees have been established within the framework of the conference to receive reports and to review and refine procedures; and in ministers' plenary sessions there have sometimes been set occasions for the making of funding pledges.

As part of this process of review, the work of the education secretariat in Marlborough House was also scrutinised and mandates for future activity handed down.

The second main concern of the conferences, which became more prominent from the mid-1970s onwards, was to exchange views and experience on a selected issue of pressing concern to policy-makers. It was at the sixth CEC in Jamaica that a theme appeared for the first time – in that case 'management of education'. In retrospect one can see that the mid-1970s represented a substantive shift in the nature of the conferences. Ten or 15 years after many countries had achieved their independence from Britain, recruitment or replacement of expatriates was no longer developing countries' main interest or concern; rather it was the management and improvement of systems that were now led and staffed by nationals. The dialogue shifted away from donor-recipient relationships to exchange of professional experience. The change was expressed succinctly by Professor Lionel Elvin at Kingston in 1974:

> *I am very struck by the contrast between this Conference and, I think I might say, all five of the preceding Conferences, in that here in Jamaica I have felt for the first time that we have all been taking part equally. The First and Third World polarity is getting modulated; at least in the sense that the frequency of interventions of participants bears no relation to the size or wealth of the countries they represent. We are all really working together now. I notice the growth of interchange of experience, to say nothing of persons, between countries of the so-called Third World. I also note that the myth that First World countries have no educational problems has disappeared. But above all the donor-receiver concept ... is ceasing to be the dominant one and is giving way to the proper one, that of collaboration.*

The conference themes often reflected international concerns at the time. Thus, themes of the last four conferences have been 'the vocational orientation of education' (1987), 'improving the quality of basic education' (1990), 'the changing role of the state in education' (1994) and 'education and technology' (1997). In the list of CECs/CCEMs in Appendix 1, the keynote theme of each conference has been indicated. Normally one or more keynote speakers have been invited to introduce the conference theme. Actually the idea of inviting distinguished speakers goes back further than the adoption of conference themes. As early as 3CEC in Ottawa in 1964 two guest speakers were invited: Professor Mathai from India to talk about Commonwealth Scholarships and Sir Willis Jackson from the UK on priorities in technical education.

The conferences generally conclude with an agreed communiqué and eventually a report (the Gaborone Conference is alone in lacking a report to date). On most issues it is not difficult for ministers to reach consensus, but the conferences have not been strangers to sharp controversy. The issue of full-cost fees for Commonwealth students stirred strong emotions and brought confrontation between Commonwealth sending countries and the principal hosts, particularly Britain; it dominated the conferences in Colombo and Nicosia. Tensions with Britain were exacerbated by the UK's decision to leave UNESCO, a decision from which Commonwealth countries strove to dissuade her. High Commissioners in London called on the British Foreign Secretary in an attempt to avert the decision. So fraught was the situation on these two questions in 1984/85, that Commonwealth ministers went so far as to hold a special meeting in Sofia, Bulgaria, at the UNESCO General Conference in 1985. Tensions with Britain over educational issues were of course part of a wider pattern of strained relations at Commonwealth summits, where differences continually surfaced over how to deal with apartheid South Africa.

Later in the 1980s there was a discernible divergence of views over the creation of new Commonwealth mechanisms for co-operation, especially the Commonwealth of Learning, but also higher education interchange more generally. Developing-country members tended to favour the creation of collective multilateral institutions and programmes for co-operation, in whose governance they would have a voice; whereas industrialised countries, liable to be asked to foot most of the bill for such initiatives, tended to prefer bilateral arrangements giving them more control over programmes.

5 Secretariat and Budgets

It was decided at an early stage to create machinery to promote co-operation in education and in Oxford it was agreed (as already noted in Section 3) to establish a small liaison unit. It seems to have been the New Zealand delegation, led by the renowned educator, Dr C. E. Beeby, which fought hardest for this. The unit was created with a handful of staff under the direction of V. S. Jha from India, who served until 1963, when he was succeeded by a Canadian, Freeman Stewart. The unit was housed in Marlborough House which the Queen had assigned to be a Commonwealth Centre, following the death in 1953 of her grandmother Queen Mary, who had lived there.

The CELU with its small staff helped to arrange the next two Conferences in 1962 and 1964. In 1965 Commonwealth leaders established a Commonwealth Secretariat to take over functions from the British Commonwealth Relations Office of organising Prime Ministers' Meetings, and it was decided in 1966 that the CELU should be merged into the new Secretariat as one of its divisions (the others being administration, conferences, economic affairs and international affairs). It was now accountable not to the CELC, which became more purely advisory, but to the Secretary-General and through him to Commonwealth governments.

Perhaps reflecting its historical primacy in ante-dating its new parent body, education enjoyed a high status in the Secretariat and had its own Assistant Secretary-General (ASG) for Education, supervising the work of the divisional director and his staff. The Assistant Secretary-General's post was held by, among others, Hugh Springer, later the Secretary-General of the Association of Commonwealth Universities and Governor-General of Barbados; Y. K. Lule from Uganda, who later briefly became President of his country; and James Maraj, who went on to be Vice-Chancellor of the University of the South Pacific and first President of the Commonwealth of Learning. Later, Professor Murshid from Bangladesh held the post, which survived until the early 1980s when an Assistant Secretary-General for Human Resource Development was appointed. Below the ASG (Education) served a succession of Directors. There were four in the first eight years of the Secretariat's existence; but then two Nigerians, Sam Cookey and Rex Akpofure, each had a longer tenure. None of the directors was a woman, but the longest-ever serving member of the professional staff, Amu Krishnaswamy, was. Of the support staff, Leilani de Silva (Packer) served with three directors over 20 years to 1991, valuably providing much of the continuity and institutional memory of the division/programme.

The twin notions of co-operation and assistance were comfortably merged during these early years, no sharp distinction being made in Secretariat budgets between the consultative function and that of development aid. This changed with the creation in 1971 of the Commonwealth Fund for Technical Co-operation, which took over the provision of experts and funding of training. The Fellowships and Training Division of CFTC was the largest in programme terms and its remit was later to expand substantially with its special programmes of Commonwealth support for the countries of Southern Africa – Rhodesia/Zimbabwe, South-West Africa/Namibia, South Africa and Mozambique. It has been through CFTC that Commonwealth multilateral assistance to individual countries' education systems has flowed.

More problematic for the so-called functional divisions of the Secretariat was that they now ceased to have their own budgets for programme activity; instead they had to rely on funds from the CFTC, which had a special vote on which Secretariat divisions could draw for activities deemed 'developmental'. This became an increasingly tight straitjacket for the Education Division which had been accustomed to regard as one of its most valuable functions that of being a catalyst for exchange of experience and the co-operative development of new Commonwealth initiatives of a regional and pan-Commonwealth kind. Support to individual countries in response to requests for development assistance had not been its prime concern. As this new dispensation for the 1970s continued and intensified into the 1980s, education in the Secretariat found that the only pro-gramme money it received directly in its own right, rather than through CFTC, was for high-level meetings (ministers' conferences and the Standing Committee of Student Mobility and Higher Education Co-operation), together with a declining travel budget. Given that the Commonwealth Secretariat did not have field offices in member countries, visits by headquarters staff for liaison purposes and to keep the Secretariat informed about issues and conditions in education were essential; but these generally could only take place in the context of seminars and training courses conducted by Secretariat staff under programmes approved by CFTC.

Two other developments were severely constraining professional activity in education. The range of responsibilities undertaken by the Commonwealth Secretariat expanded to include law, health and later women and development. New specialised institutions in the form of a Commonwealth Science Council and Commonwealth Youth Programme occupied some of the 'territory' that might previously have been expected to fall under the Education Division's remit. This meant that there was more competition for the attention of ministers and governments, as well as for budgetary funds available to the Secretariat and CFTC. These resources themselves became more constrained in the years following the 1973 'oil-price shock' when governments adopted a more austere approach to international co-operation. The net result was that the Education Division was far more constrained for programme funds by the early 1980s than had been the case ten years before. The valuable series of specialist conferences (see below) was one casualty.

An internal reorganisation of the Secretariat in 1983 resulted from the proliferation of units dealing with aspects of human resources. In keeping with new international thinking about a more integrated approach to human resources, a Human Resource Development Group was created under an Assistant Secretary-General, Manmohan ('Moni') Malhoutra from India. The group included three Secretariat units now renamed 'programmes' which were education, health, and women and development. The semi-autonomous Commonwealth Youth Programme also became a member of the Group, as did the Management Development Programme and Fellowships and Training Programme of CFTC. The Commonwealth Science Council participated as an observer. The group submitted a combined development budget for CFTC support, including some joint projects involving two or more programmes. The secretariat for the group was provided by the Education Programme. The most outstanding joint product from the group was the Pitroda Report, *Foundation for the Future*, published in 1993. Throughout its existence the group had to struggle with the tensions of divided control over some of its constituent programmes between the ASG (Human Resource Development) and other authorities, and with the reluctance of programme directors to lose their autonomy. The group did not outlive the departure of Mr Malhoutra in early 1994; streamlining of the Secretariat's structure in 1993 led to the merging of the Education and Health Programmes as the Human Resource Development Division (with an Education Department and a Health Department as constituent units), and of the Women and Development Programme and the Commonwealth Youth Programme into a Gender and Youth Affairs Division.

After more than two decades in the east wing of Marlborough House, the Education Programme, along with its partners in the Human Resource Development Group (HRDG), was in 1982 relocated in the drearier office block opposite, Quadrant House, where it has occupied the bulk of the second floor for the past 18 years. Soon after the creation of HRDG, Peter Williams from Britain assumed the directorship of the Education Programme in 1984, becoming the first Director in 1993/94 of the Human Resource Development Division. On his departure, he was succeeded after a year's interregnum in 1995 by Stephen Matlin, also British, who served until 2001, being assisted as Head of the Education Department by Cream Wright from Sierra Leone.

The resource constraints intensified. Although the Education Programme took on a heavier work load and until the mid 1990s maintained a staff establishment of nine or ten professional posts, which was at times supplemented by three or four officers attached for particular projects, its programme budget contracted. In real resource terms the funding received from CFTC at the time of writing is equivalent to only about a quarter of what was available from that source in the early 1980s. For a long time the crisis has been held at bay by successfully seeking co-funding from other development co-operation agencies, in many instances bilateral agencies of non-Commonwealth aid donors, or international organisations. The marriage of their funding with the Secretariat's professional resources and access to Commonwealth developing-country networks has had productive results. Nevertheless, it has become progressively more difficult for the Secretariat to take on temporary staff and more ominously, the regular staff establishment of professional posts has been severely reduced.

6 Substantive Themes of Consultation and Co-operation

The review of conference business in Section 4 explained that two types of subject matter have engaged the attention of ministers. First, there have been the joint Commonwealth co-operative programmes and institutions in education, and second there have been themes on which they have wished to exchange experience and concert views.

a. Co-operative Institutions

Commonwealth co-operative programmes in education were launched with the Commonwealth Scholarship and Fellowship Plan already referred to and more fully described in Chapter 7, and this was supplemented in the 1980s by the creation of new institutions and programmes of co-operation at tertiary level. For good reasons, tertiary education is the level where collaboration has been most developed. The specialisation of branches of knowledge and technology means that national higher education systems cannot be self-sufficient. Higher education takes place in English in most member countries, making interchange easier. The exchange of relatively small numbers of academics and researchers can make a significant contribution to institutional development. There are strong professional networks through the Association of Commonwealth Universities and professional bodies. Senior academics have played an influential role in developing Commonwealth education co-operation, and the Secretariat has invariably designated one or more staff members as responsible for tertiary education.

When the first steps in official Commonwealth education co-operation were taken, the staffing of emerging national education systems was a serious challenge. Particularly in Africa, there was a shortage of secondary-school teachers and of college and university staff, and a need to establish systems for staff training and development. Because of this, attention was given to elaborating frameworks for the recruitment of expatriate teachers, and on the training side Britain launched a major assistance programme in the form of Commonwealth bursaries to train tutors for teacher training colleges. Training places in Britain under the Bursaries Scheme were as numerous as Commonwealth Scholarships, reaching 500 at a time. This was bilateral assistance in a Commonwealth framework. The early CECs devoted considerable attention to teacher supply and teacher training, usually establishing a committee of the conference to discuss them. By the end of the 1970s, however, these topics had disappeared from the agenda of joint Commonwealth programmes of collaboration, reflecting the substantial progress made by developing countries in localising the teaching service; and the Commonwealth Bursaries were discontinued by Britain.

A third area in which co-operation has been institutionalised is distance education. Commonwealth countries were pioneers in correspondence education and external degree programmes, but it was only in the 1980s that their common interest crystallised as the Commonwealth of Learning. A number of factors, including rapid development of new information and communication technologies, combined to bring about the creation of this new organisation. The increasing cost of physical mobility of students directed the attention of the Commonwealth Standing Committee to new approaches to learning across national frontiers; one of its members was Anastasios Christodoulou, Secretary-General of the Association of Commonwealth Universities, who brought to the committee his experience as founding Secretary of the Open University in the UK. In 1984 for the first time the Secretariat appointed a specialist in distance education to its staff.

Canada's interest in distance education and the happy coincidence that, as host of the Heads of Government Meeting in Vancouver in 1987, it was glad to sponsor a concrete new initiative in Commonwealth co-operation, helped to bring the new institution to life. Imaginative proposals by a committee chaired by Asa Briggs (Lord Briggs), strong advocacy by the Commonwealth Secretary-General and generous pledges from Brunei Darussalam, India and Nigeria to supplement promises from the governments of Canada and British Columbia all combined to turn dream into reality. Chapter 6 gives a description of COL's work and development.

b. Themes of Consultation and Joint Activity

The institutions described above are independent of the Commonwealth Secretariat, even though generated through intergovernmental conferences and enjoying support from the Secretariat/CFTC. But the Secretariat has launched a wide array of other co-operative initiatives for exchange of experience and joint activity in education, using its own staff and modest budgetary resources to bring Commonwealth representatives together and to mobilise Commonwealth action. The range of mechanisms available to the education branch of the Secretariat for such purposes has been limited, consisting mainly of consultative meetings, training workshops and seminars, and working groups, very occasional study visits and attachments, and the publication of directories, studies, surveys and reports, frequently in the form of resource manuals for use by practitioners or of handbooks of good practice. Direct funding of follow-up operational activity has always been the responsibility of governments, with support where appropriate of consultancies and training provided by CFTC.

Secretariat activity, which is mandated by ministers and Heads of Government, at their periodic conferences and meetings has focused on a number of different issues. A good guide to the priorities in the first two decades, the 1960s and 1970s, is the list of themes chosen for the expert or specialist conferences which took place in between the Commonwealth Education Conferences (see Appendix 2). Secretariat staffing, activities and publications were to a large degree clustered round the issues about to be addressed, or recently addressed, in the specialist conferences. The nine conferences held between 1961 and 1979 discussed: teaching of English as a second language; teaching of science in schools; education and training of technicians; mathematics in schools; education in rural areas; teacher education in a changing society; educational broadcasting; materials for teaching and learning; and non-formal education for development. This series of conferences only ended in 1983, when financial difficulties meant that the Secretariat had to ask member countries to pay a higher share of the costs of attendance, which resulted in fewer countries notifying their intention to be present.

Among these themes, technical and vocational education was prominent from the very beginning and was the subject of one of the four main committees at the Oxford Conference (along with CSFP, teacher training and teacher supply). It has continued to figure largely in Secretariat concerns up to the present, but it was only in the mid-1970s to mid-1980s that there was a specialist officer in post. Science and mathematics education, teacher education and in-service training, materials and book development, including low-cost publishing and provision of library services, and non-formal education all received a good deal of emphasis in the 1970s and early 1980s. A wide range of practical resource books and reports was published on these themes, some of them going into repeat editions in response to demand. More detailed information about Secretariat work in these areas will be found in Chapters 4 and 5.

In the period from the mid-1970s to mid-1980s, covering the sixth to the ninth conferences, the themes chosen by the Commonwealth ministers for their conferences addressed political, social and economic issues in education, including questions of financing and management, rather than professional concerns over schools and schooling. The termination of the series of specialist conferences, and the onset of the student fees crisis, reinforced this trend, as did the formation in the Commonwealth Secretariat of the Human Resource Development Group already referred to. Considerable attention was given to higher education and distance education in those years, and a higher education unit was formed within the education programme. In 1990, higher education co-operation through the Commonwealth Higher Education Support Scheme (CHESS) programme was – with basic education – mandated by ministers as one of the two main thrusts of the Secretariat's work programme in education. This was complemented by a strong new-found interest in education development of small states – a subject of obvious Commonwealth interest and comparative advantage, particularly after Commonwealth membership expanded in the 1970s and 1980s to include many newly independent small island countries. Following an influential seminal meeting in Mauritius in 1985, a series of training workshops, practical studies, professional networks and exchange visits was developed.

After the mid-1980s, however, a special effort was made to balance these new concerns by a return to issues concerning processes and content of education, the curriculum, teacher quality and morale at school level. The themes of 10CCEM and 11CCEM concerning the vocational orientation of education and the quality of basic education served to redress the balance somewhat. At 11CCEM in 1990, the year of the Jomtien World Conference on Education for All, it was decided that improvement of basic education should be a priority for Secretariat work and that a major focus of this should be teacher management and support activities. That programme started in Commonwealth Africa, originally an initiative confined to the Commonwealth, but later partially subsumed within the spectrum of activities orchestrated by the Association for the Development of Education in Africa (ADEA) and complemented by a programme in francophone Africa. It included an important strand of headteacher training. The Commonwealth Secretariat became the lead agency for ADEA's Working Group on the Teaching Profession, and more recently also of the Working Group on Non-formal Education. In the early 1990s, when the Education Programme had nine established posts, its activities spanned basic education, science and mathematics education, student mobility and higher education co-operation, the work on small states, distance education, entrepreneurship, community schools and human resource development. All of these to a greater or lesser extent received international recognition and attracted co-funding.

c. Commonwealth Student Mobility

A subject that dominated the last two of the four decades was Commonwealth student mobility. This issue gave rise to a sharp conflict of views, but at the same time generated creative ideas about the potential for practical co-operation in education among Commonwealth countries. The vehicle for this thinking was the Commonwealth Standing Committee on Student Mobility, chaired by Sir Roy Marshall. The profile of student mobility has been so high in the last two decades that it is the subject of a later chapter. Here only highlights of the debate ensuing from the introduction of full-cost fees will be sketched.

The initial fateful shots in the battle over student mobility were fired at the time of the first Wilson government in Britain, in the aftermath of the 1963 *Robbins Report on Higher Education in the UK*. It was decided for the first time to charge differential tuition fees for students from abroad in British higher and further education. A high proportion of the students affected were from newly independent Commonwealth countries, which had been accustomed to sending students to Britain for courses not available at home. At one level of analysis the introduction of differential charges for students from abroad can be seen as a question of education finance, of reducing the public subsidy to higher education; but it was also part of an ongoing process of differentiating Commonwealth from British citizens and turning the former into part-aliens in what they had hitherto regarded as the 'mother country'. The level of the British differential charge rose over the next decade and was substantially increased by the Wilson-Callaghan governments from 1974 to 1979. In 1979 the Conservatives were returned to power under Margaret Thatcher and resolved on introducing full-cost fees for students from abroad (other than those from the European Community). Eventually, after concerted lobbying through the Overseas Students Trust and others, a series of partial relief measures (the so-called 'Pym Package') in the form of additional scholarship awards was introduced.

The Commonwealth response to the new fees was one of dismay and the Secretary-General set up a Consultative Group on Student Mobility under the chairmanship of Sir Hugh Springer, the retiring Secretary-General of the ACU. When this Group reported in 1981 it was decided to establish a Standing Committee on Student Mobility under the chairmanship of Sir Roy Marshall. The committee, with ten to twelve members drawn from different Commonwealth regions, met annually between 1982 and 1986, and again in 1989 and 1992. It produced a series of seven reports that monitored the level of fees and the volume of student interchange in the Commonwealth, and made recommendations for action on the part of the Commonwealth Secretariat, Commonwealth governments and higher education institutions. In recognition of the wide scope of the Committee's concerns its title was broadened by adding 'and Higher Education Co-operation' in 1987.

On student mobility itself, the Standing Committee may have had some modest influence in relation to the reporting systems on mobility and in encouraging the greater supply of scholarships and awards – in particular the increase in size of the

CSFP in the years after 1984. But in general it failed to secure any significant changes in the fee policies of the principal Commonwealth host countries; on the contrary, it had to witness the introduction of full-cost fees in Australia, followed later by New Zealand, and the raising of fees in some Canadian provinces. In the lifetime of the Standing Committee, only India among the major Commonwealth host countries refrained from discrimination against students from abroad and from substantial rises in the level of tuition fees in its higher-education system. What the committee called the 'final frustration' was the rejection at its Seventh Meeting by the group of Commonwealth industrialised countries of a package of five modest measures proposed by the Secretary-General as constituting 'a favourable fee regime' which would give relief to developing-country students.

The effect of full-cost fee regimes on Commonwealth student mobility was initially dire, causing a sharp decline in Commonwealth students going to Britain. Later however, mainly in the period after the Standing Committee was disbanded in 1994, there was a surge in the number of international students in Australia and Britain, including a rise in Commonwealth students. It would seem that provision of strong financial incentives to cash-strapped higher education institutions to undertake international student recruitment caused them to market their courses vigorously and effectively.

Among the less desirable effects of making international study expensive have been difficulties experienced by countries that are low on the UN's human development index in participating fully in Commonwealth student mobility. Intra-Commonwealth flows have been heavily concentrated on a few countries as hosts (Australia, Britain, Canada and to a lesser extent India and New Zealand) and a few countries as senders (mainly four relatively wealthy countries from south-east Asia).

The Standing Committee never failed to emphasise the links between, and complementary nature of, student mobility and higher education development. This led it to explore alternative patterns and modes of student and knowledge mobility, and to focus on new possibilities of Commonwealth co-operation to promote the development of higher education in member countries. The Standing Committee adopted a consistently wide view of the linkages between different aspects of higher education co-operation and advocated the notion of a Commonwealth Higher Education Support Scheme to bring together the different elements of student and staff mobility and staff development awards programmes like CSFP, inter-university and inter-college links, and the nurturing of regional centres of excellence in Commonwealth developing countries. The committee's seven reports, and the papers commissioned by the Secretariat to support its work, are replete with useful analysis of these matters.

The committee's most substantial legacy consequently lies not so much in Commonwealth consensus on fees, which it failed to achieve, as in innovative programmes of higher education co-operation. It deserves its share of the credit for the development of the Commonwealth of Learning, the Commonwealth Higher Education Management Service, and the Commonwealth Universities Study Abroad Consortium. It gave impetus to the Secretariat's work on gender and higher education development, availability of journals, and supply and maintenance of equipment in higher education.

7 Building Education Infrastructure

In the four decades reviewed by this paper, the Commonwealth succeeded in creating a number of successful, and in some senses pioneering, institutions for educational co-operation. They include the Education Department of the Commonwealth Secretariat whose work was described in Section 5. The Secretariat's programme in education, and the two major institutions of Commonwealth official co-operation in education – CSFP and COL – are reviewed periodically by ministers at their conferences. A further group of higher-education co-operation programmes, initiated by the public agencies of the Commonwealth, are now largely sustained and managed by the Association of Commonwealth Universities. COL is the subject of a separate chapter and is also discussed in Chapters 3 and 4; it is only mentioned briefly here.

a. Commonwealth Scholarship and Fellowship Plan

The Commonwealth Scholarship and Fellowship Plan was established at the first Commonwealth Education Conference at Oxford in 1959 and quickly grew in reputation and prestige to become the 'flagship' of educational co-operation. It expanded quite rapidly until 1993, but has since suffered a period of serious decline in awards held, from a peak of 1800 awards then to only just over 1000 now. The reasons for the decline are to be found partly in less enthusiastic policies of particular countries (for example Australia) and partly in a reassessment by donors of priorities in the education sector, with much greater support for basic education. Growing differences in living standards between industrialised and developing countries has made traffic in persons more expensive than hitherto. Within the plan, the number of individuals receiving new awards has declined less than the total of award-holders on course at any one time, reflecting new policies by the principal donors, Britain and Canada, of making a higher proportion of short-term awards under CSFP.

CSFP operates through bilateral agreements within a common multilateral frame. Countries control the offer of awards to each other, but follow agreed principles, criteria and procedures. The guiding principles for the plan laid down at Oxford were that it should represent distinctiveness and additionality in relation to other award schemes; mutuality and the sharing of experience; a Commonwealth-wide character but be based on bilateral arrangements; and commitment to the highest standards of intellectual achievement. Flexibility in terms of diverse and changing needs was a further defining principle, and one that has been actualised by allowing countries lacking a tertiary education institution to request undergraduate places for their students, even though CSFP is essentially a programme for postgraduate awards.

Every member of the Commonwealth at Oxford pledged awards, but subsequently the Commonwealth perhaps 'missed a trick' by not making participation in the plan an unwritten condition of joining the association. In 1967 there were 14 awarding countries, but in the 1990s there have never been more than nine at any one time. Among developing countries, India and Brunei Darussalam have recently been the largest contributors. In 1999 Britain gave 685 out of 1021 awards and Canada gave 244. Virtually every one of the 60 or more Commonwealth countries and dependent territories has received awards. Awards to women have increased as a proportion of the total, now standing at 40%,

A constant concern of members has been the non take-up of some offers by developing countries. This would appear to have been due in some cases to unattractive terms and sometimes a lack of welfare and support for visiting scholars. Another continuing concern has been that scholars might not go back to their countries on completion of their studies. Preliminary data from an ACU survey of British award-holders shows that the vast majority do return home and many attain prominent positions in their own societies. Over the first 40 years of the plan there has been a subject shift among scholars going to the UK away from arts and science and towards social and business studies.

Among new possibilities now being considered are more short-term awards and the possibility that awards might be available for studies in a distance mode. There is also an observable tendency for assistance agencies to put more emphasis on the 'training for development' dimension of CSFP, involving a progressive – and to some, controversial – prioritisation of the instrumental purposes of CSFP over its academic-interchange aims.

b. Higher Education Co-operation: CHESS, CHEMS and CUSAC

The Commonwealth Higher Education Support Scheme was formally launched by ministers of education in Barbados in 1990, having been first conceived in the Standing Committee on Student Mobility and Higher Education Co-operation. The committee was aware of many different programmes and efforts through CSFP, CFTC and bilateral agencies and thought that more impact might be made through planned collective effort. An expert group chaired by Professor James Downey of Canada met before and after the Barbados conference to hammer out the details. Essentially CHESS was intended to be a framework for activity in which bilateral and multilateral agencies, national governments and higher education institutions, could all participate, mobilising wider co-operative effort for higher education development programmes than single agencies could generate independently. In practice, CHESS has always had to be more of an ideal than a reality because governments decided not to create any central higher education support fund, nor any administrative body separate from the Higher Education Unit in the Education Programme of the Secretariat, to activate the Scheme. In the event, many of the activities under a 'CHESS' label have been managed by the ACU.

Three priorities were chosen for CHESS: books and materials; higher education management; and staff development. The main thrust of the work undertaken on books and materials in the period 1991 to 1994 was a series of reports and meetings aimed at making academic journals more accessible to developing countries, trying to give developing-country higher education institutions the benefit of the marginal costs of larger print runs. Unfortunately, resource constraints at the Secretariat prevented progress with some of the promising possibilities explored. Useful work was undertaken in staff development, much of it in conjunction with ACU and UNESCO, focused particularly on staff development for women in higher education which was part of wider concern in the Commonwealth with advancing the role and status of women (see Chapter 3).

Management was accorded perhaps the highest priority of all, and protracted staff-work and negotiations with the CFTC eventually brought about agreement to establish the Commonwealth Higher Education Management Service (CHEMS) in 1994 with funding support from the Commonwealth Fund, and facilities made available by the Association of Commonwealth Universities where the service was based. It was directed by John Fielden for the six years of its operations, but has now been subsumed under other ACU programmes. CHEMS has delivered consultancy services to several countries and has published a wide range of guidelines and briefing notes, as well as more substantial publications on education management. A major obstacle was the requirement that as far as possible it 'breaks even' financially. This compelled it to offer its services more to reliable payers, and less to needy developing countries and institutions, than had been intended by the original advocates of the service.

Another new programme developed at the same time as CHEMS, and also seen as a component of CHESS was the Commonwealth Universities' Study Abroad Consortium, launched in 1993. Like CHEMS, this was developed within the ambit of Secretariat work on higher education, in which the Association of Commonwealth Universities participated: it was later (1999) taken over and managed by ACU, which also provides some financial support. It is an international consortium of Commonwealth universities which, within the framework of a common agreement, exchanges students and staff for short stays, agreeing to give credit for study abroad and wherever possible waiving fees. There are now about 70 participating universities, and 200 students were involved in the programmes in the year 2000. The emphasis is on low cost (insofar as fees are waived), an agreed framework of quality control and the benefits to students and staff from spending a period abroad. An executive committee is drawn from member universities.

c. Commonwealth of Learning

The Commonwealth of Learning, based in Vancouver, was the first intergovernmental organisation devoted to distance education. It is unique in Commonwealth terms as the only major Commonwealth agency to have its headquarters away from London. It is an agency responsible to governments but run by a board of governors, which gives it a certain independence and continuity. It has a small staff headed by a president (chief executive). COL reports to education ministers at CCEMs and to Heads of Government at their biennial meetings.

The original report in 1987 of an expert group chaired by Lord Briggs envisaged that COL might have many of the functions of a university institution, including the ability to validate degree programmes offered by other institutions and perhaps even to offer its own degree courses. But Commonwealth governments working through a committee chaired by (now Sir) John Daniel, which met in the first half of 1988, later decided to depart from this model and to create COL as an agency for co-operation in distance education. The Memorandum of Understanding to establish COL was approved on 1 September 1988 and the institution began work by the end of that year. Following the required evaluation and review in 1993, certain changes were made to streamline the constitution.

The budget is funded by voluntary contributions from governments. Canada initially pledged £6m, and there were additional promises of £3m from Brunei Darussalam, £1.5m from Nigeria and £1m from India. Britain originally insisted on making its contribution mainly in kind by offering services at the International Centre for Distance Learning of the Open University, but later agreed to give more flexible financial support and has become, after the governments of Canada and British Columbia, the host province, the largest contributor. India is the next largest contributor and altogether 19 developing countries provided funding in 2000. Currently the organisation has a budget of $C6m. (about £2.8m) per annum, of which $4.4m is in contributions from member governments. Three quarters of the expenditure is on projects.

In its promotion of distance education, and distance education co-operation, in Commonwealth member countries, the ten substantive areas in which COL works are:

- creating and developing institutional capacity

- programmes in distance education

- information and consultancy

- staff training and management

- communication links

- evaluation and applied research

- access to teaching materials
- adapting and developing teaching materials
- recognition of academic credit
- support services to students.

In pursuing these tasks, COL has to date delivered more than 600 projects valued at $C45 million, and has trained 1200 individuals and employed 400 short-term consultants from 39 countries. Most of its work is through working with and energising the capacities of its partners

8 Bilateral and Non-governmental Co-operation

This survey has focused on intergovernmental Commonwealth relationships in education. These were what were inaugurated at Oxford and they form the part of Commonwealth education co-operation that is best articulated and recorded, and so most amenable to a synoptic view. But the official programmes bearing a 'Commonwealth' label account for only a small part of the totality of Commonwealth educational interchange. Official bilateral co-operation between individual member countries of the Commonwealth far exceeds in scale anything that is done through Commonwealth channels. Moreover, there is an extensive range of voluntary, professional and private commercial activities and linkages, including spontaneous and unplanned movement of individual students and teachers. Regional co-operation amongst Commonwealth countries constitutes a further element worthy of note.

a. Bilateral Co-operation in Education

A significant tranche of Commonwealth educational co-operation takes the form of bilateral flows within a multilateral framework. This has always been the status of Commonwealth Scholarships and Fellowships under the CSFP. Much British assistance for Commonwealth education in the early days followed a similar pattern. Thus the Commonwealth bursaries for teacher education were conceived within the framework of the CECs and progress was regularly reported to ministers even though their administration was solely in the hands of Britain and her partners. Britain's Aid to Commonwealth English (ACE) programme and her Aid to Commonwealth Technology and Science (ACTS) were of the same kind.

About £4–5 million annually is spent on multilaterally-administered Commonwealth education co-operation, half through the Commonwealth Secretariat in London (where a large part of the expenditure consists of staff posts at headquarters) and half through the Commonwealth of Learning in Vancouver. This is only a fraction of what some individual donor countries spend bilaterally each year in support of education in Commonwealth developing countries. One might calculate, for example, that Britain's budgetary share of Commonwealth multilateral co-operation in education is about £1.5 million; its annual contribution to the CSFP is eight or nine times as great at around £13 million; but it probably spends in the region of £100 million per year in support of education in Commonwealth developing countries under the bilateral programme. Indeed, annual spending on some of the huge individual basic education projects assisted by the UK Department for International Development (DfID) in India or Commonwealth Africa dwarfs the total annual budgets for all multilateral Commonwealth education co-operation put together.

Other Commonwealth 'industrialised' countries, such as Australia, Canada and New Zealand, are also active in bilateral co-operation with developing Commonwealth countries, Canada having especially close links with the Caribbean and certain African countries, while Australia and New Zealand pay particular, but not exclusive, attention to south-east and south Asia and to the Pacific. The list does not by any means end there. Ghana, India, Nigeria, Malaysia, Pakistan and South Africa have all had their own programmes for technical co-operation, involving provision of teachers or of study and training awards.

b. Private and Voluntary Resource Flows for Education

Government-orchestrated exchange in education is complemented by a significant amount of interchange through private and voluntary channels. This includes:

- Commercial for-profit activity by suppliers of educational goods and services to other countries. This may take the form of supplying education-related goods such as laboratory equipment and workshop machinery, computers for classroom and school-office use, or of publishing and selling books and materials for use in the classroom. It can include the supply of services like consultancy, examinations and qualifications, recruitment of teachers, or provision of study and training opportunities. In recent times many universities and colleges in the more developed countries of the Commonwealth have become hardly distinguishable from private profit-making companies, at least in terms of the commercial motivations and behaviour driving their revenue-earning overseas operations.

- Activities of numerous voluntary and religious non-profit NGOs which sponsor schools and education programmes abroad, supplying teachers, giving scholarships, and operating co-operation and exchange schemes. They include churches, missionary societies and religious charities; philanthropic foundations like the Nuffield Foundation and Leverhulme Trust; bodies like Oxfam, Action Aid, Save the Children; or professional organisations.

- Mobility through privately made arrangements, involving international service abroad as teachers or study abroad for education and training. Intra-Commonwealth student mobility at the higher education level was estimated at around 100,000 in 1995/96, since when it has undoubtedly grown.

- Linkage and exchange agencies operating programmes to support and facilitate twinning of education authorities and schools; or (as for example the League for the Exchange of Commonwealth Teachers), to support interchange of teachers and other educators.

- Professional and other associations/organisations which link education institutions and individual education professionals across the Commonwealth. They include the Association of Commonwealth Universities, the Commonwealth Association of Polytechnics in Africa (CAPA), the Commonwealth Institute, the Commonwealth Council for Educational Administration and Management (CCEAM), the Commonwealth Association of Science, Technology and Mathematics Educators (CASTME), and the Commonwealth Association for the Education and Training of Adults (CAETA). The most prominent of these is the ACU with its mainstream programmes of scholar exchange, recruitment services and information networking. Membership stands at over 460 universities, almost four times as many as the 121 members at the time of the first Commonwealth Education Conference.

- Finally, there is the phenomenon of distance learning, through print and correspondence, audio and video links, and more recently through on-line computer-based programmes. Increasingly in future co-operation may take the form of mobility of knowledge and virtual education programmes, teacher and teacher, learner and learner, learner and teacher across the Commonwealth's great physical distances.

c. Co-operation among Commonwealth Countries at Regional Level

To complete the picture, there is extensive multilateral co-operation involving Commonwealth countries at the regional level. In the Caribbean and South Pacific there are regional universities, the University of the West Indies and University of the South Pacific, subscribed to in each case by several Commonwealth governments. Regional examination bodies, most notably the Caribbean Examinations Council and the West African Examinations Council, have long records of service to member countries. Regional groupings of countries, in the Caribbean (Caricom), south Asia (South Asian Association for Regional Co-operation), South Pacific and Southern Africa, bring together Commonwealth members in various kinds of co-operative endeavour, including education programmes. These regional institutions also include a small minority of non-Commonwealth members. Although economies of scale and geographical contiguity are a major part of their raison d'être, the shared language and common institutional heritage derived from a colonial past and Commonwealth membership are important underpinnings of effective activity.

In aggregate, these different facets of Commonwealth interaction through education constitute an impressive array of co-operative endeavours. They build on a heritage of shared language in English, similar structures and practices in educational organisation, and many shared understandings about appropriate professional roles for administrators, inspectors, heads and teachers, or about the relative autonomy to be enjoyed by higher education institutions. They provide a strong foundation for co-operation and exchange and for the fruitful sharing of experience.

9 Assessing the Impact of Official Co-operation

What conclusions might one draw about the overall effect of the official programmes of Commonwealth educational co-operation described in this chapter, and about the extent to which they have had a beneficial impact on education in member countries?

Any assessment has to take account of the broad context of international activity and resource flows. External influences and resources are small in relation to the complete range of influences and expenditures on education by Commonwealth member countries. Moreover, the Commonwealth's own contribution, within the total international flow of resources for development, is tiny. The combined budgets of Commonwealth official institutions, for all sectors and purposes, amount to the equivalent of about $50 million p.a., compared with annual World Bank resource commitments 100 times as large, and a British government aid budget 80 times as big. The United Kingdom is the largest aid donor among the 54 Commonwealth countries but only channels 1% of its multilateral contributions to and through Commonwealth institutions. For these reasons, the separate and specific impacts of Commonwealth initiatives are likely to be difficult to disentangle from other influences, and are likely to be small in relation to the problems targeted.

In this regard, one should distinguish between influence and resources. As explained above, the Commonwealth has not been a major channel for resource flows compared with other agencies. The only real exceptions to this are the Commonwealth Scholarship and Fellowship Plan and, while it lasted, the Commonwealth Bursaries Scheme. Each of these activities, it should be noted, was bilaterally funded within a multilateral Commonwealth framework. Both programmes were conceived at a time when staffing deficits in newly independent Commonwealth countries were a real constraint on development. The opportunities provided by CSFP for advanced study, particularly in the period when modern university development was in its initial stages in Africa and other developing areas, and when postgraduate study provision was limited, were exceedingly valuable and a significant proportion of senior staff in the new universities of former British colonies was able to benefit. As university systems have developed and grown, the relative significance of CSFP in quantitative terms has naturally diminished, though it remains as one of the larger scholarship programmes benefiting the developing world. In the same way the education bursaries were, while they lasted, of real significance in building up the cadres of education professionals, particularly in teacher education but also in curriculum development and management and administration of Commonwealth developing countries at a critical period. Any survey of senior professional staff in the education systems of Commonwealth Africa, the Caribbean, Malaysia and the South Pacific would show that large numbers of them acquired professional qualifications and experience through the Bursaries Scheme.

In the 1990s, the Commonwealth of Learning has occupied a 'niche' position as a source of technical assistance and advice in distance education. Its resources are not substantial, but COL is visible, specialised and today relatively well-known. In its own field it has had considerable impact in helping countries to take the early steps in familiarising themselves with, and exploiting, the potential of distance education.

In much of the rest of its work, the Commonwealth's influence on educational development has been less in terms of resources than in providing a forum for creating awareness about international issues and in giving leadership in developing new thinking. This is indeed the proper role for any secretariat which is potentially well-endowed with professional expertise but short of programme funds.

At the policy-making level of ministers and ministries of education, the Commonwealth contribution has probably been most important in making developing countries aware of common problems and shared interests, and in helping them to articulate their views on international issues in education. In that regard, the work of specialist groups on student mobility and higher education co-operation, on distance education and human resource development were especially useful. The Secretariat analyses on major conference themes like education financing and resource use, vocational orientation of education, quality of education and the changing role of the state in education were highly regarded by policy-makers, as have been the syntheses of country experiences.

In a number of areas of professional work, Commonwealth activity has been influential. In the 1970s and early 1980s well-valued resource books were produced on, for example, low-cost publishing, teachers' centres, in-service teacher education, community libraries and non-formal education. Unfortunately, the impact of some of these was limited because of the ineptitude of the Secretariat in marketing its publications. A later series of publications on community contributions to education and shift schooling, and particularly the resource materials on teacher management and support and headteacher training, were far better disseminated. In some cases this resulted from the use of commercial publishers and in others from a partnership with international bodies like UNESCO who co-published with the Secretariat.

Generally the Secretariat's work over much of its existence has suffered from the disease, which also besets much of UNESCO activity, of 'tokenism'. A topic becomes fashionable in international dialogue and an agency is open to criticism if it fails to include a mention in its programme. A small activity such as a consultative meeting or a commissioned study is then included in the programme but without sufficient resources for proper impact, dissemination or follow-up. There is no discernible trace of the activity five years later. This fate befell many Commonwealth initiatives.

Where the Secretariat has achieved critical mass of resources, selecting a key theme and creating a more substantial sub-programme of activities around it, there has been considerably more impact and the Commonwealth has become a leader in the field. At the end of the 1980s, in response to resource shortage, a conscious effort was made to cluster activity around fewer main themes with generally beneficial results. This same resource shortage had the effect of driving the Secretariat to seek co-funding partners for its work and this had the paradoxical effect of making Secretariat work known more widely.

It is possible to give a few examples of Commonwealth Secretariat work in education which benefited from concentration of resources and/or partnership with others, consequently achieving deeper impact. The work of the Standing Committee over more than a decade in addressing both Commonwealth student mobility and capacity-building in Commonwealth universities and the follow-up work leading to the creation of CUSAC, was one; and the work on distance education, leading to the creation of COL was another. Others included higher education co-operation activity involving collaboration with the ACU and UNESCO on staff development for women; the extensive series of activities on education development in small states of the Commonwealth; and the substantial work, mainly in Commonwealth Africa, on teacher management and support. The pioneering work of the Commonwealth on these last two themes, where the Secretariat had an international leadership role for many years, has been taken up by other agencies like UNESCO's International Institute for Educational Planning (IIEP), which have since made them major planks in their own programmes.

10 Challenge and Constraint

After attempting to assess impact, it is logical to move on to an analysis of strengths and weaknesses of Commonwealth co-operation in education, and the opportunities and threats it now faces. The analysis will be tackled mainly in terms of official pan-Commonwealth programmes.

a. Strengths

From many points of view, Commonwealth education co-operation gives the appearance of being in good health. Commonwealth Heads of Government regularly affirm their commitment to education and its importance to the Commonwealth. Education ministers' conferences are well attended and produce a warm glow of approval for the principle of education collaboration among Commonwealth countries, enunciated more formally through the Halifax Statement on Education in the Commonwealth, *Education for our Common Future*, in November 2000.

There is an array of institutions and programmes bearing a Commonwealth education label, both intergovernmental and non-governmental. The creation of the Commonwealth of Learning just 12 years ago, followed by CHEMS and CUSAC, represents further development of the co-operation infrastructure. New initiatives are being taken in the area of school networking via electronic links. A Commission on Commonwealth Studies reported three years ago. The number of students moving between Commonwealth countries appears to be at record levels.

The Commonwealth has significant comparative advantage in educational co-operation. Common possession of English as the major world language and a heritage of shared institutions make the interchange of experience and personnel both fruitful and relatively easy. Many of the Commonwealth's institutions like the Commonwealth Scholarship and Fellowship Plan, the Commonwealth of Learning, the Commonwealth Fund for Technical Co-operation and the Association of Commonwealth Universities are envied in other parts of the world and provide a platform for building future developments. There is also a strong Commonwealth infrastructure for educational collaboration at regional level, in the shape of shared university institutions and examination bodies in Africa, the Caribbean and the South Pacific.

The comparative intimacy and friendly informality of ministerial conferences, with round-table dialogues and working groups, may have been diluted somewhat by the growth of Commonwealth membership, but still stand in sharp and welcome contrast to the rostrum-cum-assembly-hall model that has to prevail in larger international gatherings. Over the years, the Secretariat has developed procedures for backing debate with good documentation and for ensuring that discussion is purposeful and productive.

The fact that Commonwealth membership spans the industrialised–developing country divide, yet contains a great majority of developing-country members, makes its deliberations both relevant to developing countries and reflective of their concerns on co-operation issues. It is natural that the Commonwealth should have focused so much of its activity on South–South co-operation, third country training, capacity-building and regional and sub-regional dialogue. Smaller countries, too, can feel confident that their particular problems and constraints are in the minds of discussants. All of this gives a greater sense of ownership to developing countries. And while nearly all members enjoy good relations with the United States, many find it refreshing to meet in a truly international forum where the business is not built around, or unduly influenced by, American agendas and interests.

The official multilateral Commonwealth picture is reinforced by strong traditions of co-operation through bilateral relationships and by the activities of NGOs. The United Kingdom, particularly, has sharply increased bilateral educational assistance, mainly at basic education level, to individual Commonwealth recipients like India, Kenya, Uganda, Zambia and South Africa, and has recently announced its intention to establish a fund which will ensure access to basic education for every child in the Commonwealth. Canada and Australia are also important sources of assistance. Of particular significance for the future are the smaller but growing assistance programmes of countries like India, Malaysia, Nigeria and South Africa, which are simultaneously recipients and donors. Non-government agencies like Oxfam have also become much more heavily involved with education in recent years. There are active pan-Commonwealth NGOs in the education sector which provide professional networks with a potential to serve as partners with official agencies in international co-operation. In both Gaborone and Halifax the ministers' conference deliberations have been enhanced by dialogue with other parts of civil society through 'parallel events' in the form of a symposium and trade fair.

b. Weaknesses

Commonwealth educational co-operation clearly has much going for it, but at the same time operates considerably below need and potential. Need is everywhere apparent, and in the years immediately following the EFA Conference in Dakar, Commonwealth members are chastened by the realisation that Commonwealth Africa and south Asia contain a large proportion of the world's out-of-school children. Response must mainly be the responsibility of national governments; beyond the reference in the Halifax Statement there is little sign that the Commonwealth collectively sees the situation as a spur to common action.

In terms of potential, the Commonwealth has a formidable educational infrastructure, but one that is starved of resources. As we have seen, the Commonwealth Scholarship and Fellowship Plan had only seven donors among 54 Commonwealth member countries in 1999, and the number of awards, which stood at over 1800 in 1993, has declined to a little over 1000 today – a far cry from the 2000 awards that Chief Anyaoku set in 1993 as the target for the millennium. The Commonwealth of Learning, which has pioneered Commonwealth co-operation in distance education, has been forced to work with a budget considerably smaller than in the years immediately after its foundation. The Commonwealth Fund for Technical Co-operation and Commonwealth Foundation both operate well below capacity and the same is true of the Commonwealth Secretariat's education team, where experienced professional staff lack the resources to implement the good ideas and intentions of member countries. Failure to use existing proven capacity is in some ways more tragic than failure to build new capacity.

The separation within the Commonwealth of responsibility for strategic and policy work undertaken by the Education Department, and the allocation of assistance resources to education by CFTC, represents another awkwardness in current arrangements. Education ministers are not asked to advise CFTC on use of its resources to support the education sector, nor do they receive a report on past use for education of CFTC funds.

The very structure of the Commonwealth is part of the problem, containing as it does only a small proportion of industrialised countries and few sizeable middle-income ones. As a result, the 'ABC' countries (Australia, Britain, Canada) are asked to carry a high proportion of the burden of Commonwealth educational and other co-operation. Britain and Canada, just two out of 54 Commonwealth members, provide 90% of the CSFP awards, 60% of the funding of CFTC and two-thirds of the resources available to COL. In such circumstances it is tempting to argue for 'no representation without taxation', particularly in relation to CSFP with its seven donors in the latest year; and perhaps even in the case of COL, despite its success in attracting 23 donors in 2000.

Present Commonwealth structures do not assist continuity and leadership in the field of education. Because of domestic political processes, only a few Commonwealth ministers of education survive from one triennial conference to the next: those that do – like K.P. Morake of Botswana, Ranil Wickremesinghe of Sri Lanka, Dzingai Mutumbuka of Zimbabwe, Nahas Angula of Namibia, Burchell Whiteman of Jamaica or John Horne of St Vincent – can bring previous experience to the ongoing debate but they are too few in number to provide the necessary continuity and to develop a collective will. So each CCEM is as much a learning process for the inexperienced as an occasion for the exercise of leadership and the formulation of policy and new initiatives.

Civil servants and professionals have a longer 'life' than their ministers, but existing Commonwealth structures may largely marginalise them, given that their ministers are properly the spokespersons for their countries in the triennial Conferences. The Board of Governors of the Commonwealth of Learning is a useful model, blending ministerial, public service and academic representation and thus giving responsibility and providing continuity. The Secretariat's two valuable mechanisms for applying commitment and expertise on a continuing basis to educational co-operation have both been 'de-commissioned'. One was the Commonwealth Education Liaison Committee in its heyday in the 1960s: the other was the Standing Committee on Student Mobility. It can be argued that the most creative periods of Commonwealth education activity coincided with active work of these bodies. The experience suggests that for Commonwealth co-operation to flourish it requires its 'champions'; and thought needs to be given to the kinds of structures which will provide roles and opportunities for such people to make a creative contribution. What seems to be needed is a new 'education think tank' of distinguished sympathetic educators from around the Commonwealth, constituting a semi-permanent senior group to assist ministers and the Secretariat in education and advise on the direction of Commonwealth activity in education between the ministerial conferences.

This is all the more desirable in that in recent decades the highest echelons of the Secretariat have been staffed by diplomatic-service officials. Nurturing the professional and cultural foundations on which the strengths of the Commonwealth rest may not be their 'forte'. This is a very different situation from that in the 1960s and 1970s when education had its own representative in the highest councils of the Secretariat. Given that politics and economics understandably dominate in CHOGMs, it becomes all the more important to ensure that education co-operation does not languish by default.

A closely related issue is the difficulty of orchestrating constructive professional dialogue at senior level on a Commonwealth-wide basis. The former structures with their pre-conference meetings of civil servants and professionals, and the specialist conferences in between the CECs, provided more occasions for senior professionals to interact than exist now. University vice-chancellors meet under the auspices of ACU, but there are fewer opportunities for other university staff, for members of the school-teaching profession, and local and central government education administrators, other than in regional and sub-regional workshops. A few Commonwealth NGOs exist in education, but they mostly have restricted reach and lack the resources to develop effective programmes; the paltry sums (in relation to need) made available to the Commonwealth Foundation preclude it from assisting such NGOs on any substantial scale. There has been no Commonwealth association mobilising the largest group of professionals, the teachers. In this respect education is in a weak position compared with professions like law and medicine which have more private and independent practitioners, and many more 'well-heeled' members able to pay their own way when necessary.

c. Threats

The biggest threat to co-operation in education is lack of interest in the Commonwealth and in educational co-operation. In part this results from historical processes of closer regional integration in Europe, in Asia and the Pacific and in Africa, diverting attention and interest from the kind of association that the Commonwealth represents. The low level of representation of some industrialised countries at CCEMs may reflect a sense that their peers in education are other OECD countries, rather than their Commonwealth partners. In part, lack of interest reflects a failure to engage young people with the Commonwealth and its values, a neglect of Commonwealth studies and of teaching and learning about the Commonwealth in schools. Some have observed that CHOGMs give less attention than global political fora like the G8, UN Assembly or World Bank/IMF to education issues. It seems anomalous that education should be near the top of national agendas and yet apparently so low in the list of the Commonwealth's collective priorities.

This anomaly was apparent in the recent high-level review of the Commonwealth undertaken by Heads of Government which failed to accord education a place as one of the priorities for the coming period. In the Halifax conference communiqué it was affirmed that 'Ministers intend to make a formal representation to the High-Level Review Group and in so doing emphasise that the promotion of Commonwealth education co-operation should remain a key and discrete function of the Commonwealth Secretariat'. This case, that education is at the heart of Commonwealth concerns and of crucial importance to Commonwealth survival, will need to be made strongly by the wider education community in member countries, by youth and business leaders. The erosion of so many institutions concerned with education co-operation, and with education about the Commonwealth, shows how real is the danger.

It is clear that Commonwealth co-operative institutions cannot survive on the basis that they will be funded voluntarily by a handful of wealthier countries. Developing countries must carry a greater share of responsibility for the budgets of Commonwealth programmes and must do their bit in the CSFP. It is a case of 'casting one's bread upon the waters'. The effect of substantial developing-country donations to a cause found to be important was shown in Vancouver in 1987, when the readiness of Brunei Darussalam, India and Nigeria to promise substantial financial support to the establishment of COL gave a significant boost to Canadian and other efforts to get that organisation off the ground.

Ministers and others need to confront and debate the issue of whether Commonwealth co-operation in education is essentially a form of development aid or is based on interchange between equals and the concept of sharing. Current financial structures make far more resources available for direct assistance to individual member countries and not enough for consultation, analysis and the development of common positions through working groups and studies as the basis for action. Lying behind this is an uncertainty as to whether the Secretariat exists mainly to facilitate bilateral exchange between its members, or to promote collective Commonwealth action and institutions.

The same tension exists between those who distrust secretariats as inefficient bureaucracies intent on keeping themselves in business, and those who see secretariats as necessary instruments for balancing the interests of different parties on any issue and for promoting common endeavour. There is certainly a danger that staffing of the Education Department in the Secretariat will fall below the critical mass of six to ten professionals that are necessary to service the mandates handed down by ministers. The cry for greater efficiency and effectiveness is in danger of going too far, with creative professionals hamstrung for lack of funds and expected to spend too much time in meeting reporting and evaluation demands and in seeking to raise money from non-Commonwealth partners that ought to be provided by Commonwealth governments.

The commercialisation of education and of other public services represents both a threat and an opportunity. The recent CEC/UKCOSA report on Commonwealth student mobility shows how, on the one hand, commercial incentives have been important in expanding mobility, but that they have, on the other, also given rise to growing inequality. In the important area of information technology, too, there will be a need to safeguard the common public interest in the face of commercially-driven developments. On such issues, Commonwealth institutions are well-placed to orchestrate consultation and identification of acceptable common ground.

d. Opportunities

The opportunities for the Commonwealth in educational co-operation stem from its comparative advantages of shared language and institutional forms and its potentially strong institutional framework for advancing its common interests. Its inclusiveness in terms of countries of different sizes, cultures and levels of income mean that it is well placed to exploit the dynamics of diversity. In seeking to advance and protect the public interest of a wide international community, these are valuable assets.

The Commonwealth has special experience in regional co-operation in education, bringing about economies of scale and a sharing of costs and benefits. This has been most apparent in regional universities and examination arrangements and in the shared consultations on regional education issues. This experience should be analysed and more widely shared with a view to exploring its applicability elsewhere. It has a particular value in the context of small states, of which the Commonwealth has an abundance, making it especially well placed to explore the particular challenges that small-country education systems face. But successful experiences of regional co-operation have lessons for relationships among larger states too. Exchange of experiences between large multi-jurisdictional member countries about interrelating and co-ordinating the work of different authorities would be valuable as well.

The possibilities of further developing co-operation in the application of distance education and new communication technologies are immense, and a field where the Commonwealth has special strengths, both at national level and in the Commonwealth of Learning. The new information and communication technology are prominent among the areas where the Halifax themes of 'expanding access' and ensuring 'opportunities for diversity' need urgently to be put into practice.

The obverse of the coin of commercialism in education is that private sector companies involved in manufacturing and publishing, providing services to public education, or running parallel independent systems of non-government schools, have expertise and resources to share with public systems. Commonwealth countries have much experience of private sector involvement in education and the Commonwealth would be well placed to develop protocols and guidelines on beneficial partnerships between public and private sectors, and to generate case studies of best practice.

Focused attention needs to be given to achieving greater synergy within the Secretariat between the professionals in education and the resources of CFTC; between London-based institutions and the Commonwealth of Learning in Vancouver; between Commonwealth multilateral institutions and bilateral assistance; and between the world of official activity and the private sector on the one hand, and professional associations and NGOs on the other. Some have suggested that there might be a useful role for a Commonwealth Education Council or Forum, in some sense analogous to the Commonwealth Business Council.

What is clear is that there is great latent energy and potential among the various public and civil-society agencies engaged in promoting Commonwealth co-operation in education. As the fifth decade of such co-operation rolls in, an attempt to chart a new course seems timely and the Halifax Conference and Statement constitute a useful starting point since the high-level review proved to be unable, in the time available to it, to map out roles and productive relationships between the different agencies and programmes in the education sector, ministers of education might themselves usefully take the initiative in doing so.

Part Two
Themes and Concerns

Chapter 2

Education for All in the Commonwealth: What are the Issues?

John Daniel

1 Preliminary

This chapter is based on a lecture given at the Palace of Westminster, London on 14 March 2002, under the auspices of the Council for Education in the Commonwealth and the UK National Commission for UNESCO. It is included here because it moves forward from the past achievements and challenges surveyed in Chapter 1 to suggest what will be the main education issues to be confronted by the Commonwealth in the next decades.

I was pleased to be invited to pose these ideas (in the Mother of Parliaments) by the Council for Education in the Commonwealth. I particularly admire the way that the Council involves parliamentarians in its membership and activities. At UNESCO, as we try to increase the momentum of the movement towards education for all, we are discovering how important the support of parliamentarians can be. Parliamentarians have one foot in government and the other in civil society. One of our key principles in the campaign for education for all is the involvement of civil society. Sadly, there are still countries where the notion of civil society is still regarded with suspicion. However, those countries often have the beginnings of functioning parliaments and the parliamentarians are eager to get involved in issues outside the legislature like education.

To give a concrete example, the MINEDAF VIII meeting of the ministers of education of Africa held in Mauritius in December 2002 also saw the launch of the Forum of African Parliamentarians for Education. Groups of parliamentarians from each sub-region of Africa met for a planning meeting in Dakar, Senegal in January and showed tremendous enthusiasm for this development. Such initiatives help to strengthen democracy by involving parliamentarians in real issues and also promote the advancement of education by multiplying the number of informed supporters.

This was the first time that I addressed a Commonwealth body since joining UNESCO in 2001. However, I felt that I was among friends. I am a citizen of two Commonwealth countries, Canada and the UK, and am proud to have played a small role in the creation of the Commonwealth of Learning. The decision to establish COL was taken at the Vancouver Commonwealth Heads of Government Meeting in Vancouver in 1987. Subsequent to that meeting I was asked to chair the planning committee for COL and was later briefly a member of the COL board until I moved to the UK in 1990. Over the years I had many contacts with the Education Department of the Commonwealth Secretariat and was delighted that people who had contributed to the important work of that department were present when I gave my original lecture, from which this chapter derives.

2 The Commonwealth and the Drive towards Education for All

At the Dakar Forum held two years ago, UNESCO was charged with co-ordinating the complex process of ensuring progress towards Education for All. That responsibility is at the heart of my duties as UNESCO's Assistant Director-General for Education. The CEC's invitation made me ask myself what is special or different about the Commonwealth in the drive towards education for all. Are the 54 member states of the Commonwealth simply a typical subset of UNESCO's 186 member states or does the Commonwealth have a special profile as far as EFA is concerned?

My remarks will examine this question and will be in four unequal parts. First, I shall look at the Commonwealth and compare it to the wider community of nations in terms of key indicators. Second, I shall turn to the educational indicators. Are the countries of the Commonwealth doing better or worse than the others in progressing toward education for all? Third, I shall recall the goals of the campaign to deliver Education for All and comment briefly on the strategy for achieving them. Does the Commonwealth have a comparative advantage in this vital endeavour? Finally, I shall look in a general way at the goals of education. Should the current geopolitical climate, notably the preoccupation with terrorism, lead us to change our priorities for education and, if so, how?

3 The Commonwealth within the World Community of Nations

I start with a few words on the Commonwealth in the context of the global community of nations. The 1.7 billion people of the Commonwealth represent 30% of the world's population. The 54 states of the Commonwealth make up a similar proportion of the nations of the world. Some readers will be more expert on the Commonwealth than I am, but it seems to me that the states of the Commonwealth are, in most ways, a pretty representative sample of the membership of the UN. The Commonwealth has rich states and poor states. It has states with very large landmasses and others that are tiny islands. These islands have very small populations, yet at the other end of the scale several Commonwealth members have very large populations.

The ministers of education of the nine most populous developing countries meet regularly under the auspices of UNESCO, calling themselves the E9. Four of those states are in the Commonwealth: Bangladesh, India, Nigeria and Pakistan. (The others are Brazil, China, Egypt, Indonesia and Mexico.) The E9 is an example of various groups that meet under the auspices of UNESCO. Other examples are the regional meetings of education ministers, such as the grouping of African ministers, MINEDAF, that I already mentioned.

Less visible to me are the more informal groupings of nations that are convened in Paris by the countries' permanent delegates to UNESCO. I am thinking of regional groupings, such as the EU group, but also subsets of countries such as the group of 77. I understand that there is a Commonwealth group as well. These groups are not very visible to the staff of UNESCO because we tend to deal with states either individually or regionally – this is as it should be.

However, my final general point is that working within UNESCO makes one realise the considerable assets of the Commonwealth group of nations when you compare the Commonwealth to the community of nations as a whole. I refer to the statement on the Commonwealth website which reads:

> *With a common working language and similar systems of law, public administration and education, the Commonwealth has built on its shared history to become a vibrant and growing association of states in tune with the modern world.*

As I sit in UNESCO meetings with simultaneous translation going on in six languages I realise what an advantage it is to have a common working language. As I work with my UNESCO staff colleagues, and observe the variety of cultural assumptions we bring to the functioning of the organisation, I understand how much easier discussions are if you have similar systems of law, public administration and education.

4 Education: The Commonwealth and the Rest Compared

An interesting question, which brings me to the second part of these remarks, is whether these shared features of the Commonwealth give its members a different profile of performance as regards education. Obviously, such comparisons are very tricky because of the great diversity within the Commonwealth. With that caveat, however, I make some observations.

First, let us look at the old Commonwealth – Australia, Canada, New Zealand and the UK; they are all placed well in the results of the Programme for International Student Assessment published last year by the OECD. The programme measured reading literacy, mathematical literacy and scientific literacy, and these Commonwealth countries ranked high on all three.

Second, as regards the newer states of the Commonwealth, my colleague Hilaire Mputu at UNESCO has made some comparisons among those states that are working to achieve Education for All within the framework set by the Dakar Forum nearly two years ago. He judges that most Commonwealth developing countries are in a better situation as regards EFA than their counterparts who are not Commonwealth members.

Net enrolment ratios in most Commonwealth developing countries are over 80% and many of these countries are either on the point of attaining – or have already attained – the goal of universal primary education (UPE in our jargon). This is important because research by the World Bank and others shows very clearly that getting most of the population to complete primary education of decent quality is the foundation for economic development. Until a country reaches that threshold, attempts at sustainable development will not succeed.

Let me put some figures to the comparisons between Commonwealth and non-Commonwealth in sub-Saharan Africa. As regards access to school, enrolment rates are higher in the Commonwealth group than in the rest of sub-Saharan Africa. From 1990 to 1998, the median net enrolment ratios rose from 78% to 87% in the region's Commonwealth countries. The rise in the remaining countries was from 51% to 56%.

Another very favourable indicator for the Commonwealth African group, which relates to my comment about the importance of completing primary education, is that Commonwealth countries show low levels of repetition compared to the others, which have high levels of repetition. This means that the Commonwealth group has higher internal efficiency in education, by which I mean low drop-out and low wastage, compared to the rest of sub-Saharan Africa. I would be interested to have others' explanations as to why both old and new Commonwealth countries per-form well on educational indicators compared to non-Commonwealth countries. After all, Britain itself – or at least England – was rather a laggard in bringing a decent education to all citizens.

However, the Commonwealth picture is not all rosy. It will not surprise you that most of the low-achieving Commonwealth countries are in sub-Saharan Africa. We are particularly concerned that some of these countries, such as Cameroon, Gambia, Lesotho, Mozambique, Sierra Leone and Tanzania, risk not attaining the EFA goals for 2015. I shall come to those goals later in this chapter. We also worry that some countries, which have made significant progress in the past, now show signs of faltering or even slipping back. I refer to Cameroon, Ghana, India, Kenya, Kiribati, Pakistan, Papua New Guinea and Zambia. However, the good news is that other countries, such as Malawi and Uganda, have achieved dramatic progress in expanding enrolment and reducing gender disparity.

But there are no grounds for complacency. One of our problems is that collect-ing reliable data takes time. We can only compare countries on the basis of data for enrolments and repetition rates that are several years old. Yet we know that recent events, such as the continuing spread of the AIDS pandemic and the multiplication of conflicts, are likely to have moved the figures for some countries in the wrong direction.

5 Education for All: Where are We?

This brings me to the third section of this exploration of the issues we must address in achieving EFA in the Commonwealth. Let me now draw back and look at EFA in the world as a whole.

The simplest way of expressing the bad news is through the raw absolute numbers. Today there are over 100 million children, 60% of them girls, who never go to school at all. At least an equivalent number do start school but drop out – or are taken out for economic reasons – before they have learned anything useful. The unschooled children of previous generations are today's adult illiterates and we estimate there are 850 million of them, 500 million women and 350 million men. In our contemporary world one woman in four is illiterate.

However, other absolute numbers also contain some good news. The total number of primary school pupils rose from an estimated 500 million in 1975 to more than 680 million in 1998. If this pace of increase were to continue, the number of pupils in the world's primary schools would reach 700 million in 2005 and 770 million in 2015. Nearly all this increase in demand for school places, if satisfied, would occur in developing countries, notably in southern Asia and sub-Saharan Africa.

It is easier to understand the challenge if I express it in proportionate terms. For most developing countries, school enrolment growth of 5% per year until 2015 would achieve the target of Education for All by that year. However, several countries would have to grow at 10% annually, which is quite a challenge. That would leave at least 32 countries that are unlikely to meet the 2015 target of Education for All without very special efforts. Nearly half of these countries are, or have until recently, been embroiled in conflict.

Sub-Saharan Africa is of particular concern, because enrolment there will have to increase at almost three times the rates achieved in the 1990s in order to meet the 2015 target. Almost half of the additional school places that the world requires are in this region. As I said earlier, the Commonwealth countries are generally in better shape than the rest, but there is a long way to go.

6 What is Being Done?

So what is being done to ensure that we go the distance? Education for All was set as a goal in the UNESCO constitution of 1945. The countries that signed that declaration stated their belief in 'full and equal opportunities for education for all, in the unrestricted pursuit of objective truth, and in the free exchange of ideas and knowledge'.

In 1990 the goal of Education for All was restated at a conference in Jomtien,

Thailand. In 2000, 164 countries came together in Dakar, Senegal for the World Education Forum. They declared:

> We re-affirm the vision of the World Declaration on Education for All (Jomtien 1990), supported by the Universal Declaration of Human Rights and the Convention on the Rights of the Child, that all children, young people and adults have the human right to benefit from an education that will meet their basic learning needs in the best and fullest sense of that term.

But what assurance do we have that anything will be different this time round? Doesn't it begin to look as if Education for All, like tomorrow, is always talked about but never comes? Without denying that the task is very challenging, I do believe that the current situation is different. The Dakar Forum drew some lessons from the relative lack of progress towards EFA in the decade after Jomtien. It did not merely set new targets. It outlined a strategy and put in place a series of follow-up mechanisms. In my work at UNESCO I am right at the heart of those follow-up mechanisms and therefore have a good overview of the considerable efforts being deployed.

Let me start with the targets and then comment on the strategy and mechanisms. There are six targets, which I find it helpful to remember with the acronym GET EQUAL.

The first target concerns *Girls and gender*. The goal is to eliminate gender disparities in primary and secondary education by 2005 and achieve gender equality by 2015 – with a special focus on ensuring full and equal access for girls to basic education of good quality. This is also one of the UN's Millennium goals to which the Commonwealth Heads of Government recommitted themselves at their CHOGM meeting in Coolum, Australia in March 2002.

E is for *Elementary or primary education*, where the deadline is to ensure that by 2015 all children, especially girls, children in difficult circumstances, and from ethnic minorities have access to and complete free and compulsory primary education of good quality. This is also a Millennium Development Goal.

T is for *Training*, to ensure that the learning needs of all young people are met through equitable access to appropriate learning and life skills programmes. This obviously relates to the strong emphasis that the recent CHOGM put on youth.

The next *E* is for *Early childhood*. The goal is to expand and improve comprehensive early childhood care and education, especially for the most vulnerable and disadvantaged children.

QU stands for *Quality*, without which all the rest is pointless. The Dakar Forum charged us to improve all aspects of the quality of education to achieve recognised and measurable learning outcomes for all – especially in literacy, numeracy and essential life skills.

Finally, *AL* stands for *Adult Literacy*, the challenge of achieving a 50% improvement in levels of adult literacy by 2015, especially for women, as well as equitable access to basic and continuing education for adults.

So there are three quantitative targets with deadlines and three that are qualitative. The whole package is called EFA. One of our challenges at UNESCO is to keep the focus on the package as a whole. It is legitimate that particular countries, agencies or donors should focus on a particular goal. This does not mean, however, that universal primary education, to take the most common example, represents the totality of EFA.

What is the strategy for achieving these goals? The first principle is that the primary responsibility for achieving Education for All lies with national governments. International and bilateral agencies can help, but the basic drive has to come from the country itself. In Dakar all countries committed themselves to developing national plans for Education for All by 2002 at the latest. The international community promised in return that no country seriously committed to Education for All would be thwarted in its achievement of this goal by lack of resources. Getting these plans finished, and calling in the promise about resources, is at the heart of my work at UNESCO at the moment.

The promise about resources needs to be kept in perspective. At present 97% of the resources devoted to education in developing countries come from the countries themselves and only 3% from the international sources. The challenge for the planners in these countries is to chart a sustainable strategy for achieving education for all. For most this will mean some reallocation of resources to education from, say, military expenditure. It will often mean reallocation of resources within the education budget to basic education and away from other levels. Some African governments, for instance, at present spend one hundred times as much per capita on university students as on pupils in primary school.

What will be the total bill for achieving Education for All? This is, of course, a complex calculation that is very dependent on the assumptions that you make. OXFAM and UNICEF estimate the cost at an extra $7–8 billion per year. UNESCO and the World Bank have figures in the range of $13–15 billion. Although these figures differ by a factor of two they do give us the scale of the problem. We all have our favourite comparisons. The US has just increased its defence budget by $48 billion. One third of that increase, applied year on year, would take care of Education for All. But let's not pick only on the Americans. I gather that the amount of money that Europeans spend each year on bottled mineral water would also cover the cost of achieving Education for All.

The events of September 2001 and their sequel will have an impact on progress towards Education for All. We now live, in Charles Dickens' famous words, in the best of times and the worst of times. It is the best of times because there has never been a greater awareness that the disparities between people are not just bad for the poor, but also dangerous for the rich. It is the worst of times because old habits die hard. Having raised the cry of 'terrorism', America is now encouraging other states to attempt a military response to the global social problems and injustices that breed discontent.

Of course, another problem in all areas of development is that the industrial countries engage in much self-cancelling expenditure. On the one hand, western countries eagerly sell arms to the parties involved in the world's many conflicts and civil wars. On the other, they wring their hands about the difficulty of educating children in situations of conflict. Or take agriculture. Rich countries, through their foreign aid budgets, attempt to alleviate rural poverty in the developing world. Yet the rich countries subsidise their own farmers to the tune of $1 billion per day, which is more than six times their entire foreign-aid budget. These subsidies to rich farmers have the direct effect of throwing millions of farmers in the third world deeper into poverty.

However, we have to deal with the world as we find it, contradictions and all. We are finding that the greatest challenge in ensuring progress towards Education for All is, as so often, the challenge of co-ordinating the efforts of the various players. We try to help countries that want to achieve Education for All to translate their political will into an effective plan. But that plan is not an end in itself.

Funding EFA is not the reward for a perfect national plan. It has to be part of the dynamic national planning process led by the ministry of finance. That process has, in turn, to be set in the complex framework of arrangements by which the World Bank and the IMF apply debt relief and concessionary loans to the general goals of poverty alleviation and development. It is a world of acronyms, such as HIPC (Highly Indebted Poor Countries), PRSPs (Poverty Reduction Strategy Papers), UNDAF (United Nations Development Assistance Framework) and CCAs (Common Country Assessments).

Fortunately, I do believe we are making progress. The World Bank is engaging more and more resolutely with this process and has brought out proposals for a financing framework for EFA. The G8 Summit in 2002 played a helpful role in making all the EFA processes flow together. The Canadians, who were the G8 hosts, took an admirably open and transparent approach to the preparation of the educational agenda for the summit, consulting a range of NGOs on their proposals, which are also available on the web for comment by the general public. The G8's education task force has also linked up with meetings on the World Bank's proposal for a financing framework.

The governments of rich countries, such as the UK, can play a vital role in ensuring that the various international bodies work together effectively in processes like EFA. For example UNESCO has been given an overall co-ordinating role, the World Bank is obviously best placed to put together a financing framework, UNICEF is taking a special interest in girls' education and the FAO has a special interest in rural education. Making sure that all these efforts kick into the same goal is a considerable challenge. I would like to pay tribute to the UK government and in particular to Clare Short, former Secretary of State for International Development, for the part the UK has played in ensuring that the international community does work together as it is meant to.

Viewed from Paris, the UK Department for International Development looks a very impressive operation and I notice that other countries, including the USA, defer to its maturity and experience in development matters. I should also like to commend and thank the UK for the recent announcement of a Jubilee Fund of £10 million for EFA in the Commonwealth.

Readers will form their own judgements on the attention paid to EFA within the various Commonwealth forums. I was very pleased by the communiqué that came out of the last Conference of Commonwealth Education Ministers held in Halifax, Nova Scotia in 2001. What particularly pleased me was its support of the Dakar goals and its commentary on EFA in that framework. The 15-year timeframe of the Dakar goals is clearly a long period in the context of politics. There is always a temptation to want to make a new declaration or to cut a new ribbon. However, all the evidence shows that achieving EFA requires a long-term sustained commitment. That is why progress is slower than we would like. But the answer is to commit to the long haul, not to change objectives every few years.

I was also pleased that the Commonwealth ministers started from the belief that education is a human right. This is very much our position at UNESCO. Education is also, of course, a key tool for economic and social development but it is, first and foremost, a human right.

Amartya Sen has put these aims together very well in his inspiring book *Development as Freedom*. He shows that development and human rights are two sides of the same coin. He defines development simply as the process of expanding the real freedoms that people enjoy. Freedom is central to the process of development for two reasons. The first is an evaluative reason. The central criterion for the assessment of progress is whether the freedoms that people have are enhanced. The second reason relates to effectiveness. It is primarily through the free agency of people that development is achieved. So the expansion of freedom is both the primary end and the principal means of development. Basic education, in turn, is central to the expansion of freedom.

I am less clear about what to make of the communiqué and declarations that came out of the Coolum CHOGM. In my quick reading of those documents I could not help thinking that the drafters had worked very hard to keep the word 'education' out of the texts! Certainly there is a good focus on youth – and mention of youth leadership education – but there is very little about education more generally. I hope this does not signal any lessening of the importance of education in the minds of Commonwealth leaders, but simply that they trust their ministers of education to get on with the job.

7 What Kind of Education?

I come now to my final section and some comments about what kind of education we aspire to bring to all. One of the Dakar goals is to improve all aspects of the quality of education in order to achieve recognised and measurable learning outcomes for all – especially in literacy, numeracy and essential life skills.

The World Bank has been doing some good work on the question of quality by asking the simple question, 'how much education does it take to make a difference?' The answer, in the Bank's inimitable language, is that 'countries may be trapped in a low-returns equilibrium until their level of human capital accumulation rises beyond five or six years of schooling. Once the threshold is passed, countries seem to achieve a higher steady-state growth path.'

In simple language this means, as I have already noted, that getting a decent proportion of kids to complete primary school is more important than worrying about gross enrolment rates. Quality education means working at reducing repetition rates so that completion of primary school is something that parents and children can aspire to.

Since the Dakar Forum we have had 9/11. Many believe that those attacks make it even more urgent to reduce the disparities in today's world, notably through education. But many are also asking 'education for what?' Even before 11 September, ministers of education were asking themselves whether, in assessing the quality of education, the habitual focus on individual student performance needed to be balanced by attention to the role of good education in contributing to the creation of harmonious communities.

The part of the Halifax communiqué where Commonwealth ministers talk about education in indigenous languages and the importance of inclusiveness and cultural sensitivity is encouraging in this regard.

The challenge in education, it seems to me, is to achieve a proper balance between the creation of human capital and the creation of social capital. Human capital means the individual knowledge and skills that make a person more autonomous, more flexible and more productive. It is the personal capital that you or I can invest in finding fulfilment in our lives. But human capital is not enough by itself. No man is an island. We also need social capital, which is trust in other people, networks of contacts and the coming together of people for a common goal that creates communities. The Commonwealth itself is a good example of the creation of social capital on a global scale. But there is a good analogy for this blend of human and social capital in a new phenomenon that is outside the Commonwealth, at least for the time being. I refer to the new Euro banknotes. On one side of each note there is a depiction of a window or a door. This can be a symbol of the creation of human capital as education allows us to look out on the world, to understand it and to prepare to take our place in it. On the other side of each note – and each note represents a particular era of architecture from Rome to the 20th century – a bridge is depicted. This can be a symbol for social capital, the creation of links to other people and other communities that allows us to live together constructively in societies – in other words, a symbol for education that helps us learn to live together.

Earlier I said that the Commonwealth countries were generally ahead of the pack in progress to EFA. Are they ahead of the pack in helping their people learn to live together? Certainly the Commonwealth itself has been an invaluable mechanism for helping to resolve disputes once they arise. However, recent and current events in India, Sierra Leone and Zimbabwe, to mention but three Commonwealth countries, show that conflict surfaces in the Commonwealth all too frequently. This is a big challenge to us all.

Chapter 3

Gender in Education: Overview of Commonwealth Strategies

Jasbir K. Singh

1 Introduction

Although some progress has been made towards achieving equality for women, the situation in the main is one of unfulfilled expectations. .... Social and economic disadvantages experienced by women across the globe continue to be reflected in and reinforced by political institutions which are in the main defined and controlled by men.

1995 Commonwealth Plan of Action on Gender and Development: 3

Over the last 30 years, the Commonwealth has increasingly given priority to enhancing the status and participation of girls and women in the development of their countries through improved access to educational opportunities. The educational needs and interests of girls and women have been gradually but firmly placed on the agenda of national governments and development agencies.

The Commonwealth's vision of the role of women in society has been articulated by its highest consultative body, the Commonwealth Heads of Government Meetings, and brought to fruition through the work of its various development agencies, in collaboration with other international development agencies and Commonwealth non-governmental organisations.

Commonwealth Heads of Government first formally recognised the importance of women's active participation in all aspects of the development process during the 1970s. Attention to girls' and women's participation in development gained some momentum during the 1980s with Commonwealth Heads of Government acknowledging the multi-faceted nature of women's contribution to the development process (*1987 CHOGM Communiqué*). The 1990s brought a new emphasis with the acknowledgement that women's and girls' issues were cross-cutting and central to development. These issues could not be considered in isolation; there was a need for a broad gender policy which took account of the varying impact of policies and their outcomes on the lives of both boys and girls, and women and men. There was an evident shift towards mainstreaming a gender perspective in all sectors.

In 1996 a report commissioned by the Commonwealth Secretariat (Leo-Rhynie, 1996) proposed guidelines for mainstreaming gender in the education sector, in particular formal education (primary, secondary and tertiary education) of Commonwealth countries. The consultant found inadequacies from a gender perspective in the Secretariat's own education programmes, as reported to the 1990 and 1994 Conferences of Commonwealth Education Ministers. Similarly, the report noted that member countries' own development plans tended to identify problems without offering solutions. The report put forward methodological guidelines for conducting a gender impact analysis based on the identification of a number of critical indicators, and also reviewed process and strategies for mainstreaming gender in education.

Principal among the Commonwealth agencies which have pushed forward the agenda for girls and women are the Commonwealth Secretariat based in London and the Commonwealth of Learning in Vancouver. The Secretariat and COL have made a significant contribution to closing the gap and reducing disparities in the opportunities for education and training between the sexes through a range of programmes of their own and through collaborative efforts with other international development agencies. These include UNESCO, the Forum for African Women Educationalists (FAWE) and the Association for the Development of Education in Africa, formerly known as the Donors to African Education (DAE).

Commonwealth governments set up the Commonwealth Secretariat in 1965 as a central body to organise their consultations and carry out agreed programmes. Within the Secretariat, specialist departments and divisions that have focused on education and girls, women and gender issues are the Women and Development Programme which, following a process of restructuring within the Secretariat, became the Gender Affairs Department within the Gender and Youth Affairs Division (GYAD); and the former Education Programme, later renamed the Education Department (EDD), within the Human Resource Development Division (HRDD). Both portfolios are now subsumed under the Social Transformation Programmes Department (see Chapter 1).

The Secretariat organises intergovernmental consultations, services Commonwealth meetings and committees, conducts programmes of co-operation and acts as a clearing-house for information. The Secretariat has focused on women and development issues as a priority concern in its consultative and functional activities. Such activities include advocacy with the relevant ministries of Commonwealth governments; national and regional workshops with relevant stakeholders; commissioned studies on gender stereotyping and on improving participation of girls in basic and higher education; publications and their distribution; networking; and co-operation with non-governmental organisations throughout the Commonwealth.

Commonwealth education ministers have regularly endorsed the directives of the Heads of Government and suggested to the Secretariat's education officials that attention be given to continuing to address gender concerns in the educational system, paying attention to the problems of both boys and girls (*Report of 13CCEM*: 9).

The Commonwealth of Learning is described in Chapters 1 and 6. When it was created in 1987, Commonwealth Heads of Government asked COL to pay attention to two special areas: women in development and the environment. The central emphasis of the agency remains the improvement of national capacity for human resource development through increasing access to education. Within its mandate from the Heads of Government, COL has emphasised the relationship of girls and women to the new communications technologies. To this end it has mounted a number of regional workshops on gender and technology. It has also initiated other discrete projects related to gender, such as the recent development of a United Nations and Commonwealth-wide system database on gender-related training materials.

The focus of this chapter will be on Commonwealth initiatives within the formal education sector both at school and tertiary level. The paper's coverage excludes aspects of training which Commonwealth agencies have undertaken in a broad spectrum of areas pertaining to women: violence against women, sexual harassment, enhancing the participation of women in industry and exports, gender planning in macroeconomic policies, income generation and entrepreneurial skills, environmental management, natural resource management, and women and sustainable development. All these combine with educational initiatives to encourage transformation towards gender equity.

The chapter will focus on work in gender and education carried out by the Commonwealth Secretariat (in particular the work of the Education Programme/ Department) and COL, either alone or in partnership with other Commonwealth and international development agencies that have a common agenda. Programmes that will be examined will be those pertaining to gender in basic education, in science and technology education and in higher education. The activities of COL, many of which are cross-cutting across the sectors, will be described separately from those of the Commonwealth Secretariat.

To start with, broader Commonwealth policies on gender will be outlined, as the setting within which education policies have been laid down.

2 Commonwealth Policies on Gender and Development

The Commonwealth has played a prominent role in placing the issue of gender equality on the agenda of developing countries through its proposals and programmes for mainstreaming a gender perspective into all aspects of national development. Nevertheless, the 'reality for most women is still a long way from the vision' (Chief Emeka Anyaoku, Commonwealth Secretary-General, *1995 Commonwealth Plan of Action*).

a. First Steps to Gender Equality

Commonwealth Heads of Government first raised their concern about women and development at their meeting in Kingston, Jamaica in 1975. At the following meeting in London in 1977, they recognised that 'unless women are active participants both in contributing to the process of development and as beneficiaries, the goals of social and economic growth would not be fully realised'. They proposed that 'all programmes of the Secretariat should reflect this awareness and contribute to the full integration of women in the development process' (*CHOGM Communiqué*, 1977).

The first concrete step to advance equality between men and women was taken in 1979 with the decision by Heads of Government, meeting in Lusaka, to appoint an adviser to the Commonwealth Secretary-General on women and development. In response, a Women and Development Programme was established within the Human Resource Development Group of the Secretariat to be a focal point for women and development issues throughout the Secretariat and to co-ordinate assistance to member countries in addressing the issues.

In 1985, on the eve of the Third United Nations World Conference on the Decade for Women, Commonwealth ministers responsible for women's affairs met for the first time in Nairobi to review and appraise their achievements and to share ideas. Ministers recommended a shift from *advocacy* to *integration,* and that the Secretariat should adopt a policy statement on women and development to facilitate this process. The policy statement was approved by Heads of Government at their meeting in Nassau in 1985, with the further request to the Secretariat to prepare a detailed Plan of Action to ensure effective implementation of the Statement. The Nairobi meeting was a precursor to the triennial Meetings of Commonwealth Ministers Responsible for Women's Affairs (WAMM), which now serves as the major consultative body for the Commonwealth on gender issues.

At the 1987 WAMM meeting in Harare, the *Commonwealth Plan of Action on Women and Development* was adopted and forwarded to Heads of Government who endorsed it at their meeting in Vancouver that year. The *Plan of Action* consisted of initiatives which individual member governments agreed to undertake, as well as action by the Secretariat. The 1987 *Plan of Action* succeeded in focusing the attention of the Commonwealth on the problems that arise when women's issues are not central concerns in development efforts.

b. The Harare Declaration

In 1991, at their meeting in Zimbabwe, Commonwealth Heads of Government drew up the Harare Declaration which provided clear directions and priorities for the Commonwealth as a whole and reaffirmed equality for women so that they may exercise their full and equal rights. Two years later in Cyprus, Heads of Government renewed their commitment to the Harare priorities, and stressed their dedication to building 'a world in which women enjoyed their full rights and were equal partners in shaping the economic, political, social and cultural development of their countries'. They also recognised that women's rights are an 'integral and indivisible part of human rights' and that men's violence against women is a contravention of basic human rights. Heads of government agreed to promote women's rights through special measures to increase women's participation at all levels of political and decision-making processes (*CHOGM Communiqué*, 1993).

During 1992–93 the Secretariat undertook a restructuring process with the aim of making the organisation more focused and efficient in areas where it enjoyed comparative advantage over other institutions. The Secretariat evolved a three-year strategic plan based on the Harare priorities. The Women and Development Programme and the Commonwealth Youth Programme merged into a composite **Women's and Youth Affairs Division**. A special programme on **Gender Equality** was formulated to provide assistance and advice to member governments and the Secretariat on gender issues.

The fourth Meeting of Ministers Responsible for Women's Affairs (1993) examined progress on implementation of the Plan of Action. Ministers decided the Plan would benefit from review and updating in view of recent Secretariat restructuring and the changing international development context. Although the cross-cutting nature of gender issues was recognised in the plan, the process of mainstreaming gender concerns into all Secretariat programmes was not fully developed. In view of the forthcoming United Nations Fourth World Conference on Women in Beijing, timely renewal of the Plan was suggested.

c. The *1995 Commonwealth Plan of Action on Gender and Development*

The *1995 Commonwealth Plan of Action on Gender and Development* gave reality to the pledge made by Heads of Government in the Harare Declaration that equality for women would be one of the areas of priority action for the Commonwealth. The plan represented the new Commonwealth vision for women towards the millennium and beyond. It was taken to the World Conference on Women (Beijing) and contributed to the development of a global agenda to bring women into the twenty-first century. It represented a blueprint for Commonwealth action to achieve gender equality, providing a framework within which governments and the Commonwealth Secretariat can harness their resources to transform the Commonwealth vision for women into reality. An innovative and forward-looking plan, it mainstreamed gender issues into all policies, programmes, structures, processes and activities of governments and the Secretariat, to ensure social justice, equality and fulfilment for all (*1995 Commonwealth Plan of Action on Gender and Development*: 1).

The plan set out *new directions* for both Commonwealth governments and the Secretariat:

- *From women to gender:* The gender and development approach seeks to integrate women's needs into the wider picture, calling for the different life courses of men and women to be considered at an early stage and emphasising the need to monitor the different impact of policies and programmes on women and men, girls and boys;

- *Focus on results:* The plan seeks to accelerate the achievement of women's empowerment, focusing more on achieving results than establishing rights and obligations;

- *Strengthen national women's machineries (NWMs):* NWMs include ministries for Women's Affairs, focal points for gender issues within ministries, commissions and departments;

- *Integration of gender issues into the mainstream of all government and Secretariat activities:* This ensures that decision-makers and those implementing policies and programmes in all areas of member governments, together with the Secretariat itself, are equipped to build gender issues into their activities;

- *Equality and equity of outcomes for women:* Policy commitments must be delivered. It therefore recommended monitoring and evaluation at the highest levels to turn the vision into reality (ibid: 6–7).

Special *terms and techniques* were evolved to meet the objectives of the plan.

- *Gender management system:* this included two key elements:

  1. Development of gender management and development action plans which provide a framework for establishing what interventions are necessary to integrate gender into development policies and programmes within a particular country;

  2. A system for managing the integration of gender in mainstream policies and programmes to ensure that the plan's objectives are met;

- *Gender budgeting and accounting:* the purpose here is to identify and monitor the flow of sufficient resources to ensure that women and men are equal beneficiaries of programmes, and to specialist projects aimed at benefiting women only;

- *Positive and affirmative action:* 'Positive action' referred to taking specific temporary measures to achieve equality. Affirmative action referred to giving special privileges to compensate for a long history of discrimination and inequality (ibid: 8–9).

For member governments and for the Secretariat, the plan identified *strategic objectives* which provide a framework for Commonwealth action at two levels: strengthening institutional capacity to mainstream gender issues into all sectors of society; and focus on a limited number of critical gender issues for Commonwealth action in the areas of political and human rights and social and economic development. *Women and human resource development* was one of the key issues identified for Commonwealth action (ibid: 10).

Fifteen areas considered desirable components of the *1995 Commonwealth Plan of Action on Gender and Development* were identified for government planners and implementers. The plan also clearly stipulated how functional divisions within the Secretariat should respond to the plan.

Since 1995, the Commonwealth Secretariat has adopted special measures to strengthen its capacity to provide gender-inclusive and women-specific functional and technical assistance to governments in key programmes affecting women. The principal action points are listed in the box below.

d. Advancing the Commonwealth Agenda into the New Millennium

A recent development has been preparation of *An Update to the 1995 Commonwealth Plan of Action on Gender and Development for the period 2000–2005* (Commonwealth Secretariat, 2000). This refines the focus of the *1995 Plan* by more closely defining Commonwealth priorities for action on the basis of its areas of comparative advantage, for example gender mainstreaming through the Gender Management System approach, gender integration into macroeconomic policies, gender and human rights, politics, peace and conflict prevention. It recommends a more strategic advocacy, brokerage and catalytic (ABC) role for the Commonwealth's GYAD. It concentrates Commonwealth efforts on resources – to ensure greater effectiveness and impact of outcomes through more innovative and cost-effective strategies and approaches. The *Update* identifies gender mainstreaming processes as the cornerstones for advancing gender equality, as well as stressing the need for effective monitoring of impacts and capacity-building actions.

3 Implementing the Plans of Action

At various stages of policy evolution, the Secretariat took positive steps to implement Plans of Action on Gender and Development, 1987 and 1995.

The *1987 Plan* impacted on Secretariat programmes, including education programmes, by increasing the level of gender awareness among policy-makers and programme staff. Divisional planning for project activities, policy-making and technical assistance to governments were all affected. Consultation with member countries through points of contact regularly included reference to improving women's involvement in Secretariat initiatives, and planning within the Secretariat often ensured that the gender dimension was taken into account when Secretariat activities and workshops were implemented.

Implementation of the *1995 Plan of Action* was managed through the *Gender*

Steering Committee. The administrative Divisions were the 'front line' of the Secretariat where strategic direction was transformed into meaningful action and as such they represented an integral part of the mainstreaming strategy. Two Secretariat Divisions played a key role in overseeing that the objectives of the plan were met within Secretariat operations:

The *Strategic Planning and Evaluation Unit (SPEU)* co-ordinated gender training for all staff; reviewed proposals for expenditure to determine whether a gender intervention had been effectively included in the proposal; evaluated the gender component of project activities; and assisted with the mainstreaming of the Commonwealth mandates on gender in the Secretariat.

The 1995 Commonwealth Plan of Action on Gender and Development: The Secretariat's Response

- Inclusion of gender issues in all Commonwealth and divisional mandates, action and strategic plans.

- Gender training workshops to develop the capacity of in-house professional staff for gender planning and gender analysis.

- Appointment of consultants and experts, who either have, or will acquire, the capacity for gender analysis and planning.

- Equal and equitable participation of women and men in all Secretariat activities.

- Collation of gender-disaggregated information related to implementing the Plan of Action.

- Use of this information to monitor the effectiveness of each Division in implementing the Plan of Action.

- Gender accounting that identifies and allocates resources to facilitate gender integration as well as undertaking women-specific projects and initiatives to help women 'catch up'.

The 1995 Commonwealth Plan of Action on Gender and Development

---

The *Gender and Youth Affairs Division (GYAD)* took responsibility for co-ordinating the implementation of the *Plan of Action* and developing a gender mainstreaming strategy for the Secretariat. GYAD prepared a guide to gender mainstreaming to assist Commonwealth policy-makers, planners and implementers consider the special needs and interests of women in all areas of planning. This presented a range of planning tools designed by Commonwealth countries and international organisations to trigger concerns for gender equality in the development and analysis of policies, programmes and projects. The guide defines gender, provides a conceptual framework for gender equality, identifies partners in policy-making, provides an outline for the type of data and information necessary to the development of gender-sensitive policies, programmes and projects. It sets out socio-economic indicators of equality, provides a framework for assessing the needs of women in development projects and suggests gender planning tools (*Engendering the Agenda*: 2).

To further assist Commonwealth agencies and governments to implement gender mainstreaming through the Gender Management System, the Secretariat has published a series of handbooks for all stakeholders in the process. The GMS Series includes a *GMS Handbook* which is a reference manual; a quick guide to gender mainstreaming in development planning; a manual on use of gender sensitive indicators; and a GMS manual for the public sector.

Following the Harare Declaration, it is taken for granted that all Secretariat Divisions have taken steps to mainstream gender throughout their activities. From the outset, all projects must bear in mind the special needs and involvement of women. In the assistance the Secretariat gives with education, trade promotion or the application of new technology, the role of women and the relevance of the assistance to their needs is borne in mind. So too is the need to open the doors of recruitment and promotion to the female half of the human race, whose talents and energies have too often been stifled by the weight of tradition (ibid: 3).

4 Gender in Basic Education

The Commonwealth has focused on the needs of girls in basic education as a fundamental right. Access to basic education is recognised as a prerequisite to the enhanced participation of girls and women in higher levels of education as well as to better employment opportunities.

a. Early Concerns

The issue of girls and their special educational needs received little or no attention in the early work of the Commonwealth as an international organisation. That the education of women and girls deserved the highest priority in Commonwealth programmes was first acknowledged by the eighth Commonwealth Education Conference in Colombo, Sri Lanka, in 1980. Ministers noted examples of gross discriminatory practices in developing countries. In 1976 it was estimated that 79% of the 712 millions girls in the world under 15 years of age were in the developing countries. Very few of them had sufficient access to education or skills training.

There was also a very high rate of female wastage through girls dropping out of the school system. Even in countries where educational opportunities were more plentiful, there was still a preference for giving education to the boy rather than to the girl if a choice had to be made (*Report of 8CEC*).

Ministers recognised that in order for women to acquire the knowledge and

---

Impact of the 1987 Plan of Action on Commonwealth Work

- Workshops, seminars, training courses and policy-oriented research – included women and development issues in agenda, background papers and research.

- Provision of educational and training opportunities – CFTC fellowships and CSFP; request to governments to make special efforts to nominate women; encouragement to point of contact in national governments to set targets for women in fellowship and training opportunities; investigation of factors inhibiting participation of women; and monitoring and reporting on the participation of women in Secretariat-sponsored training.

- The provision of technical assistance ensured that women and development concerns feature in projects.

- Women and Development Programme crucial and central in the implementation, monitoring and evaluation of the Plan of Action by all divisions and programmes in the Secretariat.

- Secretariat staffing policy aimed to increase representation of women in professional positions.

- The Secretariat Committee on Women and Development was established to co-ordinate and monitor the implementation of the Plan of Action by individual programmes/divisions.

The Commonwealth Plan of Action on Women and Development: 1987:2–4

---

skills necessary to participate fully in the development of the community, there was urgent need for large-scale and sustained programmes of public education for the masses, especially in the developing countries. This required both re-orientation of male attitudes as well as the preparation of women psychologically and socially for education and change.

Rather than conducting research into the causal factors, which were well understood, ministers proposed that a more useful activity would be the interchange of information on strategies that could be adopted to reduce the disparities between the sexes in the utilisation of educational opportunities. The Commonwealth Secretariat was urged to assist the exchange of information about successful measures by member countries to reduce: (a) gender disparities in participation in education; and (b) the incidence of early leaving or dropping out of school (*Report of 8CEC*).

Despite these recommendations, it was only in the 1990s that basic education was given priority and the position of girls within this sub-sector was identified as a critical issue.

Divisional Steps to Mainstream Gender

- Directors identified critical/priority areas in their strategic and operational plans for gender mainstreaming.

- Directors in collaboration with Gender Focal Points identified the obstacles and limitations to mainstream gender in their respective divisional activities with special attention to be given to procedural obstacles.

- A gender mainstreaming strategy to be developed for each Division.

- Continued support to be given to development of the role of professional staff (especially Gender Focal Points) in each division by identifying the training needs for divisional staff.

The work of the Commonwealth Secretariat has emphasised three aspects of gender in basic education:

- Increasing girls' access to basic education both in the formal and non-formal education sector, identifying and advocating modalities which target a large number of girls;

- Improving the quality of the teaching force, the key to improved quality of basic education, by ensuring better terms and conditions for teachers with a special focus on the service conditions of women teachers, who can play a pivotal role in the education of girls in many developing countries; and

- Greater sensitisation of teachers to gender issues.

b. Access: the Commonwealth Response to Education for All

The year 1990 began a decade of the special significance for basic education. It marked International Literacy Year when the world community sought to extend opportunities to acquire literacy. In March, in Jomtien, Thailand, the World Conference on Education for All provided a new impetus to the goal of universal access to education at the basic level. In tune with international concerns with basic education, the Eleventh Conference of Commonwealth Education Ministers in Barbados (1990) adopted the theme 'Improving the Quality of Basic Education'. In their deliberations, ministers noted the recommendation from the World Conference on Education for All to 'ensure access to, and improve the quality of, education for girls and women, and to remove every obstacle that hampers their effective participation' (*Report of 11CCEM*).

Educational needs identified by ministers were literacy and numeracy; education to provide job skills; preparation and supply of materials; and use of teaching techniques appropriate for out-of-school learning. It was agreed that education

65

that was intended to increase employment skills needed to go beyond jobs that were the traditional preserve of women 'to embrace subjects where the job opportunities are widening, including such areas as growth industries and information technology' (*Report of 11CCEM*: 17). Ministers concurred that in all countries improvement of the quality of teachers was central to the delivery of quality basic education.

c. Improving the Quality of the Teaching Force

Improved teacher education, and teacher management and support (TMS) were identified as important ingredients of good basic education. Within strategies for better teacher management and support, the role, status and training of teachers from the gender perspective were considered critical and have occupied a significant place in the work of the Commonwealth Secretariat.

The Commonwealth's principal thrust in improving the quality of basic education focused on improving the quality, delivery and working conditions of teachers in Africa. As a result, in Botswana, Lesotho, Swaziland, Uganda and Zambia the Secretariat's Education Programme worked with ministries of education on a range of issues related to teacher management. These have included teachers' record systems, discipline and codes of conduct for teachers, and the place of women in the teaching service (*EDD Annual Report 1991/2*: 4).

d. Gender Sensitisation of Teachers in Africa

Wide gender gaps exist in the teaching profession in Africa. In most cases it is women who tend to be disadvantaged. This was recognised, particularly in relation to teacher training and educational management, by participants at the first Teacher Management and Support Colloquium for Anglophone Africa and Mozambique, held in Dar es Salaam in 1993. They identified access, equity, the curriculum and sexual harassment in teacher training institutes and the workplace as issues creating crucial barriers to the effective quality participation of females in the teaching profession. Participants emphasised the urgency of integrating gender concerns into all aspects of the TMS programme. Affirmative action was recommended as a key strategy to redress the prevailing gender imbalances.

It was also resolved in Dar es Salaam that Commonwealth action on women's issues should be undertaken in collaboration with the DAE Working Group on Female Participation and the Forum for African Women Educationalists. These bodies have consistently given financial aid and material support in the cause of gender sensitisation in education and have placed gender mainstreaming firmly in the Teacher Management and Support Programme in Africa (*Wamahiu*: iii).

In the TMS work, a gender perspective was adopted rather than a focus on women alone. The perceived advantages were:

• It is comparative, encompassing the perspectives of both men and women;

- It helps to identify the disadvantages suffered not only by women but also by men;
- It recognises the heterogeneous nature of human society;
- It involves women and men in finding solutions to the problem.

This meant the institutionalisation of a gender perspective into all levels and sectors of organisational and development planning and implementation of TMS. Three strategies for mainstreaming gender into the TMS Programme were adopted: problem diagnosis, needs assessment and gender sensitisation.

A needs assessment survey was planned for each country to identify specific groups and issues that required targeting, and to assess the local resources available to support sensitisation initiatives (ibid: 1–2). Because considerable animosity was noted towards the idea of gender mainstreaming among key actors in the development of education in Africa, gender sensitisation of various target groups was identified as integral to the successful programming of TMS activities in all countries. As a result, a gender sensitisation plan was proposed for TMS member countries during 1995–96.

A gender sensitisation needs assessment survey in 1995 identified gender issues within the teaching profession, giving attention to the extent of imbalance and perceived causes. It revealed the need for the training of gender specialists and the adoption of a more balanced approach to gender issues (ibid: 6–8).

During 1995–96, gender-sensitisation workshops were conducted in Zanzibar, Botswana and Lesotho. A training of trainers workshop was held in Malawi during 1996. The impact of sensitisation workshops was felt in terms of attitudinal change; personal commitment to change the status quo as soon as possible; commitment to the development of action plans; the acceptance of gender discrimination in African classrooms as an indicator of poor quality teaching; the strengthening of intersectoral and subregional links; and the creation of a critical pool of sensitised personnel, comprising senior education decision-makers and practitioners able to effect changes in education at national and sub-regional levels (*Wamahiu*: 1–12).

e. Commissioning of Studies

The Commonwealth Secretariat has sponsored a number of studies on gender and basic education which have illuminated the problems encountered, and have proposed solutions to enhancing the participation and performance of girls at the basic level of education.

Making a Difference in Girls' Education

The Commonwealth Secretariat, in conjunction with the Girls' Education Team of the Human Development Network of the World Bank, commissioned two studies that provided powerful evidence for change and successful strategies in two countries, Malawi and Baluchistan, Pakistan. These cases, serving as possible models for other countries, outlined how to make a difference in the education of girls. The two studies sought:

> *... to examine the process by which education policies targeting girls were implemented and to assess whether the desired outcomes were achieved...* [they were] *also especially interested in examining whether and how policies aiming to improve education quality and curriculum relevance had taken account of the gender dimension.*

Wolf and Kainja: 3

Commonwealth Secretariat and FAWE Gender Sensitisation Activities 1995–97

- Needs assessment survey in eastern and southern Africa.

- A national gender sensitisation workshop for TMS Country Working Group (CWG) in Zanzibar.

- Regional gender sensitisation workshops for CWG representatives from Botswana, Lesotho, Malawi, Swaziland and Zanzibar.

- A national gender sensitisation workshop for CWG members and other key educational personnel in Lesotho.

- A regional gender sensitisation training of trainers workshop for CWG representatives and other key education personnel from Botswana, Lesotho, Malawi, Swaziland, Tanzania and Zanzibar.

- The development of a gender training manual in Zambia.

- A gender sensitisation needs assessment in West Africa.

- Assessment of the integration of gender into the training modules adapted and translated from the Commonwealth Secretariat 'Better Schools' series for head teachers in Mozambique.

Wamahiu: 4

The findings of these studies show that 'very real and significant progress is being made in improving girls' access to education'. They also reveal a need to 'shore up these achievements with efforts to improve the quality of education and ensure that both instructional content and instructional methodologies are adapted to be more appropriate and consistent with girls' and their families' educational expectations' (ibid: 3).

The report on Malawi (Wolf and Kainja) portrays the progress made by girls since 1990 from the perspective of access (which doubled between 1990 and 1997), retention and achievement; and parental attitude to girls' education that revealed that priority was given to the education of boys. The report focused on changes that had come about since 1990 due to the efforts made by Malawian women with political and institutional power, beginning in the 1980s, and to international interest in girls' education. Wolf and Kainja have described the factors which supported girls' education in Malawi (see box). Other factors that played a crucial role in creating change were an atmosphere within the country which set the scene for educational change and government strategies (ibid: 4–25).

Strategies which succeeded in supporting girls' education in Malawi

- Fee waivers for primary school girls.

- Creating more school spaces for girls.

- Training more female teachers and improving teacher distribution.

- Scholarships for secondary school girls.

- Improving girls' retention in school by readmitting girls after pregnancy.

- Social mobilisation campaign – bringing girls into school early.

- Establishing girls, clubs, reforming girls' initiations, encouraging positive role models.

- Eliminating school uniforms.

- Improving girls' achievements in school by gender appropriate curriculum and textbooks, changing classroom practices, gender streaming mathematics.

Wolf and Kainja: 11–24

Non-formal Education for Out-of-school Children
Studies in Bangladesh, India and Pakistan were commissioned by the Commonwealth Secretariat in an effort to document their interesting experiences in providing education and training for large numbers of children who either never go to school or who drop out before completing basic education. These reports gave accounts of the special programmes and measures being taken by these countries to enter into partnerships with NGOs, and to deal with the issue of providing basic education to out-of-school children in general and to girls in particular. The majority of these children are girls. The studies also point out the strengths and achievements of these programmes and the constraints experienced in attempts to achieve universal basic education. Among the non-formal education programmes reported were those of the Bangladesh Rural Advancement Committee (BRAC), the Social

Work Research Centre (SWRC), night schools in India and the Hafizabad Literacy Promotion Programme (HLPP) in Pakistan. The results of these studies were published in 1994 and widely distributed.

Teacher Management and Gender

A Secretariat publication on teacher management (Halliday: 1995) highlights gender issues that persist in schools. It points to unequal gender balance in school admissions; higher drop-out rates by girls from school; gender stereotyping through inherited curriculum structures and vocational guidance; sexual harassment of girls and women teachers; inequalities in promotion arrangements; and timing of extra-school activities which disadvantages working mothers.

Issues which could improve the provision for girls were also identified: the importance of putting in place curriculum structures showing that education is as relevant to the needs of girls as it is to boys; the availability of bursaries and/or grants; physical facilities for girls; personal, social and vocational guidance programmes; and parental roles in school policy formulation.

Strategies to Improve the Role and Status of Women in Education

- Conditions of service for women teachers should be same as for men. Service agreements should not disadvantage women.

- Sexual harassment cases should be treated as a matter of priority and investigated impartially.

- Educational policies should be carefully framed so that teachers are sensitised to policies which seek to redress gender and other inequalities.

- Appointment and promotion policies ensuring that both sexes can rise through the education system without discrimination.

- All subjects in the curriculum are freely and equally available to both genders.

- Approved textbooks do not reinforce traditional roles.

Halliday: 88–89

If equal opportunity legislation and regulations are to be monitored effectively, it is essential that appropriate statistics are collected by gender. The required data would include information on pupil attendance, drop-out rates, promotion rates from primary to secondary school, teacher appointment, teacher promotion, teacher utilisation, cases of harassment, officers in districts, the inspectorate and other ministry of education cadres. Without this data it is impossible to provide answers when questions of alleged discriminatory practices are raised in public debate.

f. Contribution of the Forum of African Women Educationalists

In Africa, FAWE, a unique group of influential African policy-makers, has been well-positioned to stimulate broad policy reform and create a conducive environment for increasing parental demand for girls' education. FAWE is a membership organisation that brings together African women ministers in charge of education systems, women vice-chancellors of African universities and other senior women policy-makers. It was founded in 1992 and registered in Kenya in 1993 as a pan-African NGO. FAWE has 60 full members from 34 African countries, associate members comprising male ministers of education and permanent secretaries, and 31 National Chapters. Although FAWE has more extensive and substantial programmes than the Commonwealth Secretariat, and includes many non-Commonwealth countries in its membership and activities, its initiatives in collaboration with the Commonwealth Secretariat have made significant impact on girls' education in Africa, especially in Commonwealth countries.

FAWE's overall goal is to increase access and retention, as well as improve the quality of education for all girls within the school system and for women in universities. To achieve this, FAWE has distilled seven strategic objectives: policy and data analysis; advocacy; interventions; empowerment of girls; partnerships; strengthening of organisational capacity; and monitoring and evaluation.

FAWE programme activities aim to help FAWE members, many of whom are also Commonwealth members, to analyse, plan, guide and effectively implement external and internal investment in the education sector to redress gender imbalances. FAWE's overarching goal is to use its forum as an intellectual resource to assist in the development of member countries' national capabilities to evolve, implement and improve strategies that have the potential to accelerate female participation in education (*FAWE News*, Vol. 8, No. 1).

In 1999 FAWE produced a five-year strategic plan which charts FAWE's future strategy and which relies on its comparative advantage and strengths. The plan emphasises the need to empower girls themselves. The education of girls remains a priority area, not only for advocacy, but for specific action to promote development (*FAWE News*, Vol. 8, No. 1: 3).

The Secretariat has worked with FAWE to influence as many ministries of education as possible and Secretariat personnel have been regular attenders at major FAWE meetings. FAWE collaborates with the Commonwealth Secretariat in defining many of its policies and in implementing on-the-ground training and sensitisation activities. As a result of the intensive advocacy work of both agencies, ministerial speeches and declarations across Africa have recognised the importance of girls' education and have placed it on the map. A realisation has also emerged that positive female role models are a powerful tool for raising awareness and inspiring girls. The situation has also been helped by the growing number of girls' education programmes across Africa (ibid: 5). However, the gender gap in school enrolments has not narrowed. FAWE therefore emphasises the need for going beyond the focus on numbers. It advocates review of the curriculum, changes in pedagogical practice and school culture, and the need for gender sensitisation and training. Attention is shifted to programme planning, as well as to implementation, with a need for quantitative as well as qualitative baseline data – as in the case of the second phase of the African Girls' Education Initiative (AGEI).

5 Women in Science and Technology Education

Gender discrimination and under-representation of women in technical and vocational programmes and courses, as well as the participation of girls in more diversified vocational education, has been of special concern to the Commonwealth. As an aid to policy development in Commonwealth countries, the tenth Conference of Commonwealth Education Ministers (1987) requested the Commonwealth Secretariat to examine these problems, together with the measures which were being undertaken by member countries and their impact. In response, over the last decade the Education Programme/Department has addressed the specific problem of the dearth of girls and women in science and technology courses and occupations.

a. Barriers to Girls in Science and Technology

The Commonwealth Secretariat's Education Programme/Department began by examining the barriers that prevent girls entering and performing well in science and technology subjects and courses. Analysis of the problem revealed that for cultural and traditional reasons girls and women continued to be under-represented in comparison with men in science- and technology-based occupations and in the education and training courses that lead to them. Many countries still need assistance in developing strategies to promote positive attitudes towards science and technology for girls and women.

Principal barriers to girls'/women's participation in science and technology were identified as:

- Stereotyped and outdated attitudes held by girls, their parents and teachers about girls' abilities and occupational choices;

- Gender stereotyping in textbooks and other educational materials;

- Girls' poor performance in mathematics, constituting a barrier to learning science (especially physical sciences) and technology;

- A perception by both parents and the girls themselves of science and technology as male subjects.

To overcome these barriers and to enhance the participation of girls in science- and technology-related courses and occupations, the Secretariat launched a series of initiatives in the following areas.

Stereotyped and Outdated Attitudes

The Commonwealth Secretariat aimed to raise awareness of gender biases in science, technology and mathematics education in Africa through a regional workshop held in Accra, Ghana in January 1987. The workshop identified outdated stereotyped attitudes as one of the biggest barriers preventing women from entering science and technology. The Secretariat acted on this signal. Women scientists and technologists were identified, interviewed and photographed. Tapes of the interviews were used to create the profiles of women included in a Secretariat booklet and to prepare a programme made available for use by local radio stations. It was hoped that publicising women scientists and technologists in this way would provide role models to girls in schools in order to challenge the stereotyped assumptions of their parents and teachers. Girls' clinics were initiated in Ghana where over 200 girls were brought to a camp for a week. They listened to lectures by eminent women scientists and technologists from all over Africa. Girls had the opportunity to interact with them, and visit research institutions and industries in which women played prominent roles (Wolf and Kainja: 4).

To combat stereotyped attitudes, the Secretariat initiated the concept of a Science and Technology Roadshow for girls, which would move from city to city, and region to region, carrying a message to girls about opportunities for them in scientific and technical careers. Such a series of exhibitions, practical activities, publications and co-operation with female role models had already been tried out in the clinics held for top science students in Ghana's secondary schools. But a fully-fledged model of roadshow activities remained to be devised when the Commonwealth Secretariat Education Programme invited offers from African ninistries of education to act as hosts for such a roadshow. The Ministry of Education of Botswana agreed to pioneer the event with support from UNESCO and SIDA (the Swedish International Development Agency). The Roadshow was held in Gaborone and Francistown, Botswana, 12–18 August 1990 (*Roadshow Report and Manual*: 1).

The aims of the roadshow were to:

- Convince women and girls that they could succeed in many more areas of employment if they sought appropriate qualifications and training in science and technology;

- Make an impact on the attitudes and myths that prevent girls and women from taking advantage of today's opportunities in science and technology;

- Provide information to parents, teachers, employers and the general public on the country's need for scientific and technological manpower and to encourage them to change their attitudes towards women in these fields.

The roadshow was attended by secondary school students in all Southern Africa Development Community (SADC) countries, accompanied by their teachers.

Women working in science-based professions and occupations in Botswana, Ghana, Nigeria, Kenya and Zambia served as resource persons and role models. The activity was fully supported by local industries and by a number of government departments willing to open their doors to enable the girls to see women in action.

The major outcome of the Botswana Roadshow was the development of a manual that could help others in organising events of this kind, supported by a video made during the roadshow entitled *Righting the Imbalance*. The manual and video were distributed to all interested member states. To complement the roadshow, a regional resource book was published, *Women Too in Science and Technology*, which focused on Africa. Two commissioned studies were published: *Measures Increasing the Participation of Women and Girls in Vocational and Technical Education and Training: A Caribbean Study* and *Gender Sensitivity in Primary School Mathematics in India (Education Programme, Annual Report 1990–91*: 8).

In support of the participation of girls and women in science and technology, the Programme has continued to disseminate the idea of roadshows and clinics. The video, *Righting the Imbalance*, has been in great demand. The publication *Women Too in Science and Technology*, originally published in 1990, was reprinted in 1994 (*EDD Annual Report 1992–93*: 11–12).

Gender Stereotyping in Textbooks and other Educational Materials
Textbooks occupy a central place in curricular materials in all countries, especially in developing countries. The gender biases and stereotyping found in textbooks have therefore contributed greatly to the perpetuation of gender inequalities in society. Such stereotyping reinforces discriminatory attitudes and discourages girls from studying or performing well in subjects traditionally seen as more appropriate for boys, such as mathematics and technology.

Among the strategies stressed at the meeting in Nairobi was the inclusion in curricula, at all educational levels, of examples and discussions of the contribution that women have made, and are making, to the economy. Teaching materials 'should demonstrate clearly the equality of the sexes' and be 'rewritten to ensure that they reflect positive, dynamic and participatory images of women'. Incentives and counselling should be provided to encourage girls to study scientific and technical and managerial subjects at all levels (Harding and Apea: 1–2).

A Commonwealth study of primary mathematics in India found that 'in its traditional form mathematics was deeply gendered and [has] pathologised girls and women over many centuries, leaving females learning mathematics in a no-win situation' (Harris: 2). The study by Harris reviews the literature; provides a framework for gender analysis of primary textbooks which could be applied to textbooks in use in India; and makes practical suggestions for the in-service training of teachers and teacher educators that address gender sensitivity and could help to develop locally available material for primary mathematics education (Harris: Preface).

Girls' Poor Performance in Mathematics

Educationalists have questioned the reasons behind girls' poor performance in mathematics. There was little evidence, but a strong perception, that poor understanding of mathematics prevented girls from doing well in science and technology subjects. It was not clear whether it was mathematics or the way in which schooling was constructed that was blocking girls' entry into the study of science. The way mathematics was taught and the ways in which teachers of mathematics and science were prepared could influence girls' learning of science (Goel and Burton: 9–10).

In 1996 the Commonwealth Secretariat orchestrated a pan-Commonwealth conference on the issue in Ahmedabad, India. The symposium pointed out that the difficulty was caused not by the nature of mathematics, but the way in which mathematics was packaged and delivered. A cluster of issues to be addressed were identified: there was need for comparative studies in different country contexts using qualitative methods; changes were needed at different levels of the system – teacher education, classrooms/schools/community groups, policy-makers and pedagogy; the time devoted to teaching for girls needed to be increased; guidance and counselling should be made available to girls; mathematics teaching should be relevant to the daily needs of girls; and more female role models were needed (Goel and Burton). The follow-up study by Harris revealed a situation where men were doing valued, and women less-valued, things throughout the mathematics sector (Harris).

b. From Research to Action

The work of the Commonwealth Secretariat in gender, and science, mathematics and technology (SMT) has been complemented through collaboration with FAWE's project on Female Education in Mathematics and Science in Africa (FEMSA). FEMSA has made significant inroads into understanding and devising interventions into the problems that keep girls lagging behind boys in science- and mathematics-based subjects. FEMSA's goals are:

- To improve the participation and performance of girls in science, mathematics and technology (SMT) subjects at both primary and secondary levels;

- To stimulate ministries of education and policy-makers to make the necessary adjustments in curriculum, teacher training and examinations, to ensure fuller participation and performance in SMT by both boys and girls.

The Secretariat and its partners have succeeded in placing the issue of women's participation in science, mathematics and technology on the agenda of most countries and agencies in the Commonwealth. There is certainly greater awareness of the need to recruit students into all levels of education to ensure better representation of girls and to direct efforts into removing traditional gender stereotypical attitudes from instructional materials.

FEMSA'S Project on Science, Mathematics and Technology

In the first phase of the project's work, Cameroon, Ghana, Tanzania and Uganda completed country profiles on boys' and girls' participation and performance, perceptions of students, teachers, parents, teaching method, syllabuses, examinations, and past and ongoing interventions aimed at improving girls' participation and performance in SMT. This was followed by sensitisation seminars.

In the second phase eight new countries have completed country profiles and FEMSA has moved to action on:

- Advocacy for reform in the key areas of curriculum development, and teacher education and examinations; and

- Interventions concentrating on sensitisation of all stakeholders; motivational activities to promote girls' interests in SMT; teacher in-service training; development of relevant instructional material; and mobilising communities to support school facilities.

FAWE News, January–March 2000: 14

---

6 Women and Higher Education

The Commonwealth Secretariat and the Association of Commonwealth Universities have played a vital role in enhancing the participation of women in higher education. Their efforts have concentrated on two fronts:

- Enabling more women to obtain higher education, in particular post-graduate education, through greater access to Commonwealth awards and fellowships; and

- Improving the participation and status of women in higher education management.

a. Commonwealth Scholarships and Fellowships

The Commonwealth Scholarship and Fellowship Plan which was instituted in 1959 following the recommendations of the first Commonwealth Education Conference in 1959 is, as Chapter 1 has already made clear, the flagship scheme of Commonwealth higher education co-operation. The awards are for 'men and women of high intellectual promise who may be expected to make a significant contribution to life in their own countries on their return from study overseas' (*Report of 1959 Commonwealth Education Conference*: 6). Within the scheme, attention has gradually been given to the poor participation of women and to measures to alleviate the obstacles that have prevented better uptake of the awards by women.

Throughout the early operation of the plan, female participation was extremely poor. In 1962, only 10.4% of the scholars were female. Almost a decade later, in 1970, female uptake still accounted for only 12.4% of the awards. The first ten-year review of the plan took note of this and proposed the removal of gender-based discrimination in the payment of marriage allowances. These recommendations were endorsed by the 1974 Jamaica Commonwealth Education Conference (*Report of 6CEC*: 31–32). The eighth conference in Colombo (1980), by which time female representation had risen to 20.7%, took up the issue once again and urged scholarship agencies to nominate an adequate number of women applicants for awards so that more of them could be selected for scholarships under the Plan (*Report of 8CEC*: 18).

A second ten-year review of the Plan, conducted on the 25th anniversary of the CSFP, reported to 9CCEM at Nicosia, Cyprus, in 1984. By this time women took up 23.3% of the awards. Several of the receiving countries expressed the strong hope that sending countries would submit more nominations of women candidates so that the proportion of women Commonwealth scholars would be increased. Suggestions for a separate award scheme for predetermined quotas for women were discussed. Though no recommendations were made, it was recognised that there was a need for women to win more awards (*Report of 9CCEM*: 40–41).

The concern of ministers with the continued poor representation of women (20–25%) during the 1980s, was again highlighted at the 11CCEM in Barbados. The CSFP report showed that while there was a small proportional increase over the decade, the absolute number showed a net drop. A number of awarding countries expressed their desire to make more awards to women but pointed out that this was dependent on their being put forward as candidates by nominating countries. A suggestion was made that awarding countries should provide better family support to women scholars through the day-care and other social services which some universities now offer.

In some cases, awarding countries agreed to waive the usual academic requirement (upper second pass) if a nomination was supported by sufficient evidence of the quality of the candidate and his or her ability to carry out advanced academic work. A number of delegates expressed concern that age limits tended to discriminate against candidates with work experience or against women who had stepped out of academic life to raise families. The UK gave special consideration to candidates who had had to postpone their entry or re-entry into higher education (*Report of 11CCEM*: 29).

By the time of the third ten-year review in 1993, it was reported that 33% of the scholars were women. The percentage had risen from 25% at the time of the last CSFP ten-year review, the whole of the improvement having occurred between 1989 and 1993. While this was considered an encouraging phenomenon, there was a need to go further (*Report of Third Ten-Year Review Committee*: 14). There was some evidence of affirmative action succeeding. In 1991–92, 25% of scholarship applications were submitted by women, the percentage of female nominations was 31% and the percentage of women among those actually taking up awards was 33%. One could infer from this that a modest degree of affirmative action was occurring.

Many countries reported special efforts to increase the number of women who held CSFP awards. For example, some awarding countries had implemented quotas in order to increase the number of awards to women: however there was no consensus among countries on the desirability of extending the use of quotas for the purpose of developing a better gender balance. Others suggested easing the upper age limit for anyone – male and female – who had been out of academic work but who could demonstrate ability and the commitment to return to it. This would be beneficial, especially to women who had interrupted their employment or studies to assume family responsibilities.

It was also evident that some women who had been granted awards had difficulty in taking them up, needing to be accompanied by families that included dependent children. Terms and conditions of awards needed to make special provision for scholars with dependents. There was also need for more flexible immigration procedures allowing the entry of accompanying carers for family dependents (ibid: 19).

The issue of awards remains on the agenda of Commonwealth ministers and at the thirteenth conference, held in Islamabad, ministers again noted that women consistently accounted for only about a third of awards (*Report of 13CCEM*: 5). Since then, the situation has somewhat improved in scholarships and the percentage of women scholars now stands at about 40%. The situation on fellowships is less encouraging – women currently hold around 20% (data supplied by the ACU).

In summary, progress in ensuring that women take up a larger share of Commonwealth awards has been slow but steady. Today women are still under-represented in the awards but the numerous affirmative measures have made an impact, raising women's participation from around 10% in 1962 to 40% in 2000.

b. Women and Higher Education Management

The Commonwealth project on women and higher education management addresses the Commonwealth's concern with issues of educational access and quality pertaining to women in higher education. The women's programme was identified as a priority area as it addressed two of the Commonwealth's focal areas in higher education – management and staff development.

Data from many countries made it apparent that administrative leadership remained the domain of men. Women had been and continued to be grossly under-represented in higher education management. A UNESCO-Commonwealth report showed that:

... in spite of advances which women have made in many areas of public life in the past two decades, in the area of higher education management they are still a long way from participating on the same footing as men. With hardly an exception, the 'in spite of advances which women have made in many areas of public life in the management level and at about twenty to one at senior management level. Women deans and professors are a minority group and women vice-chancellors and presidents are still a rarity.

Dines: 11

The dearth of women in senior administrative positions was viewed from two standpoints. The first was person-centred, in that the paucity of women was attributed to their psycho-social attributes, including the personality characteristics, attitudes and behavioural skills of women themselves. The focus was on the need for women to adapt – to compensate for their socialisation deficits. The alternative perspective is the structure-centred paradigm that advances the view that it is the disadvantageous position of women in the organisational structure which shapes and defines the behaviour of women. The remedy is to make a fundamental change which eliminates inappropriate discrimination in institutional policies and practices (Sheryl Bond).

The Commonwealth Response through the Commonwealth Secretariat and the ACU

To address these issues and to raise the profile of women in higher education, the Secretariat initiated a Women in Higher Education Management Programme for which the ACU offered to be the implementing agency. The programme tried to bring together the previously ad hoc activities of both organisations in a coherent range of activities.

The aim was to facilitate the development of women in Commonwealth universities so that they could use their academic, administrative and, above all, management, skills to contributing to the institutional development of universities, thus securing a significant increase in the number of management positions held by women, as universities redefined and developed their role in the twenty-first century (ACU-CHESS Steering Committee, 1993: 3).

The ACU and the Commonwealth Secretariat worked closely together in developing the remit of the Women's Programme; from 1991, when ACU, the Commonwealth Secretariat and UNESCO entered into a Memorandum of Understanding for the establishment of a co-operative programme of activities, these three organisations collaboratively planned and gave financial support to a wide variety of projects. The programme chose to make interventions on two fronts: changing the management structures of universities and enhancing the capacity of women in universities to 'break through the glass ceiling' into top management positions.

A broad range of activities was successfully undertaken to achieve the objectives of the programme:

Crucial Strategies to Sustain the Work of the Women's Programme

- The identification and development of a group of core trainers and senior women managers across the Commonwealth who can network with each other and provide leadership in future training activities/initiatives; and

- The ready availability of reliable and user-friendly training materials which could be used by other trainers.

Training Workshops

Considerable work has focused on enhancing the management skills of senior women administrators in higher education. The programme began with a series of management training courses in several parts of the Commonwealth: Bombay (1986 and 1988); Jamaica (1990); Botswana (1991); Kuala Lumpur, Malaysia (1991); The Gambia (1992); Suva, Fiji (1994); Port Moresby, Papua New Guinea (1995); Cape Town, South Africa (1996); Colombo, Sri Lanka (1997); New Delhi, India (1998); Malacca, Malaysia (1999); Kandy, Sri Lanka (1999); and Lagos, Nigeria (1999).

Support continued to be provided at the time of writing, for regional and national training workshops. Planning was underway for the next training workshops in the West Indies and in Pakistan.

Training Modules

A core focus of the programme was the commissioning of user-friendly training materials. The principal product of the activity comprised the training modules which address the key problems encountered by women in higher education management. Six themes were developed:

- *Management Development for Women: A Facilitator's Handbook,* which provides a basic level of information about good training practices;

- *Academic Leadership,* which provides knowledge and skill in the domain of academic leadership, points to a leadership style strongly associated with women and urges that women have the right and the obligation to assume leadership positions in the university;

- *Women's Studies as a Catalyst for the Advancement of Women in Higher Education,* which aims to help create and strengthen a cadre of women leaders on the various campuses who, by their involvement in research, teaching, outreach and advocacy within the university system, can transform the now present male dominated pattern of gender relations within the institution;

- *Managing Personal and Professional Roles,* which deals with the multiple roles that women play in society, and the often expressed dilemma of managing all those roles and achieving a balanced life;

- *Women and Research* which argues that research prowess enables women to take their share of professorial positions and suggests strategies whereby women can improve their research capacity and visibility;

- *Women and Governance in Higher Education*, which highlights the level of participation required to promote the advancement of women to senior positions within the University and assists women to develop their skills in committee and legislation work in order to enable them to contribute effectively to the decision-making process. Ancillary materials focus on:

  - Developing Management Skills, designed to offer women who are leaders and managers in higher education, or wish to become leaders and managers in higher education, the opportunity to develop some of the most useful and important management skills.

  - Women and Mentoring in Higher Education, which looks at the particular relevance of mentoring for higher education and argues that women, through their relatively limited access to higher management, are particularly well suited to mentoring relationships.

The Commonwealth Secretariat and the ACU have published the first six modules. Entitled *Management Development for Women in Higher Education*, the volumes comprise the training modules and the ancillary materials which provide additional resources to increase the richness and diversity of the Programme.

MA in Women and Management in Higher Education
This Master's degree programme on Women and Management in Higher Education at the Institute of Education, University of London commenced in 1998 and is the fruit of collaborative planning initiated by those involved in the Women's Programme through the early Secretariat workshops held in 1995 and 1996. The programme of study has been designed for individuals who want to:

- Understand more about the position of women in educational management;

- Have the opportunity to explore the situation of women in management in higher education;

- Have the opportunity to make informed decisions and plans about their working life.

The ACU continues to support women from less developed countries to attend this one-year MA course. Three cohorts of women had passed through the programme, at the time of writing, including participants from South Africa, Guyana, Sri Lanka, Trinidad, Kenya, Nigeria, Ghana and Namibia. Several of them have returned home to promotions in their universities, to enrol on PhD courses or to take up new policy-making roles.

Pacific Charter for Women Managers in Higher Education

The University of the South Pacific Council adopted the Pacific Charter for Women Managers in Higher Education on 21 October 1996. This represents a major initiative by Pacific women and a landmark charter to ensure gender equity in higher education in the Pacific.

Surveys and Studies

The programme undertook a number of surveys and studies which have illuminated the status of women in higher education, highlighted the problems they encounter and suggested ways in which the role and status of women in higher education can be enhanced. Prominent among the studies was a book jointly planned and published in 1993 by the Commonwealth Secretariat and UNESCO, under the title *Women in Higher Education Management*. Edited by Elizabeth Dines, it analysed the career paths of women in higher education in the context of national higher education environments.

Other studies have included:

- *Review of Training Workshops:* In 1996, the ACU commissioned a review of the training workshops which had taken place since the inception of the programme in1985. The review was in part financed by funds from UNESCO.

- *Gender Management Systems:* With funds from the Commonwealth Secretariat, a handbook of good practice in gender management in the higher education sector was commissioned. The aim of the handbook, which is based on a general review of the literature on gender mainstreaming and on country case studies, is to increase awareness and knowledge of strategies and mechanisms used across the Commonwealth and elsewhere to mainstream gender equity into higher education development. The handbook also provides governments and ministries of education with a user-friendly guide to mainstreaming gender integration into all aspects of planning, implementing and evaluating higher education development projects.

- *Equal Opportunity Officers (EOOs):* With the support of a grant from UNESCO, a survey was undertaken to provide comparative information about what had prompted the establishment of EOOs in the university sector, their methods of operation and the impact they have had on their institutions, with special reference to gender. The resulting data were analysed to ascertain the key factors relating to the establishment, management and impact of EOOs.

- *Female Staff in Commonwealth Universities:* In 1998 the Commonwealth Higher Education Management Service undertook a survey of female staff in Commonwealth universities. Its report, *A Single Sex Profession?: Female Staff Numbers in Commonwealth Countries*, portrays the low level of participation by women academics in universities in general (24%) and the very low level of participation in senior management of universities (about 10% of professors and 7% of vice-chancellors/presidents).

Reports and Publications

The workshops and projects of the women's programme have generated a large number of reports which are useful resource materials for those working in this field. Publications by associated agencies include:

- A regular feature in each issue of the *ACU Bulletin*, containing articles, reports, news and views about women in higher education management;

- A handbook on good practice in the field of 'Women and Higher Education Management' prepared under the auspices of UNESCO's Special Project – Women, Higher Education and Development. The handbook has brought together examples of international, regional, national, institutional and class-room strategies and practices, which advance the aims of the Special Project and which strengthen the access and participation of women in higher education and in leadership roles both within this sector and in society as a whole.

Special Projects

Two special projects deserve mention. In 1995 and 1996, a three-way exchange project enabled three women academics representing the University of Adelaide, the University of the West Indies and SNDT Women's University (Bombay) to carry out two-week study visits at each other's institutions looking in particular at the teaching of gender studies and at ways in which networks could be developed between the universities to their mutual benefit. The second project, initiated in 1994, was a review and report on strategic development plans to enhance the contribution of women to universities in Southern Africa.

Commonwealth Women's Networks

Pan-Commonwealth and national level networks and contacts have been established to provide mutual support and information to women in higher education in the Commonwealth. The principal network is the *ACU Women's Network*, an electronic network operated from Malaysia. The network circulates information about appointments, successes, publications and research; shares views about women in higher education; publicises events such as conferences, meetings and workshops; poses problems and seeks help and solutions. There are currently about 100 Commonwealth women in this network. The network links up with other national and regional level Commonwealth networks for women in universities. Principal among these are the Colloquium of Senior Women Executives in Australian Higher Education; the Senior Women Academic Administrators of Canada (SWAAC); the Australian Technology Network (ATN); the Forum for African Women Educationalists, South Africa (FAWESA); the Professional Women's Development Network (PWDN) in the United Kingdom; and the Network of Women in Higher Education in the Pacific (NetWHEP).

Future Activities
The project expects to move towards:

- Mainstreaming gender concerns at all levels of higher education through a Gender Management System for the tertiary education sector;

- Extensive advocacy work with those in a position to effect change;

- Instituting gender sensitisation programmes training for both men and women in higher education;

- Extending the network of senior women managers;

- Developing more link and exchange programmes between women's study centres.

7 The Commonwealth of Learning: Gender in Open and Distance Learning

The overall aim of COL's programme for women in development is to improve the status of women through widening access to education. COL sees distance education as a means of enabling more women to improve the quality of their lives, to play a more active role in their communities, and make a greater contribution to their countries' development.

COL Report to WAMM, 1990

The Commonwealth of Learning is committed to removing barriers to women's access to education through the delivery of gender-balanced programmes and projects, as well as through initiatives that are specifically targeted to benefit women and girls. COL is also committed to participating fully and actively, within the framework of its mandate, in the implementation of the *1995 Commonwealth Plan of Action on Gender and Development.*

Open and distance education, because of its flexibility and openness, has the potential to reach the previously 'unreached', such as the disabled and rural poor, and girls and women with quality education. By making learning available at times and places suitable to the particular needs of the student, distance education overcomes many of the barriers faced by girls and women trying to access conventional education systems. Therefore gender issues, especially with respect to equitable access to quality education and training, feature prominently on COL's agenda.

Following on the recommendations of Commonwealth Heads of Government in 1987, COL began to develop programmes relating to women in development. The central emphasis of COL's work focused on improving national capacity for human resource development through better access to education and training. COL identified a comparative advantage in being able to apply open and distance learning methodologies to meet the special educational needs of women. Distance education 'provides them an opportunity to re-enter the educational mainstream or, for those who completely missed formal school, an opportunity to make a start'. COL also saw the need to help women to improve their education and skills for work; to be better home-makers; to re-enter the work force; and to prepare for positions of leadership and responsibility. With the flexibility it offered, open and distance learning 'allows women to study alongside their responsibilities' (*COL Report to WAMM*, 1990).

A conference of women vice-chancellors organised by COL in May 1990 identified open and distance learning as a means of educating both rural and urban women in areas such as basic and functional literacy and legal and health education, as well as providing training in entrepreneurship. It was regarded as important to identify strategies for the empowerment of women in all walks of life, as well as to ensure that modern-day technology was harnessed for the advancement of women (*COL Report to WAMM*, 1990).

a. COL Initiatives 1990–93

Following the initial report to Ministers Responsible for Women's Affairs at Ottawa (1990), COL developed a strategic action plan to address the educational and training requirements of women. The provision of adult education for women and access to education and training was recognised as an essential prerequisite for female participation on an equal basis in society. Attention was focused on those aspects of education where women's needs are most critical, such as literacy, teacher-training, and gender and development.

Literacy

Attention was first directed to enhancing literacy among women, a fundamental channel to access education and training, which has been denied many women, particularly in the Commonwealth countries of the South. COL, in conjunction with Pakistan's Allama Iqbal Open University (AIOU), one of the few Commonwealth institutions offering literacy programmes for women through distance education, hosted a Symposium on Women's Literacy Programmes – The Role of Distance Education in Islamabad, 23–27 September 1991. Its purpose was to orient senior level personnel engaged in literacy and post-literacy programmes in the Asia-Pacific region to methods and techniques of planning, implementing and evaluating such programmes, and to highlight how literacy could be approached through the use of open and distance learning techniques. Presentations and discussions of literacy programmes emphasised the importance of literacy for women as a basic human right and the way to empower women.

In Ghana COL contributed to the Mass Literacy Programme (Masslip), a huge government literacy programme aimed at raising functional literacy, providing technical advice on the management of the programme, field recording equipment and technical training in the use of recording equipment. Women formed a large percentage of those accessing the classroom instruction, which was facilitated by the government's organisation of free childcare in rural areas.

Gender-Sensitive Statistics

Realising the far-reaching significance of training in statistical analysis and application, the COL agreed to collaborate with the UN International Research and Training Institute for the Advancement of Women (INSTRAW) in a South Pacific training workshop to sensitise both users and producers of statistics on the issues and problems relating to statistics and women.

With financial assistance from COL, the New Zealand Open Polytechnic produced a workshop resource book. This was designed to enable participants to identify information available from existing statistical collections, develop key indicators, and present data in a comprehensible form, while assessing the adequacy of existing data.

Teacher and Higher Education

The Government of The Gambia, wishing to upgrade existing teachers, called upon COL to complete a profile of teachers in the education system. The report revealed that a large percentage of untrained teachers were women. This information was used by the government to develop a programme to meet the needs of women teachers.

Statistics in the South Pacific revealed that too few women were accessing the University of the South Pacific's (USP) extension programmes. A group of graduate Pacific women recommended that the university undertake a research survey to identify barriers faced by women in the region in accessing and completing credit courses and programmes offered through distance education by the university.

COL assisted Makerere University, Uganda to establish a Bachelor of Education programme implemented with open and distance learning methodologies. This was completed under the guidance of a female senior lecturer and staff from the University of Nairobi. As a result, an increasing proportion of women have enrolled in the Bachelor of Education courses.

In Malawi, Zambia and Zimbabwe, COL was involved in a refugee teacher training programme with the aim of identifying suitable teaching materials for teacher training in the refugee camps, the majority of whose occupants were women.

In the Caribbean, the COL Teacher Education by Distance Project in Jamaica had an original enrolment of 205 people, 203 of whom were women. Two of the three key personnel involved in the Guyana Distance Education Network project supported by COL were also women, both of whom received special training under COL sponsorship.

Fellowships
In the award of Fellowships, COL paid special attention to ensure that an equitable gender balance was achieved. Of the visiting fellowships awarded, the overall percentage awarded to females was 37.5%. Nominations for visiting fellowships were requested from ministries of education, who were asked to give particular consideration to nominating women. Of the outgoing fellowship awards that send British Columbia educators to developing countries, 27.2% were female.

b. COL Initiatives 1993–96
During this period COL was engaged in preparing materials, conducting research and training related to gender.

Distance-Education Materials
COL published the following materials:

- *Theoretical Perspectives on Gender and Development* (1996), a core module which focuses on the theoretical justification for examining the specific roles and contributions of women to development initiatives;

- *Sensitive Learning Materials: Handbook for Educators* (1995), a handbook designed to be used by those developing distance learning materials to assist in identifying bias concerns and improving capacity for addressing them.

Research
In addition to producing and disseminating the educational resources described above, COL supported research in the field of women and open and distance learning, for example the production of an occasional paper, 'Barriers to Participation of Women in Technological Education and the Role of Distance Education' (1994). COL also provided funding toward a collaborative effort resulting in a University of the South Pacific/COL co-publication, *South Pacific Women in Distance Education* (1995).

Training
COL was also involved in training educators in the techniques of open and distance learning, women and the media, and technology training. In its budget year 1996/97, COL gave high priority to areas which included open schooling, non-formal education and technical teacher training.

c. COL Initiatives 1997–2000
At their 1996 meeting in Trinidad, Ministers Responsible for Women's Affairs consistently emphasised the need for more training to raise awareness about the importance of gender issues and to strengthen the capacity for gender mainstreaming.

Ministers also considered gender sensitisation and training in gender planning and analysis vital for key stakeholders. In response, COL's efforts complemented the efforts of other Commonwealth agencies, governments and NGOs in implementing the *1995 Commonwealth Plan of Action on Gender and Development*. COL integrated gender issues into its programming both at a broad level and through the development of discrete programmes. In the first instance, COL ensured that its programmes were gender–balanced and worked towards improving access to education and training for girls and women, particularly where imbalances had been identified.

Supporting Basic Education

Programmes to improve conditions for women and children have received priority through the development and implementation of appropriate open and distance learning materials, particularly in support of basic education. Efforts in this area have focused on initiatives to promote open schooling, non-formal education and teacher education, such as:

- Encouraging the development of open schooling systems through collaboration with UNICEF, UNESCO and local institutions. COL has convened regional workshops in Asia, Africa and the Caribbean, as well as a national workshop and an international symposium in India on the potential of open schooling for increasing access to basic education for girls and women;

- Working with the Bangladesh Open University to develop a pilot programme to increase the business skills of rural women and to encourage them to become self-employed;

- Working with eight Southern African countries to upgrade teachers, most of whom are women, of upper primary and junior secondary science, mathematics and technology and general education using open and distance learning methodologies;

- Co-ordinating a materials development and training initiative in Southern Africa to provide a suite of high-quality learning materials comprising the core curriculum at the junior secondary level common to the nine countries involved;

- In conjunction with Domasi College and the Malawi Ministry of Education, developing materials to professionally upgrade 3,500 teachers currently teaching without the requisite training.

Other Areas of Work

- Assistance from COL enabled the Women's International Network (WIN) to publish a book on how women can use technologies for open and distance learning.

- COL carried out an environmental scan of the literature and barriers encountered by women in accessing the new information and communications technologies. The scan identified challenging issues on a regional basis. COL initiated regional meetings to discuss regionally specific issues and to identify strategies to address them. The meetings were held in New Delhi, November 1998 (in conjunction with the British Council); Barbados, November 1999; Tanzania, March 2000, and Australia (for the Pacific region), 2001.

- Development and implementation of an electronic database on gender-related training materials available within the UN system and from the Commonwealth Secretariat. Designed to encourage inter-agency collaboration on the design, use and review of materials that support capacity building on gender equality issues, the Steering Committee was composed of representatives from three UN agencies – UNICEF, UNIFEM and UNDP. The database is directly accessible through the UN WomenWatch website (the UN Internet gateway on the advancement of women) in conjunction with a best practices website, COL's website, and the Gender link on the Commonwealth Secretariat's website. The database's main purpose is to organise training material into a readily accessible resource base that provides useful and strategic links to agencies, and their materials, with experience in gender training. COL undertook the design and implementation of this project with the continued guidance of the Steering Committee. The database was showcased during the year 2000 review of the Platform for Action (Beijing +5) as a demonstration of a co-ordinated response to the Beijing strategies and actions. This meeting took place in New York in June 2000.

- The need to increase literacy levels, particularly among girls and women, remains one of the pre-eminent educational challenges facing developing Commonwealth nations. COL, in conjunction with the UK Department for International Development, has undertaken the development of a pilot project in selected Commonwealth countries to explore ways in which literacy programmes can be enhanced through the application of information and communications technologies. The project is currently underway in India and Zambia. Its goal is to demonstrate and evaluate the effectiveness of technology-based community learning centres through which literacy workers can develop learner competencies in reading, numeracy, and the use and operation of information and communication tools. Initiated in 1998, the Implementation Plans have been developed in conjunction with the two in-country project directors to guide the project over the next three years.

d. Future Directions for COL

COL's current strategic plan builds on and strengthens its contribution to enhancing the participation of women in development through increased access to education and training. Its Three-Year Plan, 2000–2003, focuses on the application of distance-, open- and technology-mediated education in a broad range of sectors, including basic and primary education and skills development. COL also invites ministers responsible for women's affairs and their colleagues to engage COL in a dialogue on key gender issues, and to explore ways in which distance education and open learning methodologies can be adapted to address the issues of equitable access to quality education and training, professional upgrading, teacher training and retraining, upgrading of skills in those areas critical to poverty reduction and elimination and other areas which COL's expertise can be harnessed in the realisation of ministries' objectives (*COL Report to WAMM*, 1999). A broader survey of COL's work will be found in Chapter 6.

8 Strengths, Weaknesses, Opportunities and Threats

a. Strengths

The policies, structures and processes to mainstream gender into all aspects of Commonwealth development have been put in place. The Commonwealth's vision of gender in development has been clearly enunciated in its *1995 Plan of Action on Gender and Development*, which has been endorsed by Commonwealth Heads of Government and subscribed to by Commonwealth countries at the national level. Commonwealth agencies, the Commonwealth Secretariat and the Commonwealth of Learning have adopted the strategies and mechanisms recommended in the Plan of Action and formulated their programmes and projects from a gender perspective.

This chapter has shown that, in developing their educational programmes and projects, both the Secretariat and COL adhere closely to the guidelines drawn from the Plan of Action. Both agencies have included a gender dimension into their work affecting all levels of education. Commonwealth agencies have also collaborated very effectively with other agencies having similar aims. Considerable attention has been given to ensuring that the Commonwealth programmes which enhance the participation of girls at the basic level give due consideration to enabling more girls to attain basic levels of literacy and numeracy through the formal system of education, as well as a range of out-of-school initiatives. To make girls and women more competitive in the new scientific and technological fields of employment and in the knowledge industries, special attention has been paid to girls and women's access to science and technology education and to the new communication technologies. At the upper level of the education sector, women's access to the award of scholarships and fellowships encourages greater uptake by women. Women's entry into senior management positions in higher education has been promoted by the Women and Management Programme.

The Commonwealth has succeeded in creating an enabling environment for the achievement of gender equity in education. The review of policies, strategies and programmes in development in general, and education in particular, indicates that appropriate guidelines and structures have assisted the various Commonwealth agencies and their functional divisions to ensure more equitable representation of girls and women at all levels of education. The gender perspective is advocated throughout the development, implementation and assessment of education activities in the Commonwealth.

b. Weaknesses

Why then is the reality still far from the vision?

The principal obstacle within the Commonwealth agencies has been the lack of resources to push programmes forward. Over the last decade, funds available for programme implementation have gradually shrunk and budget allocations for projects have been inadequate for carrying out wide-ranging programmes that can make a real impact. Where possible, staff have collaborated with other agencies and have been able collectively to launch activities which are making a difference on the ground. However, the resources are grossly inadequate to address the enormous problem of girls' disadvantage in education. Despite the efforts of Commonwealth agencies, national governments and NGOs, and despite the strenuous efforts of UN agencies pursuing Education for All, the problems of girls' attendance in schools in many of the south Asian countries and in Africa continue to be of great concern. Exhortations by ministers of education and ministers responsible for women's affairs that more funds should be provided for the education of girls and women have not borne fruit. Faced with many competing demands on their resources, Commonwealth governments and the Secretariat are unable to match the intention to raise the level of girls' participation in education with the necessary funds.

A second, related, factor has been the slow process by which staff have been made aware of the policies, sensitised to the issues and acquired competencies to plan their own programmes from a truly gender perspective. The division responsible for this at the time (GYAD) put in place most of the structures such as gender steering committee, gender focal points and training for staff. Requirements from SPEU and the management, that all projects must pay attention to their impact on women, have again strongly influenced the planning of programmes and the presentation of project proposals. Reporting procedures have also required data to be disaggregated and the impact on women clearly noted. However, limitations of time and resources, have hindered the implementation and impact of policies and guidelines. It is expected that as more staff are exposed to the tools of gender mainstreaming, the changes in project plans and implementation will become more real than cosmetic.

c. Opportunities

The opportunities for achieving gender equity in the education sector of Commonwealth countries have been recognised and much work has commenced, marking important steps towards the attainment of this objective. In this respect, the Commonwealth has been a leading light for others to follow. The Plan of Action, together with all the work that has gone into developing strategies for mainstreaming gender through evolving gender management systems, represents a groundbreaking initiative. Much more can be expected from carrying this work forward.

The Commonwealth represents a unique model for co-operation. The Secretariat's successive teams and the COL have demonstrated their ability to achieve much with limited resources. Given more resources and continued co-operation with partners, the potential for expanding current work is enormous.

The Commonwealth also has a wealth of experience that can be tapped to assist the development of new models of co-operation and new programmes. 'Learning from each other' is an accepted Commonwealth way. While there is much evidence of this having happened in the field of education, the possibilities for more studies, greater sharing of information, building of networks and developing new models for enhancing women's and girls' education cannot be ignored.

Part Three

Spotlight on Science, Technology and Mathematics Education

Chapter 4

The Road from Oxford to Halifax: Snapshots of Science, Technology and Mathematics Education

Ved Goel

1 Introduction

The Oxford conference took place the same year the Sputnik was launched into space. This latter event caused a great deal of soul-searching about the role and importance of science education, in particular, and provided much of the impetus for curriculum change in science education in the 1960s. Shortly after this, in 1964, the then British Prime Minister, Harold Wilson, referred to the 'white heat of technological revolution', thus stressing the importance of technology as well as science.

The international context of Science Technology and Mathematics Education (STME) has changed and developed over the 40 and more years of Commonwealth education ministers' conferences but two very important themes recur throughout the period. The first of these may be described as 'continuity and change'. The records of the early CCEMs and key specialist conferences such as the 1963 conference on 'School Science Teaching' held at the University of Ceylon, show that key issues and topics identified then are still significant now. For example, the importance of teacher training and the significant role of resources for teaching, including both equipment and books, are still relevant. In the earlier stages, there was reference to the supply of teachers, often referring to the provision of expatriate specialist teachers; this is no longer a significant issue for some countries. However, in a number of Commonwealth countries there is an acute shortage of science and mathematics teachers, and expatriate teachers are still needed.

The second key issue is that of 'partnership and co-operation'. In the 40 years since the Oxford conference, an immensely wide range of activities has been undertaken in STME in the Commonwealth. None of this would have been possible without partnerships at a variety of levels, starting from the personal and ranging through institutional to governmental co-operation. In addition, the growth and development of national and international professional associations and organisations has enabled a wide range of activities.

For example, national science associations such as the All India Science Teachers Association, the Association for Science Education (UK) and the Science Teachers Association of Nigeria, international organisations such as UNESCO, donor agencies such as the Canadian International Development Agency (CIDA), DfID and the German International Development Agency (GTZ), and foundations such as the Rockefeller Foundation have all contributed in various ways to Commonwealth STME.

Partnerships between countries and institutions in the earlier years were often predicated on the assumption that models developed in the industrialised countries of the Commonwealth could be translated (sometimes with little or no adaptation) to the less developed countries. Partnerships now are much more likely to have a more equal basis – an illustration of continuity and change

The two themes of 'continuity and change' and 'partnership and co-operation' will recur throughout this chapter. The first section provides a brief historical overview of the developments in STME in the Commonwealth over the 40-year period. This gives a basis for the following section, in which some examples of the important issues in Commonwealth STME are described in more detail. The final section is about the future, since the needs of Commonwealth countries are changing and it is important not only to learn from the past but also to be able to identify and respond to future needs.

2 Overview of Developments in STME in the Commonwealth

The Oxford conference identified some important priorities for Commonwealth co-operation in education, some of which are still important 40 years later. Among the key areas identified were the training and supply of teachers and technical education, the latter largely because there was a perceived link between technical education and economic growth. The focus in teacher training was largely on in-service programmes, which could be used to help overcome teacher shortages in specialised areas such as science and technical subjects.

The priorities in STME were largely those of the industrialised countries of the Commonwealth. For example, during the 1960s and early 1970s there were very powerful movements of curriculum reform, such as the Nuffield project for the sciences, the Science Education Project (India) and 'new' mathematics. These in turn were often used as the basis for curriculum reform in the less developed countries of the Commonwealth, often drawing upon expertise made available through bodies such as the Center for Research on Education Outcomes (CREDO, later CEDO) and the British Council. There was little sense at that time of the inter-relatedness of science and mathematics, and technology was often seen as discrete and different – for example as part of an approach to craft, design and technology.

The key issues identified at the second Commonwealth Education Conference, held in India in 1962 were very similar to those originally pinpointed at the Oxford conference, but perhaps had an increased focus on the problems of textbook development and supply. The need for the training of teachers in science and mathematics was also clearly identified, as was the training of technical teachers, this latter being seen as a key priority area. At the second CEC, there was recognition of the importance of training for technicians, which has remained an area in which there has been substantial Commonwealth co-operation (see the section on Training for Technicians).

There was a useful British contribution to the provision of textbooks in the form of the ELBS (English Language Book Scheme) through which paperback versions of British texts for post-secondary education and training were made available at a reduced price.

An important recommendation endorsed by the second CEC (but proposed at the Oxford conference) was that for an expert conference, which resulted in the December 1963 conference on School Science Teaching, held at the University of Ceylon (now Sri Lanka). This was a good example of co-operation and partnership, since Commonwealth governments, UNESCO and the USA supported it. The conference was held under the auspices of the Commonwealth Education Liaison Committee.

The themes at the conference were instructive:

- Science for All (which has continuing resonance with the emphasis on Education for All at the 1990 Jomtien and 2000 Dakar UN conferences, and the continuing emphasis on primary science teaching and learning);

- Teaching Science (with emphasis on primary science, science for the more and less able, technical training, syllabus revision and practical work);

- Teacher-training and science teacher associations;

- Aids to teaching;

- Evaluation;

- Co-operative measures such as emergency training of teachers and research centres.

Each of these themes remains important, even though the emphasis may have changed.

The conference also focused on developments in science teaching in the UK, Europe and the USA – it is noticeable that there is relatively little mention of programmes and activities in the less developed countries of the Commonwealth. Co-operation at that stage tended to imply the absorption of ideas and models from the industrialised countries by the less developed countries.

One example of such co-operation was the focus on curriculum development in the 1960s and early 1970s, during which there were a number of projects, often funded by donor agencies such as ODM (UK), CIDA, UNESCO and USAID, in which science, mathematics and technical curricula were developed in various parts of the Commonwealth. Such projects included the East African Secondary Science Project, the West Indies Integrated Science project, the development of 'new' mathematics curricula in many Commonwealth countries and industrial arts curricula. Substantial work was also done at primary level, for example the African Primary Science Programme (which became the Science Education Programme for Africa).

The work of the Ceylon meeting was commended by the third Commonwealth Education Conference in Ottawa, Canada.

The key importance accorded to curriculum development in the 1960s was reflected in the establishment and growth of curriculum development centres or units as part of ministries of education or autonomous organisations in many countries. However, it became clear that it is not possible to isolate the curriculum from other components of the education system, since curriculum changes have immediate and continuing implications for assessment and evaluation, teacher training, provision of texts, and the nature and scale of equipment required. Ironically, it is still possible to find examples of education systems in which the staff members of curriculum development units and teacher training institutions have little professional contact with each other.

The third Commonwealth Education Conference continued to stress the issues identified in previous conferences. Apart from the training and supply of teachers (including technical teachers), attention was drawn to the importance of equipment. There were at least two components to this concern. The first related to the need for equipment in order to be able to teach the sciences, and this led to an emphasis in the 1970s on the production of low-cost equipment, often at centralised production units such as that at the Kenya Science Teachers College (see below). The second related to the need for different types of equipment, taking account of the development of new curricula in the sciences, technical subjects and mathematics. There was also a focus on the role of science teachers' associations, a concern that predated the founding of the Commonwealth Association of Science Technology and Mathematics Educators in 1974.

Following a recommendation of 3CEC, a conference on the education and training of technicians was held in Huddersfield, UK, in 1966, and the report of the Conference was considered by a committee at 4CEC which took place in Lagos, Nigeria. The education and training of technicians continues to be an important issue (see below). Some of the most important topics considered at the Huddersfield conference were:

- The importance of an accurate assessment of needs;
- The role of technical education within general education;
- The need for a close working relationship with industry and commerce;
- The nature of planned technician education programmes;
- Assessment and evaluation in the training of technicians.
- The training of technical teachers;
- Gender issues in technician training.

The main concerns of both the 1963 and 1966 expert conferences have remained important in science and technical education. They were followed by a similarly important expert conference on Mathematics in Commonwealth Schools, held in Trinidad in 1968. The key themes of the conference were:

- Fundamental ideas and objectives of mathematics education;
- The teaching of mathematics at primary level, including both methods and content;
- The teaching of mathematics at secondary level; (a) as a general 'core' subject; and (b) as a subject for those with specialist requirements;
- Assessment of children's progress and evaluation of programmes, purpose and method;
- Teachers: selection, initial and subsequent training;
- Resources for learning mathematics, including textbooks, films, radio and television;
- Programmed learning.

The fifth Commonwealth Education Conference, held in Australia in 1971, which proposed the expansion of the Commonwealth Secretariat's Education Division, included a specific reference to a Commonwealth Book Development Scheme. The focus of previous conferences was largely reiterated, with an increased emphasis on assessment and examinations; there had been some regional approaches to this issue, such as the West African Examinations Council and the East African Examinations Council (the Caribbean Examinations Council was founded in the 1970s).

The sixth CEC took place in Jamaica in 1974, the year of the formation of the Commonwealth Association of Science and Mathematics Education at a conference held in Jamaica in 1973. CASME incorporated Technology to become CASTME in the early 1980s. The formation of CASTME was reflection of the increasing importance placed on professional teacher associations. The section below on

CASTME provides an outline of some of the important activities of the association. The Jamaica CCEM reflected concerns about equipment in the form of kits.

Prior to 7CEC, held in Ghana in 1977, a seminar/workshop on technical education and industry was held in Hong Kong in 1976. The conference drew attention to the importance of science education (including issues of relevant equipment) and technical education, and provided the basis for the formation of the Commonwealth Association of Polytechnics in Africa, founded in 1979.

The work on low-cost equipment, which was carried out during the 1970s, was recognised at 8CEC, held in Sri Lanka in 1980. Work on mathematics education reported to the conference included the first Inter-African Seminar of the African Mathematical Union, held in 1979. A recommendation was made for a conference on STME.

STME was dwarfed by the issue of student mobility at the 1984 CCEM held in Cyprus; this is an issue that has continued to engage successive CCEMs, as explained in Chapter 1. The 1980s could be regarded as a decade of consolidation and possibly retrenchment, as resources became increasingly difficult to obtain. The single greatest achievement flowing from the 1987 CCEM (Nairobi) was the recommendation leading to the acceptance by the 1987 CHOGM in Vancouver of the establishment of the Commonwealth of Learning. This has provided the basis for a review of all the different methodologies for the delivery of education and training (see Chapters 1 and 6). However, the issue of the popularisation of science was also discussed (see below).

Science education has been one of the five key themes of the Commonwealth Education Programme. The resources available for the Education Programme during the 1980s were not large, and this was a continuing source of concern from the mid-1980s. Attention was drawn to this issue at the 1990 CCEM (Barbados) and even though resources have been made available through CFTC, the core funding available to the Education Programme has remained low. This has meant that the search for partnerships has been not just desirable but essential.

The emphasis in the 1990s has tended to reflect the emphasis on basic education of which the World Bank has been a strong proponent. The Bank holds the view that the allocation of scarce resources should contain a strong emphasis on primary education. This was reinforced by the two conferences on Education for All (Jomtien, 1990 and Dakar, 2000). The theme of the 1990 CCEM was 'The Quality of Basic Education' and this included an emphasis on science education at basic level. The professional development and support of teachers was the subject of work carried out jointly by the Commonwealth Secretariat and UNESCO. The issue of resources was again reflected at the conference – fewer resources were available for the core programme of the Education Division than at 10CCEM.

This historical overview has provided some of the context and background for the work carried out in key areas by the Commonwealth Secretariat in STME over the years since the Oxford Conference. The following sections contain brief descriptions of the work done in these areas, in order to indicate the range and scope of this work, and to emphasise the importance of the key themes of 'continuity and change' and 'partnerships and co-operation'.

3 Key Areas of Commonwealth Co-operation in STME

There has been an amazing diversity of Commonwealth activities in STME over the last 40 years or so and it is not possible to provide a full description of all of these. However, by focusing on a number of key areas in which activity took place either over the entire period (such as the training of teachers) or for a good part of it (such as resources for science teaching including equipment), it is possible to provide a framework which can be used as the basis for discussion of the future. The areas selected illustrate the issues identified by Commonwealth governments over time, and reflect their approaches to the implementation of policy on STME. For example, the focus on the training of teachers has remained a recurrent concern for many governments. The popularisation of science and technology with the objective of achieving scientific and technological literacy has been seen increasingly as a key factor in devising an indigenous STME culture, as well as providing a sound basis for the increased inclusion of girls in STME. The policy of individual governments has often reflected the concerns articulated not only at Commonwealth conferences, but also in expert group meetings.

a. The Relevance of STME

Much of the work undertaken in STME could be broadly described as being about its relevance, since there has been a continuing debate about the role of science and technology in development and the contribution that STME makes to science and technology in any given country. There would appear to be general agreement that science and technology are crucial for economic development, but there is no consensus about the specific ways in which the education system can provide the necessary skills and experiences in these fields. In the Commonwealth context, these and related issues have recurred at a variety of levels. For example, in the late 1970s there was particular concern about the need for science, mathematics and technology to be inter-related. This concern was translated into a recommendation for a specialist conference, which never took place. However, a number of papers were commissioned, seven of which were published in 1985, drawing upon expertise from various parts of the Commonwealth. The importance of the training of teachers was stressed, as was the need for appropriate local equipment. An important paper looked at the need for inter-related teaching of the subjects as preparation for the world of work. Much of the curriculum development work of the 1960s and 1970s focused on 'pure' science and mathematics, with little apparent attention to the need to relate school curricula to the world outside in appropriate ways. It was proposed in another paper that there were two ways to bring about interrelatedness:

a) By identifying related topics in the existing curricula, and then interrelating the existing curricula;

b) By signing teaching modules covering topics commonly found in all science and technology subjects.

There was an important CASTME activity in 1986 (see below), at which the issue of making STME relevant was discussed. The importance of teacher preparation was strongly advocated in one of the lead papers. In the overview paper, some of the assumptions underlying the approach to making STME relevant were reviewed. For example, it is not necessarily true that some form of STME training will enhance an person's employment prospects.

All this work was undertaken against an international background in which the relevance of much STME was being questioned, with a strong movement towards the recognition of the impact of science and technology on society manifested, for example, in 'Science, Technology and Society' courses and programmes. The continuing need to review and reflect upon the nature of STME curricula is illustrated by the increasing importance ascribed to environmental education, largely as a result of the major international conference held in Rio de Janeiro in 1992. Despite moves towards integrated science curricula at secondary level in many countries, much remains to be done in making creative and effective use of the interrelatedness of STME.

b. Teacher Education for Science, Technology and Mathematics

Teacher education has been a lead area for Commonwealth co-operation in STME, since the quality of education is critically dependent on teachers. The emphasis on Basic Education and Education for All since the 1980s has indicated not only the increasing importance of initial training, but also of continuous professional development not only of teachers but also of teacher trainers at the primary level. In addition, there has been an emphasis on the development of resources and materials for use in in-service training. This has come about in part, at least, because of concerns about the quality and quantity of science (and technology) education at the primary level, and the need to develop scientific and technological literacy for all. In-service education and training (INSET) can be a useful tool for continuous professional development of teachers and for overcoming present deficiencies, while pre service-training should provide a sound basis for an educational system in the future.

The Commonwealth Secretariat had two main partners in this area in the 1980s – the International Council for Science Committee on the Teaching of Science (ICSU-CTS) and UNESCO. Immediately after a major conference sponsored by ICSU CTS in Bangalore in 1985 a Pan-Commonwealth workshop took place on primary science. This was the precursor to a joint Commonwealth Secretariat/ UNESCO project which focused on the development of materials for use in the in-service training of teachers. The trainees would begin to develop an awareness of the role and value of science process skills both in their learning and teaching. This was intended to enable teachers to move away from both a 'nature study' approach to teaching science, and from the approach in which the emphasis was almost entirely on memorisation by rote. A planning workshop in 1986 was followed by a 1987 international seminar in Barbados on primary science teacher training. At the seminar, draft materials were used and reviewed. The participants identified both gender issues and those associated with technology as prime areas for future consideration. Workshop participants agreed to develop country-specific materials. After successful development of country-specific material in India a group of Commonwealth specialists, together with the Commonwealth Secretariat's Director of Project and Chief Programme Officer, visited India to review the material. One eventual useful by-product of this project was the UNESCO source book for science in the primary school. Further collaboration between the Secretariat and UNESCO resulted in the publication of a workshop module on professional development, 'Assessment in Primary School Science'. This material was based on intensive piloting and consultation with those who tried out the materials.

In order to sustain quality teacher training it is essential that trainers themselves are adequately trained. In recognition of this, training of trainers in science and technology education was the subject of a significant initiative in the Commonwealth Secretariat in the 1990s, with the publication of four regional editions of a handbook, *Training of Teachers in Science and Technology*. Each edition contains six monographs, with topics ranging from 'training needs in science and technology teacher education' to 'participating in science and technology education research'. Mathematics was not forgotten, with the publication of a joint Commonwealth Secretariat/National Council for Teacher Education (India) handbook in 1999 containing modules in mathematics for elementary teacher educators. These modules were later reviewed and revised at an Asian Regional workshop held in New Delhi in June 2000. The work on mathematics education was also carried out in the context of gender (see below).

The need for an emphasis on gender issues and the importance of drawing on local culture was emphasised in a meeting in Malawi in 2000 that focused on the development of resource materials for teachers in science and mathematics at upper primary and junior secondary level. This work focuses on providing useful teaching resource materials for teachers, which integrate content and pedagogy, including gender issues and the popularisation of science and technology. Thus the Commonwealth Secretariat continues to make a sustained effort in the area of teacher education and the training of teacher and this will continue to be an important part of its work.

c. Resources for Science Teaching

It is often assumed that the teaching of science requires adequate laboratory space, complemented by a wide array of equipment that will enable the learners to behave as if they were scientists. There is some doubt about this assumption, since many of the exercises undertaken by students are more like cookery, with precise instructions to be followed and a prescribed format for writing about these experiences. However, there is little doubt about the need for a wide range of experiences for effective science teaching and learning, drawing, for example, on resources available in the environment. The essential need for equipment and other aids for teaching was recognised in the 1963 conference on school science teaching, and that concern has been reiterated in various ways up to the present. One of the major problems facing less industrialised countries where there has been a massive expansion in educational provision has been that of allocating sufficient resources to enable effective science (and technology) teaching. It was therefore important to examine different and hopefully more cost-effective ways of providing equipment. One way of confronting this problem has been to examine a variety of approaches to 'low-cost' equipment. Commonwealth activities in this area were undertaken in the 1970s and 80s in particular, starting in 1975 with a general review of the various approaches to the production of science equipment. (This review was revised and updated in 1983.) This included useful information on equipment design, relevant books and the various kits that were available.

This was followed by three regional seminar/workshops which took place in 1976, 1977 and 1979 on low-cost science teaching equipment. The overall emphasis in these activities was on training for both production and use of low-cost equipment. Yet again, the need for adequate teacher preparation and training had been highlighted. The seminar/workshops drew upon an impressive range of expertise, including from the National Centre for Research and Technology (India), the Regional Centre for Education in Science and Mathematics (Malaysia), the Science Education Policy Unit (Kenya) and Professor S. T. Bajah of the University of Ibadan, who later worked at the Commonwealth Secretariat, underlining the importance of effective co-operation and partnership. The role of vibrant and effective science teacher associations was also stressed.

An issue which was almost ignored for a long time, and has only been recently addressed, has to do with the maintenance of science equipment. Another is the need to consider how to provide effective teacher preparation to enable teachers to make use of their environment to improvise equipment.

d. The Training of Technicians

The key importance of technician support for professional/technological activities has been recognised for many years. However, it has often proved difficult to translate this recognition into a convincing career structure for technicians, particularly in the public sector. This may in part reflect the superiority ascribed to 'pure' science, as against technology, in many Commonwealth countries. Good laboratory (or workshop) technicians can make the difference between an imaginative and creative programme of practical work and one in which routine procedures are the order of the day. The presence of a trained laboratory technician can mean that science teachers have more time to support students, as well as increasing the life of equipment through care and maintenance. Laboratory technicians can also ensure a safe working laboratory. The importance of identifying training needs and providing appropriate training opportunities was stressed in a survey conducted in the 1970s on technician training in Commonwealth Asian countries. It also drew attention to the need for appropriate and relevant training – there is little point in providing training on equipment and machinery which is no longer in use in the outside world.

Since the 1980s there has been an emphasis on the development and delivery of training programmes for technicians, the first of which was a joint CASTME/ University of the West Indies project on the distance training of technicians, using the UWIDITE system. This was a good example of one of the advantages of distance learning, in which the trainees did not have to leave their home countries or jobs – an interesting omen for the future. Two key players involved in this project, as in so many other facets of Commonwealth STME, were Dr M. Goldsmith (founding President of CASTME) and Mr E. Apea of the Human Resource Development Group, the Commonwealth Secretariat and latterly of UNESCO).

During the 1990s, a substantial body of work was undertaken on the training of laboratory technicians involving the Secretariat, COL and CAPA. COL obtained the rights to the use of technician training materials developed by Scitech Diol, a UK-based company. These have been the basis for the development of relevant and appropriate distance learning materials for technicians in India (through the Indira Gandhi Open University) and Sri Lanka (through the Open University of Sri Lanka), the South Pacific (through the University of the South Pacific) and in Kenya, Tanzania, Uganda and Zambia (through CAPA). Unlike Asia and the South Pacific, where universities had experience of distance learning, in Africa the Commonwealth Secretariat and COL developed the capacity of participating institutions through training courses in writing resource material for learners and in assessment and delivery mechanisms, including management of distance learning courses. Kenya and Uganda have already started offering these courses through distance methods. Work has also been undertaken on the training of technicians at university level in Africa under the auspices of the Commonwealth Higher Education Support Scheme.

The continuing need for the training of technicians draws attention to the need for a 'culture of maintenance'. When scarce resources are invested in equipment it is crucial that the equipment is properly maintained.

Provision of a distance training programme for technicians highlights the importance of institutional support, since a range of practical experiences are needed that can be properly assessed at the institutions, with some form of external moderation. Given the ongoing developments in ICT, there is little doubt that distance training of technicians will continue to be an important field of activity.

e. Popularisation of Science and Technology

Even if there is no clear relationship between science and technology education and economic development, there has been an increasing emphasis on the need for countries to provide education for all their potentially school-going population. If this is to be achieved, there is an important role for the development of scientific and technological literacy, however defined. This has been recognised by many organisations and institutions, including UNESCO, which was responsible for Project 2000 + on Scientific and Technological Literacy for All. The Commonwealth Secretariat was a partner in this project. Effective efforts to popularise science and technology could provide a basis for scientific and technological literacy for all.

The popularisation of science was the subject of a regional seminar held in Zambia in 1985. Some of the issues identified then remain relevant now, including the need for mathematics and science to be linked (see above), the role of both formal and non-formal education, the need to make effective use of the media, and the role of science fairs and science teacher associations.

A substantial body of work was undertaken in the 1990s, with three expert group meetings (Singapore, 1997; Malawi, 1998; and Trinidad, 1998) on popularising scientific and technological culture. The importance of both formal and non-formal education was stressed, as was the role of both teachers and parents. The need to demystify science and improve communication between scientists, media personnel and curriculum developers resonated in all expert group meetings. It was also stressed that information about good practice must be exchanged. As a follow-up, the Commonwealth Secretariat, in collaboration with the Asian Media Information and Communication Centre, Singapore, published *Asian Case Studies* on the popularisation of science and technology. A similar book is under preparation for Africa in collaboration with the African Forum for Children's Literacy in Science and Technology (AFCLIST). Another innovative work on the popularisation of science and technology has been the production by the Commonwealth Secretariat of *Using Science Centres and Museums to Popularise Science and Technology*, a book for museum curators and science teachers. An interesting approach of the book has been the use of all kinds of museums, not just science museums, in popularising science and technology. The Secretariat stresses the need to take careful account of the local context. In order to achieve useful results, it is important to identify relevant sources of information and also the target groups for particular activities. As in the 1980s, the role of national and regional science fairs has been stressed. CASTME (see below) has also played an important role by establishing the CASTME annual awards, which have been in existence since the mid-1970s. These encourage creative and imaginative approaches to the teaching of science, technology and mathematics and therefore contribute to the popularisation of these subjects.

If scientific and technological literacy for all is to be achieved then there will be a continuing and expanding need for the popularisation of science and technology, drawing upon a wide range of media and both formal and non-formal education. This should also also facilitate increasing participation by girls and women.

f. Technical Education and Technical Teacher Training

The 1966 Huddersfield conference drew attention to the importance of technical education and technical teacher training. Even though curriculum content has changed markedly since then, particularly with the impact of the development of ICT, this remains important. There have been a number of different approaches to technical education, one of which involved the provision of separate schools (such as technical high schools), while another drew inspiration from a Canadian model of industrial arts. There appears to be little general agreement about the ways in which technical education should be provided at the secondary and immediately post-secondary levels. This is an important issue for the less industrialised countries, since technical education is expensive and there is considerable doubt about its cost-effectiveness if it is included in general secondary education programmes. There is also a continuing debate about the relationships between technical education and the world of work, and the need to take account of developments in approaches to small business and entrepreneurship. This will be discussed in Chapter 5.

Polytechnics became an important vehicle for the delivery of technical education in the 1960s and 1970s, and this was reflected in the foundation in 1978 of the Commonwealth Association of Polytechnics in Africa (see Chapter 5). CAPA has remained a valuable source of support, experience and knowledge, even though it is very short of resources.

Technical teacher training was the subject of a seminar held in Kenya in 1980 at which the importance of identifying training needs and of staff development in training institutions was reiterated. Canada played a key role in advising on technical teacher training and in providing funding for infrastructure in support of it.

The assessment of technical education is an important issue, with the City and Guilds of London Institute (CGLI) playing a vital role in the early years, and national and regional bodies taking on increasing responsibilities in the 1980s and 1990s. The importance of ensuring a suitable role for local industry in setting standards, for example, has to be recognised.

g. Gender Issues in STME

Participation by girls in STME and their poor performance in these subjects has been a subject of concern to all Commonwealth governments. This concern has been made more manifest since the setting up in the 1980s of a mechanism for reporting on Women's Affairs. The Forward Looking Strategies for the Advancement of Women (Nairobi, 1985) provided part of the background for the Commonwealth Plan of Action, which was adopted in 1987. The 1994 Beijing

Conference provided an important platform for the discussion of women's concerns.

The subject of women in science and technology has been extensively discussed in Chapter 3, so will not be further discussed here. This is not to detract from the importance accorded to this issue in the Commonwealth over the years.

h. The Role of the Commonwealth Association of Science, Technology and Mathematics Educators

Teachers are at the heart of education in STM, and it is important to draw on and utilise a range of strategies for their continuing professional development. One such strategy is the fostering and development of professional teacher associations, first at the national and then the regional and international levels. Such an association can provide a forum, through meetings, conferences and publications, for continuing professional development. One successful national example is the Association for Science Education (UK) which now embraces technicians and primary science teachers; another is the Science Teachers Association of Nigeria. The International Council for Associations of Science Education (ICASE) provides an umbrella for national and regional associations.

CASME (it should be noted that technology was not part of the original remit) was inaugurated in 1974, with Dr M. Goldsmith as its Founding President, at a conference in London on Conceptual Development in Science and Mathematics. The precursor to this conference was a meeting in Jamaica in 1973 on Social Significance in Science and Mathematics Teaching. CASME developed into CASTME in 1982, and the latter was recognised as a Commonwealth professional organisation in the early 1980s. The focus of CASTME's work has been on the promotion of the social, human and economic aspects of science and technology through low-cost quality materials.

The work of CASTME has been very varied, focusing on issues of importance to science educators and teachers. Mention has already been made of the role of CASTME in the development of a programme for the training of technicians in the Caribbean. One of CASTME's important contributions has been to promote classroom innovations in the teaching of science, technology and mathematics in the Commonwealth through its prestigious CASTME Annual Awards Scheme for Innovations in Science Technology and Mathematics. The scheme, which started in 1974, has kept going without interruption, in spite of having few resources. A large number of teachers and teacher educators have participated and received CASTME Awards. In many countries, CASTME award winners are being used by governments to support and train other teachers. The quarterly *CASTME Journal* provides a means for STM educators to reflect on developments in various parts of the Commonwealth and to share their experiences. CASTME regional conferences enable educators in a region to pool ideas and consider issues of future relevance – in July 1998, after 13CCEM in Botswana, CASTME organised a conference on educational technology for science and mathematics education in the

Caribbean and its social and cultural relevance in the twenty-first century. This is a good example of how a professional association can make bridges between CCEM and classrooms. Another important regional conference in Asia was organised by CASTME in collaboration with UNESCO and the Government of India in Goa, India in February 2001, on the theme 'Science Technology and Mathematics Education for Human Development'. Its task was to lay down priorities and strategies in the next decade in STME for human development.

To extend its reach to a larger number of teachers and teacher educators, CASTME is establishing regional branches. A Caribbean branch started in 1998 during the Caribbean regional conference, a West Africa branch is in the process of establishment and the Asian branch was established during the Goa conference. There will be a continuing role for CASTME in the twenty-first century as STM teachers around the Commonwealth endeavour to draw upon the experiences of others in different parts of the world, with the help of developments in ICT.

4 A View to the Future

The previous sections have provided a snapshot of contributions to STME carried out by and through the Commonwealth Secretariat over the past 40 years. They illustrate the importance of two overarching themes – continuity and change, and partnerships and co-operation. Concerns voiced in the 1960s as important to STME have been shown to be important still; yet it is also important to take account of change, not only at national but also at regional and international levels. For example, the training of teachers has been continuously identified as one of the key issues for STME in the Commonwealth. This remains true, but the content of and approach to teacher training has to be reviewed on a regular basis to ensure that advantage is taken of the most up-to-date research findings. Similarly, the production of quality learning resource materials and developing the capability of teachers to produce contextual materials continue to be important in improving the quality of science teaching in schools.

Another important area, which needs development in the Commonwealth, is technology education. There is a lack of clarity on what technology education includes. Different countries interpret it in different ways. Much thought has gone into developing this area in some countries, for example South Africa. There is a need to share experiences and help countries to develop their policies on technology education.

In addition, the modalities for the delivery of training need to be considered in light of developments in ICT, which have an impact on all nations. It is now potentially possible to deliver education and training to individuals where they are, rather than taking them away from their jobs and insisting that they enter dedicated training institutions. There are many issues to be considered here, including the ability of less industrialised states to afford the hardware and software costs associated with such modern developments. Nevertheless, the training of teachers and of

109

technicians will continue to be crucial for the development of STME, and the combined resources of the Commonwealth Secretariat and COL can be important in these areas. This was reflected at 13CCEM in Botswana, where the training and motivation of teachers was identified as one area in which ICT could be applied.

Given the level of resources available to the Commonwealth Secretariat's education team, it will be imperative to develop and expand the search for meaningful partnerships, since otherwise there will be little possibility of significant work in STME. There have been many instances of co-operation in the field of education between the Secretariat and national, regional and international institutions and organisations in the past 40 years and these provide a sound basis for future development. However, it will be crucial to ensure that the work undertaken meets the real needs of Commonwealth countries.

Chapter 5

Skills for Survival: Technical and Vocational Education and Entrepreneurship

W. Bonney Rust

1 Introduction

This chapter offers a survey of Commonwealth strategies and activities in Technical and Vocational Education (TVE) and entrepreneurship over the 40 years from 1959. The story told relates very closely to the discussion of science, technology and mathematics education in Chapter 4 and inevitably refers to some of the same conference recommendations and publications. It follows on from the discussions of science and technology education and opens up a whole new field of Commonwealth activity in education and training. It directly confronts policies and ideas linking education with the world of work.

a. Education and Employment

Education may be seen as a process which begins in our earliest years by the transfer from parents to children of the skills required for survival. Those skills, in the poorest communities, may simply be those required to produce food and shelter. As communities become more complicated and sophisticated, this education becomes institutionalised. The process then involves the transfer of a given culture pattern from one generation to the next, including patterns of behaviour and the training of society's leaders, as well as teaching the skills required for the future. These skills include earning, or making a living and, hopefully, improving the standard of living from one generation to the next. It is this latter function of education, i.e. making a living, which runs through this survey of the Commonwealth's policies and practice over the 40 years from 1959 to 1999.

b. The Role of Technical and Vocational Education and Entrepreneurship in the Commonwealth

The Commonwealth comprises nations with large numbers of people living in poverty and working in the informal economy, such as Bangladesh, Zambia and Mozambique; rapidly developing countries, such as Malaysia and Singapore; and highly developed countries, such as Australia and Canada.

Inevitably, therefore, this survey covers countries at every level of development, and with a wide range of cultures, religions, languages, populations, economies and skills. Throughout the 40-year period, the aims of member governments, especially those of developing countries, have been to alleviate poverty and sustain economic improvement through human resources development. The major challenge has been to enable Commonwealth citizens to acquire the skills necessary not only to survive but to improve their standard of living. In the twenty-first century a person without marketable skills is not only likely to be unemployed, but even unemployable. This survey leads to the conclusion that TVE, underpinned by entrepreneurship, is becoming the major arena for providing those skills and for achieving the aim of sustainable development.

c. The World Context

The entire survey needs to be considered within the context of a rapidly changing world. Over the 40-year period, the effects of changing economic structures caused changing demand for skilled employees, and that caused widespread changes in the provision (and the needs) of technical and vocational education and training. Such changes occurred in courses of study in the institutionalised provision of TVE in the developing countries as well. Perhaps the prime, widespread, example is that of the provision for motor vehicle servicing, which at the beginning of the period was a relatively straightforward engineering function and at the end was a highly sophisticated exercise in electronics. This is simply one example of the decline in courses in engineering, accompanied by a rise in courses in electronics.

Over the whole of this period, economic changes in the developed countries have led to a considerable reduction in demand for workers in basic industries, such as coal, shipping, steel and textiles. On the other hand, there has been a big increase in service industries. It was estimated that by 2000, 50–60% of all TVE courses in the developed countries of the Commonwealth were providing the skills needed in service industries. Examples include the rapid rise of business studies (management, accountancy, law, economics, statistical method); courses in travel and tourism, and hotel and catering, to meet the vast increase in holiday travel; the introduction and rapid extension of computer use and information technology; the strong demand for courses in English as a Foreign Language; and the growth of courses providing skills needed in the leisure industry.

Inevitably, the differing economic circumstances of the developing countries caused variation from this pattern. The high proportion of people living in rural areas in these countries required the maximum feasible provision of courses for the improvement of agriculture and varied local industries. However, the influence of the TVE changes in developed countries affected provision in developing countries more rapidly after the political changes in Eastern Europe of 1989–90. Business studies, travel and tourism, and hotel and catering all found a place. Even additional English as a communication medium became a growing necessity for central, regional and local government administration, for growing import/export businesses and for providing skills to illiterate adults.

Organised courses were provided in different disciplines which were expected to reward success with certification. Within the Commonwealth, the UK played a pivotal role in satisfying this expectation. UK examination bodies provide certification which is widely accepted across many member countries. Such agencies as the City and Guilds of London Institute (CGLI), the Royal Society of Arts (RSA) and Pitmans' examinations offer certification for almost every technical and commercial subject. At the professional level, several UK bodies, such as the accountancy associations, the Institute of Bankers and the Institute of Chartered Secretaries and Administrators have all opened their examinations to the world. The use of the English language has made these examinations particularly suitable for Commonwealth member countries. Many Commonwealth governments would prefer to offer, and some do offer, their own internal awards. But the portability and prestige of the UK-based awards still causes many thousands of overseas Commonwealth candidates to take UK-based examinations.

A further development in TVE over the period has been the growing inter-relationship between institutional TVE and that provided as training within industry. The two systems were sharply contrasted. 'Technical education' was seen as located in one arena and 'training' as in another. However, co-operation between the two systems has steadily increased and the symbiosis was finally accepted in the UK by the formation from 1 April 2001 of the Learning and Skills Council. That body unites the organisation and funding for both technical education and training. Similar moves are beginning, or are under consideration, in many Commonwealth countries.

d. Outline of the Survey

This survey follows the developing roles of TVE and entrepreneurship from the first Commonwealth Education Conference held in 1959. That conference initiated policies which are described in Section 2. Much activity took place in TVE over the next four decades – activity largely expressed in pan-Commonwealth and regional workshops. TVE activity was stimulated by the formation of the Commonwealth Secretariat in 1965, and thereafter made steady progress. However, the progress varied from country to country. Singapore utilised TVE and entrepreneurship to expand its economy rapidly. India made great strides in training manpower with specialised skills. In some other countries overemphasis on academic education and the low social status of technical education weakened the expansion of technical skills.

Each ministerial meeting made a large number of recommendations which the Commonwealth Secretariat was expected to carry out. But the Secretariat was provided with limited resources, as explained in Chapter 1, so it was essential to prioritise and, where possible, to select appropriate recommendations (Section 3). The Commonwealth Fund for Technical Co-operation (Section 4), the Commonwealth Foundation (Section 5) and, more recently, the Commonwealth of Learning (Section 6 and Chapter 6 below) have all contributed to the support for TVE and entrepreneurship which, nevertheless, remains still seriously under-provided in several large and small developing countries. Both TVE and entrepreneurship within the Commonwealth have, over the past two decades, built up and strengthened their inter-relationship with employment in industry and commerce (Section 7).

Throughout the 40 years covered by this survey the persistence of large numbers of people working in informal economies in many developing countries has led to efforts to provide employable skills through informal methods of education (Section 8). The informal sector continues to present a massive educational and social challenge for most developing countries. Entrepreneurship deserves separate treatment (Section 9) because its full understanding and widespread application could provide a lever to raise standards of living.

For the future, Section 10 offers an 'Outlook for Technical and Vocational Education and Entrepreneurship in the Commonwealth' by employing the SWOT analysis to assess Strengths, Weaknesses, Opportunities and Threats.

e. The Colombo Plan

Preceding and running parallel to the events studied in this 40-year survey was the Colombo Plan. The plan originated in 1951. Its original formulators were a group of seven Commonwealth nations, but some non-Commonwealth countries were also involved. The plan provided assistance to the nations of south-east Asia and the Pacific in the form of educational and health aid, training programmes, loans, food supplies and technical aid. Originally conceived as lasting for six years, the plan was extended indefinitely in 1980 and still continues at the time of writing.

2 Formulating the Policies

It is a tribute to the wide-ranging scope of the first meeting of the Commonwealth Education Conference in 1959 that considerable attention was paid to Technical and Vocation Education.

Technical education was the subject of one of the four main committees established by the conference. The committee's terms of reference were: 'To consider the extent to which countries of the Commonwealth can help each other to meet their needs for the development of education and training in technical subjects, including training in industry, and the arrangements for providing such assistance' (CEC 1).

The Technical Education Committee made a series of recommendations which were adopted by the Conference. The recommendations included:

- A small information centre should be established in London to provide information about facilities for technical education and sources of advice available in the Commonwealth;

- It would be valuable to establish, preferably in association with existing institutions, regional technical teacher training colleges;

- All countries offering scholarships, other awards or facilities for education, training or research should devote to technical education in the Commonwealth a good proportion of the awards and facilities they might offer.

The Technical Education Committee set the scene for future analysis and consequential action in TVE by defining some terms. These were:

Technologist
A person holding a degree or equivalent professional qualification in science or engineering who is responsible for the application of scientific knowledge and method to industry.

Technician
A person qualified by specialist technical education and practical training to work under the general direction of a technologist.

Craftsman
Normally a person who has served a recognised apprenticeship in a trade, and who applies his skills on the shop floor.

In an interesting development, the 3CEC held in Canada in 1964 agreed to consider 'technical education' and 'vocational training' as one subject. The same conference added to the above classifications that of:

Operative
One who has developed skills in a narrow section or field of a trade or occupation, and works under close supervision.

The Commonwealth now had agreed definitions of four levels of TVE which have remained valid for 40 years.

The same conference in Canada introduced three major new concepts into their deliberations and recommendations. These were that:

- Attention should be paid to economic and manpower surveys in the planning of technical education;

- Vocational guidance and counselling services, particularly in schools, should be built up through Commonwealth co-operation;

- Among priorities was the need to obtain a better flow of suitable students into technical institutions.

Each of these concepts carries major implications for TVE. Manpower surveys, though sometimes misleading for long-term planning, had long formed part of governmental planning in the developed countries of the Commonwealth. By contrast, developing countries were often without the statistical base upon which to undertake manpower planning. The large sectors of their population working in the informal economy made the accurate collection of information impossible. However, steady progress was made in several countries. Vocational guidance and counselling was not highly organised even in the developed countries at this stage. The plea for 'suitable students' was the first, if somewhat bland, reference to the second-class status occupied by TVE which meant that it was given a low priority throughout the second half of the twentieth century.

A further addition to the TVE arena was made at the 5CEC held in Australia in 1971. The Technical and Vocational Education Committee of that conference recommended that management or supervisory studies should be incorporated in technical education at all appropriate levels.

The sequence of regular TVE committees at the Commonwealth Education Conferences was broken in 1974 at the meeting held in Jamaica, for which the theme was 'Managing Education – Innovation, Implementation and Consolidation'. This general theme precluded the conventional division into committees related to different levels of education. Instead, five working groups reported to plenary sessions. Hence, there was no specific consideration of TVE at that meeting. There was, however, a criticism of the status that societies accorded to different types of education with children being made to aspire to academic subjects as a criterion of success.

By 1977, at the meeting in Ghana, there was another general theme: 'the economics of education'. Within this framework five committees were appointed, of which one was designated for 'science education and technical education. That committee made a series of recommendations about TVE. They were that:

- A further Commonwealth regional seminar/workshop should be held on technical education and industry;

- A study should be made of the problems encountered in technical examinations;

- A meeting should be convened to consider the establishment of an association of polytechnics in Commonwealth African countries (see Section 5 – Commonwealth Foundation);

- The desirability and feasibility of a regional staff college in Africa for technical education should be explored in consultation with all interested parties;

- Proposals for a Commonwealth Exchange Scheme for Industrial Training and Experience be worked out in detail and commended to member governments (see Section 7 – TVE and the World of Work).

The 1980 Sri Lanka conference put the TVE examination system on the agenda. It recommended that a working group be set up to formulate proposals for Commonwealth action to assist member countries to overcome problems encountered in technical and vocational examinations. That role was to be undertaken by the Commonwealth Secretariat (see Section 3). The same meeting (8CEC, 1980) re-introduced sector committees, of which there were eight. Sector Committee 1 was covered 'Science and Mathematics Education; Technical and Vocational Education and Training' (see also Chapter 4). Here we see the beginnings of a strategy to inter-relate science education with technical education, especially in the school sector.

A further important addition to TVE was contained in the word 'training'. Training had historically and practically been undertaken within employment, i.e. it was on-the-job training – a concept familiar in developed countries but, at this stage (1980), limited in the developing countries to their relatively small industrial and service economies.

A much wider issue, however, was a sadly divisive topic (already alluded to in Chapter 1). As the meeting reported: 'The recent increase of tuition fees in some countries – even to the point of charging full economic cost – has become a burning issue between developed and developing countries of the Commonwealth'. This matter is treated extensively in Chapter 7. Here we need to emphasise that TVE in Commonwealth developing countries was even more severely affected by the fee increase than was higher education. In a study published in 2000, a Joint Working Group of the CEC and the UK Council for Overseas Student Affairs (UKCOSA) showed the changing position, taking the UK as indicative:

Commonwealth Students in UK Further Education

	1979–80	1997–98
Students	14,440	2,834

That is, there was an 80% reduction of Commonwealth students in UK further education over the period 1979–80 to 1997–98. By a remarkable contrast, the number of Commonwealth students in UK higher education at first dropped substantially after 1979–80, but by 1997–98 the total had actually increased by 45%.

Figures are given below:

Commonwealth Students in UK Higher Education

	1979–80	1997–98
Students	30,728	44,609

Source: CEC/UKCOSA 2000: Tables 4.1a and 4.1b

All these developments led in 1987 to the first CCEM to be planned on the general theme of 'vocationally oriented education'. It was the first of four agenda items, the others being student mobility and higher education co-operation; co-operation in distance education; and future priorities for the Secretariat's work in education

The committee on vocationally-oriented education discussed many of the issues already outlined in this survey. In particular, it welcomed a proposal for a regional workshop to be held in 1987–88 and recommended that the workshop should be the first in a series of meetings to be held over the triennium. The topics were to be 'developing the curricula for vocationally oriented education' and 'the cost-effective use of resources' for the same arena of education.

The committee also examined various views about TVE's low prestige in the educational world. These views were, in general, accepted, but the committee made an important point about prestige. It felt that there was little evidence of negative attitudes towards a vocational curriculum in countries where technical and vocational teachers enjoyed equal status with teachers of academic subjects, and where equipping pupils with vocational and technological skills was perceived as being essential for national development. In contrast, the committee discussing future priorities for the Secretariat's work commented:

> Given that vocationally orientated education was the theme of 10 CCEM (1987), the group expressed concern that the work programme proposals appeared to give insufficient priority to the theme.

Here is a gentle reminder, from an objective source, that the previous educational experience of practically all those involved in Commonwealth education had been derived from school and university education. This educational experience may have led to a mindset in which school education and university education were to the fore, whereas TVE was a less well-known field.

The Barbados Conference of 1990, on the theme 'improving the quality of basic education', provided a scenario for the improvement of school education at primary and secondary levels. TVE was a peripheral consideration, and was considered only in so far as it provided an alternative programme to academic education at upper secondary school level. Shortly after, however, a seminal study about the relationships of human beings within the Commonwealth was initiated by the Commonwealth Heads of Government meeting in Zimbabwe in 1991. They recognised in their Harare Declaration that human resource development was central to the promotion of sustainable development and the alleviation of poverty in all Commonwealth member countries, despite a wide diversity in terms of population, income and of ratings on any human development index.

A Commonwealth Working Group established to consider human resource development strategies set out in its report the core constituents required for an integrated view of human resource development. These were:

- Education and training;
- Primary health care;
- Nutrition at adequate levels;
- Population policies;
- Employment.

The report noted (para. 22) that 'Outlays on education and training represent the best possible long term investment for human resource development'. It went on:

People who cannot read, write or deal competently with numbers are severely disadvantaged; an illiterate and innumerate population is cut off from the modern world.

This statement firmly defines basic education as a necessary component of TVE.

The Working Group examined and made recommendations on five strategies which they regarded as requirements for effecting human resource development and as integral components of the human resource development process itself. The five strategies were:

- Well-managed and more professional government;
- Partnerships with NGOs and the private sector;
- Priority for women;
- Utilising resources ;
- Using technology.

This valuable analysis, offering a vision for the future, was published as *Foundation for the Future* by the Commonwealth Secretariat in 1993. It was endorsed at the Pakistan CCEM Conference of 1994 and at the Commonwealth Heads of Government meeting in New Zealand in 1995.

Partly as a result of the publication of *Foundation for the Future*, the theme for the 1994 Meeting of Education Ministers in Pakistan was 'the changing role of the state in education'. Ministers supported much of the content of *Foundation for the Future*, and agreed to pursue the five strategies outlined above. Rapid technical and technological changes underlay the theme discussions at the 13CCEM in Botswana in 1997. The theme was 'education and technology: the challenges of the twenty-first century'.

However, the education and the technology discussed were much more related to school and university education than to TVE. A major concern was that the rapid changes in technology largely led by the developed nations might widen the gap between developed and developing economies.

An even sharper forecast about future technology was made by Elifa Ngoma, Secretary-General of CAPA (see Section 5). Ngoma was addressing a conference held by CAPA in 1997 under the title 'Technological Education and National

Development'. He took the view that world trends were dealing death blows to the African polytechnic leaving it 'emaciated and utterly disorientated' (*Conference Report*, 1997). Mr Ngoma referred to several arenas which supported his thesis, and which had been discussed at an International Colloquium organised by CAPA in 1996:

- Existing training had become largely irrelevant and obsolete;

- Training programmes and curricula needed regular review to match them with rapid technological change;

- Lecturers and instructors in the African polytechnics lacked relevant skills to handle the changing environment;

- Textbooks in use were mostly outdated;

- Graduate technicians and technologists taught by the polytechnics were not aware of technologies in use by industry;

- Industry was reluctant to support the training of technicians and technologists in the polytechnic;

- Governments did not have the financial capability to fund, let alone procure, modern training equipment for the polytechnics.

Mr Ngoma was, of course, speaking for a particular region. If his strictures have parallels in technological institutions elsewhere in Commonwealth developing countries, then the 'gap' mentioned in Botswana could increase rather than diminish.

It was as a response to the needs expressed at 13CCEM that the Commonwealth Secretariat published a series of papers in January 2000 in a book entitled *Issues in Education and Technology* (Wright ed., 2002). The book made clear that:

> ... changes in education are inevitable in the face of the inexorable advance of the knowledge and information age that is being fuelled by rapid developments in ICT.
>
> Issues in Education and Technology, p.11

The book's introduction also regarded the changing role of technology as:

> ... not a matter of wholesale investment in certain new technologies, such as computers. Rather, it is about the role of technology in promoting deep systemic changes in education to meet the challenges of a new era.
>
> Issues in Education and Technology, p.12

The major theme of the Halifax meeting (14CCEM, 2000) in Nova Scotia, Canada was 'education for our common future'. Remarkably this wide framework resulted in a joint statement about educational objectives and needs agreed by delegates from many different Commonwealth countries. There was, however, relatively little specific content relating to TVE either in the proceedings or in the final statement. Nevertheless, the statement did refer to one role of education as facilitating the expansion of human capabilities, and the enhancement of competitiveness in a knowledge-based economy. The statement firmly supported the provision of learning for all, and that the private sector and non-governmental organisations should be involved in expanding access to education.

A delegate from the Association of Canadian Community Colleges attended the main sessions. The same body was strongly represented at the exhibition and symposia, together with the Canadian Centre for Entrepreneurship and Development, and the National Association of Career Colleges. This latter association is the equivalent of private sector provision for further education in the UK. The association claims to provide about half of national Canadian provision for TVE.

3 Applying The Policies

a. Structures

The first three Commonwealth Education Conferences held in 1959, 1962 and 1964 produced a considerable number of policy recommendations, but at that stage there was no institutionalised administration to apply the policies. Above that level of policy-making were Heads of Government meetings, also producing recommendations. The establishment and evolution of the Commonwealth Secretariat and its education function have been described in Chapter 1.

Arnold Smith's first report as Commonwealth Secretary-General latched immediately onto technological development. It had become obvious to him that, as a result of technological advance, the world was becoming ever more interdependent, and that international understanding and co-operation would be 'increasingly needed to find and apply solutions to problems too broad for individual states' (*Secretary-General's Report*, 1966). That was a principle which Commonwealth education ministers and the Secretariat increasingly sought to apply. As described in Chapter 1, the earliest structure of the Secretariat did not include an Education Division. However, a decision of the Prime Ministers in 1966 led to the integration of the already existing Commonwealth Education Liaison Unit (CELU) with the Secretariat to form the Education Division. The Commonwealth Education Liaison Committee (CELC) remained in being as an advisory body for the Education Division of the Secretariat.

b. The Huddersfield Conference

By 1968 Arnold Smith was reporting that, in addition to co-ordinating educational activity through its Education Division, the Secretariat was, in response to ministerial policy, organising 'periodic conferences or seminars of education experts for intensive discussion of a particular field of special interest to Commonwealth countries' (*Secretary-General's Report*, 1968). It was this activity which opened up aspects of TVE, as well as entrepreneurial studies, to groups of representatives of Commonwealth countries. For example, in 1966 a conference on the education and training of technicians took place in Huddersfield, UK.

Organised by the Commonwealth Education Liaison Committee, it was a landmark in the history of Commonwealth education, for it was the first conference to be held specifically in the arena of TVE. The conference was attended by 118 delegates and observers representing 24 Commonwealth countries and British Territories, as well as a number of international organisations. It surveyed the whole field of technical education and training. The delegates considered a broad spectrum of occupations lying between craftsmen and technologists. That spectrum they classified as technicians.

Conference working groups discussed lead papers on:

- Manpower planning and the status of technicians;
- Type, content and organisation of courses;
- Planning and equipping institutions;
- Supply and preparation of teachers and ancillary staff;
- Entrance requirements, selection and standards of attainment;
- Administration, finance, control and inspection.

No resolutions were passed, and no detailed prescriptions for administrative action were set out. This process enabled each country to apply the broad principles in its own circumstances. A full report of the conference was published, *Education and Training of Technicians* (HMSO, 1967), providing a valuable source of reference for many Commonwealth countries.

The Director of the Huddersfield College at the time of the conference of 1966 was A. Maclennan, and he was asked by the Secretariat in 1974 to review and update the report of the 1966 conference. The resulting report was published as *Educating and Training Technicians* (1975). It was no accident, as Maclennan himself reported, that his chapter headings repeated the titles of the six working groups of the 1966 conference.

c. Increasing Attention to Technical Education

The fourth CEC was held in 1968 in Nigeria. The Secretary-General reported three important aspects of that meeting. Since then, each of them has continued to influence the policies and their application. The three issues were:

- The role of education as an instrument of development;
- The importance to Commonwealth developing countries of properly balanced programmes of agricultural education and education in rural communities;
- The fact that the urgent demand for quantitative expansion of educational development had caused the qualitative aspects to receive less attention than they deserved.

In 1971, the Commonwealth Fund for Technical Co-operation was established.

It formed part of the Secretariat and served as a multilateral assistance agency. Its function was to support development by providing experts and advisers to developing Commonwealth countries, and arranging training abroad for their nationals. The CFTC remit was widened in 1972 to include help for exports, and in 1980 assistance to industry. As early as 1975, Arnold Smith was reporting that the Secretariat had begun a programme of research into how technical education could be provided for industrial purposes in developing countries. This move led to the inclusion of a section on technical education in the 1977 report of the new Secretary-General, Shridath Ramphal. The issue was included in the section on education, and was the first indication of the rising status of TVE. A TVE specialist was appointed to the Secretariat.

The technical education section of the report indicated that the Secretariat was responding to the wishes of governments in giving increasing attention to the education of technicians and their practical training in industry. It was becoming clear that there was inadequate provision for the education and training of technical teachers in developing countries, which might have to recruit such teachers from developed countries.

On the recommendation of the Accra 7CEC (1977) a working group was formed, and met in 1978, to work out detailed proposals for a Commonwealth Industrial Training and Experience Programme (CITEP). The working group surveyed the training needs of Commonwealth countries and recommended that there should be a programme providing 2000 training places around the Commonwealth for technicians, craftsmen and managerial grades. By 1981 the needs of development had led member states to give high priority to technical education and training. The Education Division of the Secretariat supported that priority by:

- Helping to establish regional associations of polytechnics;
- Assisting with technical teacher training;
- Improving the suitability of technical examinations;
- Liaising between technical education and industry.

Despite this activity, a regional meeting held in the Caribbean in 1982 concluded that the contribution which technical and vocational education could make to national development in the smaller countries had yet to be fully exploited (*Secretary-General's Report*, 1983).

On the other hand, by 1987 the Secretary-General's Report praised the extension of Education Programme's scope by the establishment of the CITEP, which was to facilitate practical training and experience in industry as well as opportunities for practical experience with advanced technologies and changing manufacturing processes. The 1989 Secretary-General's Report noted that the CITEP programme had continued to expand and had implemented more than 200 training projects over the period 1987–89. Subsequently, CITEP continued to extend its activities, and organised training programmes in advanced technological fields such as software systems, digital satellite communications, computer-aided design and computer-aided manufacture.

d. Specialist Training and the CFTC

Throughout the 1980s the Secretariat continued to support development efforts by supplying some of the specialised skills – managerial, professional and technical – which developing country governments still needed. It offered expertise in development economics, fiscal policy, law, taxation and statistics. By 1983, the Secretariat had formed a Human Resource Development Group which incorporated six different programmes. The education aspect was a major programme provider. Other specialist programmes covered health, management development, women and youth, and the Fellowships and Training Programme (FTP) of the CFTC (*Secretary-General's Report*, 1989).

The FTP had been launched in 1972 under its original title, 'The Education and Training Programme'. The objective was initially to finance the training and education of people from one developing country to another.

This objective was later broadened to enable the FTP to help Commonwealth governments to provide for their manpower development and training needs, as well as to increase the supply of trained people with the skills and expertise required to manage the machinery of government and to support national development plans.

The FTP has provided:

- Policy seminars and advanced training;
- Programmes and workshops for senior government officials and top level executives from both the public and private sectors;
- Training for middle-level technical and managerial staff;
- Training with a multiplier effect, for example the training of trainers;
- The design of customised and specialised training attachments and study visits.

In 1993 the FTP was merged with a Management Development Programme to form the Management and Training Services Division. The service continues under that umbrella utilising broadly the policies set out above.

e. The 1990s: Focus on the Private Sector

Chief Anyaoku was appointed Secretary-General in 1990. His first report, published in 1991, made it clear that one of the primary functions of the Secretariat was to help member countries build sound economic and social infrastructures through the development of skills. By 1993, Chief Anyaoku was reporting that more and more Commonwealth governments, at every stage of economic development, were seeking new ways out of the old economic impasse. They recognised that the way to future growth lay in a commitment to market principles, the development of international trade and the attraction of private capital for productive investment. Instead of trying to run businesses as instruments of government policy, many of the governments were transferring parastatal industries out of their direct control. They were seeking to provide an environment in which individual enterprise could thrive (*Secretary-General's Report*, 1993).

It is notable that the 1991 Harare Declaration had included sound economic management among its aims – thus recognising the central role of the market economy. No doubt this change of economic direction had been influenced by the break-up of the Soviet Union in 1989, and consequential changes of political philosophy within the former satellite countries of the Soviet Union. The effect in the Commonwealth on TVE, as well as on entrepreneurship, can be described as dramatic. New techniques, new structures and new styles of teaching were required to enable the rapidly developing private enterprise sector of the economy to grow. This was especially true in states which had, earlier, been highly centralised.

Consequent upon the changed attitude of several Commonwealth governments towards encouraging a private sector economy, the Secretariat developed a range of activities designed to assist that change.

- A Commonwealth Business Network (COMBINET) was launched in 1993. It aimed to strengthen the role of private business organisations by promoting investment and technology, and by helping small businesses.

- In order to support this activity, a Commonwealth Private Investment Initiative (CPII) was formed. This was a collaborative partnership with the Commonwealth Development Corporation (CDC) and the Commonwealth Secretariat. The venture was intended to facilitate a flow of investment funds to the developing regions of the Commonwealth.

- The Secretariat raised the level of the Commonwealth Business Network by providing online access to the internet in 1997. This provided chambers of commerce, industry associations and businesses with information on new technologies and training opportunities, and with direct access to market intelligence; contacts and opportunities to enter new markets.

- The Commonwealth Business Forum, established in 1997, initiated a Commonwealth Business Council which covered trade policy and facilitation; investment promotion; the promotion of good business practice, corporate governance and corporate social responsibility; e-commerce; publications and information exchange; and the young executive exchange programme (*Secretary-General's Report*, 1999).

Complementing this private sector activity was an urgent need to train skilled personnel capable of supporting private sector business. As the Secretary-General's Report of 1997 put it: 'A major bottleneck in many developing countries is the gap in key skills and expertise'. By then the Secretariat was already providing more training and more experts at the request of member countries, mainly through the CFTC. In the two years 1995–1997 the CFTC provided training to 9000 middle and top-level managers and officials in the public and private sectors in order to upgrade their skills (*Secretary-General's Report*, 1997).

Over the same period, the Secretariat met requests from 46 countries, six dependent territories, and several regional organisations serving Commonwealth countries, by placing about 650 short- and long-term experts and advisers in essential positions where qualified nationals were not available (*Secretary-General's Report*, 1997).

The Secretariat also organised a Pan-Commonwealth Workshop in India in 1996 under the title 'Partnership between government, the private sectors and NGOs in education, training and employment opportunities'. The workshop identified unemployment and under-employment as major concerns in Commonwealth developing countries. It was confirmed that the largest section of the population in most developing countries was employed in the informal sector where there was low productivity through lack of training or appropriate support services. Hence we begin to see where TVE did not reach. It failed to reach the informal sector which contained many millions of people unable to improve their low standard of living because they were not being provided with marketable skills. As the 1997 Secretary-General's Report stated:

> The Commonwealth continues to be deeply concerned about poverty – about half the world's poor live in its member countries.
>
> *Secretary-General's Report*, 1997

Reliable statistics are not available, but an informed guess suggests that at least 600 million people the Commonwealth are living in poverty.

The Secretariat was well aware of this tragic situation. It therefore carried out a major study to identify successful approaches to poverty alleviation, and initiated a series of regional workshops to promote the sharing of experience. Building on the conclusion of these workshops, the Secretariat planned to provide technical assistance and play a brokerage and catalytic role in mobilising expertise and seed capital to countries interested in self-help schemes (*Secretary-General's Report*, 1997).

f. Overview of the Secretariat's Work in the Field

This survey of 35 years of work (1965–2000) by the Commonwealth Secretariat in education reveals the dedication and immense output of the Secretariat's multinational staff. Throughout the 35 years the senior staff have struggled to respond positively to the manifold recommendations and requests arising from the triennial meetings of education ministers and from the many regional or Commonwealth-wide workshops. In addition, the impact of large-scale bilateral and multilateral aid programmes aimed at TVE in developing countries have had an effect on the

Secretariat's activity. A single World Bank project in one country might have inputs greater than the Secretariat's funding for all African member states put together. Inevitably, senior management has had to prioritise functions, and some programmes or requests have had to be given lower priority than others. It would appear from this survey that high priority has been accorded to the highest levels of TVE, i.e. the professional and administrative levels which are broadly at tertiary education level. A somewhat lower priority has been accorded to the vocational aspect in schools; and perhaps lower still to the various skill levels required by technicians and craftsmen. Beyond that level, the lowest priority appears to have been accorded to the provision of TVE for those millions of people currently subsisting in the informal economy. It may be that future ministers of education will wish to reconsider these priorities.

The record of publications provides some evidence of priorities over the 40 years from 1959. The Commonwealth Library has provided two print-outs of recorded publications. The first records the amazing output of 450 publications or papers by the Education Division, or its equivalent, over the 35 years of its existence. However, inspection of the titles indicates that less than 10% relate to TVE and entrepreneurship. A second print-out lists all publications and papers containing the word 'training'. There are no less than 235 such documents. A similar inspection of titles shows the following breakdown of subjects:

Senior officials, specialists and administrators	57%
Technical and vocational education and entrepreneurship	26%
Teachers and teacher training, including technical	14%
Others, e.g. book publishing or resources	3%
	100%

An inspection of the *Commonwealth Year Book* for 2000 shows that there are 90 listed agencies associated with the Commonwealth. No more than seven of those agencies could be regarded as related to TVE and entrepreneurship.

Nothing can detract from the massive, formidable and professional output of the Commonwealth Secretariat over its history so far. The statistical indicators, set out above, simply suggest that TVE and entrepreneurship may well need higher priority in the future.

4 The Commonwealth Fund for Technical Co-operation

The Commonwealth Fund for Technical Co-operation was formed in 1971. It was an extension of, and replacement for, the Commonwealth Programme of Technical Co-operation, which carried out similar functions but on a lesser scale, from 1967 to 1971. As noted above, by 1973 the CFTC had already prepared an update of a 1966 report on the education and training of technicians. As became customary, consultants were recruited for this task. Nigeria and UK provided the specialists for the project. The final document was published in December 1975. By 1974, the Secretary-General was already reporting that the CFTC's Education and Training Programme had become an important medium for Commonwealth co-operation in professional, technical and vocational training in the developing countries (*Secretary-General's Report*, 1974). The programme continued to grow year by year. Governments had identified the main priority as the training of middle level personnel, managers and technicians (*Secretary-General's Report*, 1979)

The same report noted that 53 people from the Solomon Islands had gone on courses and training attachments with CFTC support. Those trainees had travelled to Fiji to learn business accounting and public health nursing, and to train as forest guards. This is an excellent example of partnership and sharing of resources between two small Commonwealth countries. The CFTC awarded scholarships to enable government-nominated students and trainees to gain from training facilities throughout the developing countries of the Commonwealth. This support was mainly directed to job-related training. The scholarships were awarded for institutional courses, mainly professional and technical, but including some academic courses (*Secretary-General's Report*, 1981).

A revealing sidelight on the growing involvement of women in the CFTC training programmes was shown by the following figures published in a CFTC report of 1993. (The first two rows are taken from the CFTC report: the percentages have been added.)

Students/Trainees

	1986/7	1987/8	1988/9	1989/90	1990/91	1991/2	1992/3
Total	2649	3252	4141	4725	4884	4039	4341
Women	306	793	1094	1543	1629	1394	1604
Women as % of total	11.5	24.4	26.4	32.6	33.4	34.5	36.9

The most recent figures available cover the period 1997–99:

Students/Trainees 1997–9

Total	7185
Women	2852
Women as % of total	39.7

This report appears to show (on an annual basis) some fall in overall numbers; but it also shows a continuing rise in the proportion of women (*Skills for Development*, 1999).

By 1997 he CFTC was reporting that some 2000 training fellowships a year had been granted over the period 1993–1997. These were given to middle and senior professional, technical and administrative managers to study at some of the Commonwealth's best institutions, or to take up work attachments (CFTC, 1995 and 1997). Some of these fellowships were provided in the South Pacific region which praised CFTC in 1996 for supporting on-the-job training to foster entrepreneurship and to assist the development of small-scale industries to process locally available resources. The same report noted that women entrepreneurs and other groups newly venturing into industrial activities were the main beneficiaries of the assistance (*The Commonwealth in Action – The South Pacific*, 1996).

In contrast to the many middle-level TVE activities, and perhaps as a positive shift of priorities, the 1999 *Secretary-General's Report* stated that, to avoid duplication of effort, the Commonwealth (through CFTC) is concentrating its poverty alleviation assistance in specific areas, such as access to credit. The report also recorded that CFTC had provided regional training programmes in Cameroon on the management of micro-credit schemes for women at which participants had developed a practical and integrated approach to enterprise development. Many of the 60 to 70 enterprises receiving help were processing raw materials in one form or another. Most of them were small, privately owned and agro-based (*Secretary-General's Report*, 1999).

In 1998–99, the CFTC's budget stood at £20.5 million. The CFTC is a mutual and voluntary fund. Governments make contributions of finance, training places and expertise according to their ability, draw on these resources according to their need and govern CFTC jointly. The CFTC regards its special strengths as:

- Accessibility
- Cost Effectiveness
- Speed of response
- Flexibility
- Neutrality
- As a catalyst to bring in other agencies.

Commonwealth Year Book, 2000

Most CFTC activities are carried out by divisions of the Commonwealth Secretariat, notably the Management and Training Services Division, the General Technical Assistance Services Division, the Export and Industrial Development Division and the Economic and Legal Advisory Services Division.

The CFTC, working closely within the Commonwealth Secretariat, has played a valuable role in raising the level of skills in Commonwealth developing countries, especially at the middle areas of TVE. Experts or advisers with TVE skills were provided to fill key posts in TVE. These skills need to percolate down to much wider sections of the populace in order to have an effect upon the really poor.

5 The Commonwealth Foundation and Non-governmental Organisations

This section concentrates on the TVE and entrepreneurship-related activities of the Foundation.

The Foundation was established in 1966 by Commonwealth Heads of Government. It was designed as an intergovernmental organisation with the mission to serve, support and link the 'unofficial Commonwealth'. The unofficial Commonwealth initially consisted of mainly the professional associations. The Foundation is an autonomous body with a Board of Governors which determines its policies. The Board is made up from member governments and meets twice yearly.

In its early years the Foundation developed a programme of support for professionals, consisting of start-up and sustaining grants for Commonwealth professional associations and centres. In addition, there were responsive awards to individual professions and organisations for training, workshops and exchanges. The Foundation is the major external source of funds for the majority of the Commonwealth Professional Associations. These associations cover areas such as agricultural sciences, architecture, archives, education, engineering, geography, the disabled, human ecology, journalism, law, librarianship and literature, medicine, musicology, nursing, pharmacy, surveying, broadcasting, music and the veterinary sciences. Over the 40-year period covered by this book it was customary for the Foundation to provide annual grants for some 30 Commonwealth professional associations. Their members possess qualifications at the tertiary level. Their activities are directed towards their own professional vocations and are frequently educational.

Their importance for this study is that many, perhaps most, of the professional associations have organised training sessions for their own members. Financial help from the Foundation has contributed to the technical and vocational education of professional association members. However, of the 26 Commonwealth professional associations supported by the Foundation in 2000, only one was related specifically to TVE.

A major shift in the policies of the Foundation occurred in 1979 when the Foundation's mandate was extended to include NGOs. At the same time the Foundation was reconstituted as an international organisation.

As early as 1970 the Secretary-General's Report referred to the existence of over 250 Commonwealth-wide NGOs. The extension of the Foundation's mandate brought several hundred NGOs into a partnership relationship with the Foundation, which began to spend a growing proportion of its funds on NGOs.

The table below illustrates this change of direction.

Commonwealth Foundation Expenditure 1967–994

	1967/8	1993/94	1986/87
Funds	£250,000	£1,540,000	£1,900,000
Spent on:	%	%	%
1. Professionals	100	69	50
2. NGOs	–	15	30
3. Culture	–	16	20

Source: The Commonwealth Foundation. A Special Report, 1966–93

Total expenditure on professionals steadily declined over the period 1967–1994 from 100% to 50%, whereas expenditure on NGOs rose from zero to 30%. As a result of this change, the Special Report for 1966–93 recorded that the Foundation was supporting education for development by funding those people who were working to make education relevant to local conditions.

A subsequent report, *The Commonwealth Foundation*, covering 1996–1999, described how priority was given to collaborative activities, and to a range of development issues. These were the eradication of poverty, rural development, health, non-formal education, community enterprise, gender and disability. In the allocation of awards to individuals to support these aims, it is notable that preference for the awards was given to mid-career women and men who had had limited opportunities for overseas travel.

The same report referred to individual skill building, organisational development and Commonwealth exchange. The strategies for these activities came from support for training, technical assistance and exchanges, workshops, study visits, regional and pan-Commonwealth conferences, information sharing and networks. The same report gave two interesting examples of success from Commonwealth agencies supported by the Foundation. In India, the Commonwealth Trade Union Council's participatory training methods had enabled women to become leaders in their unions and associations. The cascading-down effect had spread the information widely because women had introduced their own training courses. Similarly, the Commonwealth Veterinary Association had organised a programme targeted at women smallholder farmers to provide information about scientific knowledge and appropriate technologies and to improve the production and safe management of animals.

In August 1991, the Foundation helped to organise the first Commonwealth Forum for Commonwealth NGOs. This event brought 170 NGO representatives from 48 countries to a meeting in Harare. Careful timing enabled the NGO meeting to put forward proposals to the Commonwealth Heads of Government meeting in Harare later in the same year. The Forum proposed that there should be a Commonwealth NGO charter to outline good practice and to chart relationships

131

with other agencies. It took some time to get this proposal under way, but in 1996 the Foundation published *Non-Governmental Organisations: Guidelines for Good Policy and Practice*. Three years later, the *Commonwealth Foundation Report*, 1996–1999 saw this event as a watershed in the developing partnership between the Commonwealth and NGOs. Further NGO forums took place in 1995 and 1999.

The twelfth Conference of Commonwealth Education Ministers (1994) agreed that the private sector, including NGOs, could play an effective role in the provision of education.

A year earlier, the *Commonwealth Foundation Report*, 1966–1993 had stressed the importance of enabling people in the expanding Commonwealth to earn a livelihood. The Foundation had therefore funded training and exchange programmes to promote income generation, self-employment and community-based development.

The same report offered the example of a southern NGO, the 'Small Industry Development' of Tanzania, and a northern NGO, 'Tools for Self-Reliance', which had worked in partnership to distribute refurbished hand tools to village enterprises and to entrepreneurs.

It is a tribute to, and a recognition of, the partnership between the Commonwealth and NGOs that the thirteenth Conference of Commonwealth Education Ministers (1997) recommended that practical strategies should be encouraged for promoting partnership between the public sector, the private sector and civil society in all areas of education and human resource development. The Commonwealth News Release of the same meeting recorded proposals to devise viable partnerships with the private sector and relevant NGOs in adapting school curricula and university courses to meet the demands of the workplace and the requirements for new means of literacy.

Early in 1999 the Foundation initiated a new project on government/NGO partnership development in collaboration with the Commonwealth Association for Public Administration and Management. This project envisaged the collection, writing and analysis of country overviews and case studies on NGO/government partnerships. It was intended to produce materials which could be used by governments, NGOs and other institutions to build understanding, skills and knowledge in this field (*Commonwealth Foundation Report*, 1996–1999).

The Foundation's support for appropriate NGOs can be illustrated by the Commonwealth Association of Polytechnics in Africa. On the recommendation of the 1977 CEC meeting in Accra, CAPA was launched in December 1978 with its headquarters in Nairobi. By 1997 CAPA had a membership of 143 polytechnics and high level technical colleges spread across 17 African Commonwealth countries. From 1980, the Association ran training workshops in different locations in Africa. For all these events the Canadian International Development Agency provided funds to supplement those of the Commonwealth Secretariat and the Commonwealth Foundation. The Education Department of the Commonwealth

Secretariat was a prime mover in promoting the CAPA projects.

In 1988, CAPA in collaboration with the International Labour Organisation, established a pilot project to address the issue of under-representation of women in technical education and training. Despite the doom-laden forecasts about the future of Polytechnics expressed by the CAPA Secretary-General in 1997 (see Section 2 above), CAPA still exists and seems set to continue to make a contribution to TVE in Africa.

A further example of the capacity of NGOs to contribute to TVE is that of the south India community colleges based in Madras. Here the vision and energy of a Jesuit Priest, Father Xavier Alphonse, initiated a survey of community colleges in the USA and of further education colleges in the UK. As a result of his researches, Father Xavier managed to obtain grants from many sources (including DfID) to set up a community college on similar lines to US or Canadian colleges. He made the project very practical by obtaining a detailed survey from all employers in and around Madras of their needs for skilled employees. These specifically requested skills formed the basis of the courses offered by the Madras Community College from 1996. The targeted clientele included school drop-outs, and students unqualified for university traditional courses; the college also offered a second chance for apparent failures.

By 1998 there were 13 community colleges in Tamil Nadu, with others being set up in Pondicherry. More such colleges are in the process of formation in south India.

All the community colleges offer a one-year diploma. The training is for 48 weeks. Of these, 18 weeks provide for life skills, 20 weeks for work skills, 8 weeks are for practical work experience and two weeks for preparation for work (Madras Centre for Research and Development of Community Education, 1999).

The Commonwealth Foundation has evolved from its earlier concentration on professional development. There is now a good mix of activities which can support TVE at several levels. NGOs have a valuable role to play in TVE, and will, no doubt, continue to receive seed-corn from the Foundation. It is partnership with NGOs which may enable the Commonwealth to tackle the TVE needs of millions of people in the non-formal economy.

6 The Commonwealth of Learning

The Commonwealth of Learning is the subject of the next chapter and aspects of it have been referred to in Chapters 1, 3 and 4. It is such a significant institution for Commonwealth education that it is not surprising it should be frequently alluded to. From the perspective of the subject matter of this chapter, the following points should be made.

From the beginning, COL was envisaged as placing an emphasis on technical, vocational and continuing education (10CCEM) and, once established, it was required to strike a balance between programmes relevant to higher education and those relevant to other levels of education and training (11CCEM). It operates by providing training materials and programme models of distance education and, as Chapter 6 demonstrates, it has helped national distance learning agencies to develop a number of innovative courses.

Specific COL activity in relation to TVE operates by merging workplace training programmes with proven distance education methods and national standards, thus overcoming traditional barriers to obtaining useful vocational skills. Examples include a technical teacher training system in the Caribbean; distance education materials to support plumbing courses in Tonga; and computerised control of curriculum, administration testing and access to training materials for vehicle manufacturing and its production line workers in South Africa (*COL Summary Report, 1994–1996*).

In a significant development, COL held a four-day workshop in Namibia in 1997 to consider the application of appropriate technologies in non-formal education and development communications. Twenty-seven people attended, representing 13 countries. Six new project proposals were put forward in the areas of literacy, basic education, agriculture, vocational skills and community development.

7 TVE and the World of Work

Industry and commerce as potential partners in the process of TVE had scarcely been mentioned at the first Commonwealth Education Conference in 1959. However, the second Conference held in India in 1962, while endorsing the TVE proposals from the first meeting, added that approaches should be made to industry by governments to see what additional help could be afforded to place students for training in industry. The Lagos meeting of 1968 also added two further relevant recommendations. These were that:

- The training of workers in small-scale industries should be given special attention in the drawing up of technical education plans;

- Industry should be closely associated with technical education in and through policy-making, manpower planning, curriculum development, provision of opportunities for industrial experience, accreditation, consultancy services, part-time courses and vocational guidance.

Analysis of the realities of the relationships between TVE and industry featured at the Canberra Conference held in 1971. The report of the main committee on TVE agreed that the chief function of technical education was to satisfy the needs of commerce and industry for various categories of technical manpower. In this respect, they argued, the needs of small-scale industries should not be overlooked. The main report went even further, for it found evidence that some countries had produced too many highly trained personnel, and too few with appropriate training for middle and lower positions in industry and commerce. It was recommended that such countries should review their existing provision in this regard.

In a widening of the economic aims of TVE, the Jamaica Conference of 1974 stated that the aim of TVE should be to contribute to increasing employment and per capita income.

These aims led the Ghana report of 1977 to state that most developing countries were faced with the paradox of having a shortage of persons with critically needed skills and a surplus of unskilled labour. This aspect was steadily becoming a feature of all economies in the world, and in developed and developing communities alike. By 1980 even the technical teachers were seen to be failing to relate their teaching to the specific developmental needs of each different country (CCEM, 1980). So the CEC urged the Secretariat to investigate the interactions between technical education curricula and associated industrial training programmes by means of a survey in member countries, followed by the publication of appropriate manuals on the subject.

By 1987, the analysis of TVE was becoming of deeper significance. The CEC held in Kenya agreed that although the cost of TVE was high, the cost of not providing it must not be overlooked. Where adequate provision for TVE was lacking, other sectors of the economy were certain to suffer, with the whole society having to bear the strain of unemployment and the loss of youth morale. In this regard an estimate made in India put the cost of not providing TVE as being 1.8 times greater than the cost of providing it.

It was relatively late, in 1984, in this 40-year period, that the conferences began to discuss an inter-relationship between schools and TVE. The 1984 meeting in Cyprus (9CCEM) recommended that a study should be made with reference to pre-vocational and vocational education of different approaches to the provision of work experience in schools. In addition, it was felt that the bringing together of school and work could help counter attitudes inherited from colonial times, i.e. that educated people should not do manual work, and that workers did not need to learn.

Going further, the same meeting suggested that there was a need to explore ways of introducing a pre-vocational element into schools and to learn from the varied and extensive experience of doing this within Commonwealth countries. One working group studied the contribution of education systems (formal and non-formal) in improving young people's access to work. The group found that terms such as employment, work and jobs need redefinition in view of the economic, social and political diversity of the Commonwealth. The group noted that the economies of developing countries were primarily based on agriculture. Up to 80% of those populations led agricultural, semi-subsistence lives. For them, life was work: work which encompassed food production, cash crop farming, home-care, house-building and road-making. This led to the question of whether all children should be taught basic technical skills as part of a broad and balanced curriculum. Increasing concern was expressed at the high cost of establishing separate technical education facilities; equipment was expensive and teachers scarce.

The working group recommended that the Secretariat should continue its initiative of providing opportunities to discuss the integration of science, technical, vocational and mathematics education in schools. The Cyprus meeting summarised the main TVE needs. These were to endow young people with the capacity to respond flexibly to changing patterns of work, and to provide for those who could go into wage employment, become self-employed, work in the traditional sector, in co-operatives and other semi-formal institutional environments. At the same time, while education needed to reflect the world of work, a narrow vocational emphasis would not meet all these ends.

All these recommendations were placed in a different context by the Kenya Conference of 1987, where ministers agreed that measures needed to be taken to overcome negative attitudes of parents, teachers and pupils towards vocationally-oriented programmes which were commonly identified as being intended for slow learners, under-achievers, drop-outs and the culturally deprived.

Already by 1987 doubts were beginning to arise about the role of the state in relation to TVE and industry. A key question was: at what point should governments inject support for entrepreneurial development and provide assistance for small-scale businesses? The 1990 meeting in Barbados was concerned that the private sector was also developing vocational institutions, and a committee on TVE recognised that it was becoming necessary to control the standards and practices of private sector TVE institutions. By the time of the 1994 meeting in Pakistan, ministers were recording that pressures on the state from different sources had necessitated a serious rethinking of the role the state played in the delivery of services. However, they felt that calls for the state to withdraw from educational provision to any significant degree were likely to be restrained. In any case, the state remained responsible for the securing of the provision of basic education as a right of all citizens (12CCEM).

Over the 40-year period to 1999 there has been a progressive development of the inter-relationship between TVE and the worlds of public and private employment. That inter-relationship seems likely to expand and improve for the future, as the possession of marketable skills becomes a prerequisite of employment.

8 TVE and the Informal Economic Sector

The informal economic sector was rarely mentioned at early meetings of the Commonwealth Education Conferences. Almost by definition, little was known about the extent and variety of the informal sector, and ministers were preoccupied with expanding formal education, especially in the developing countries. Only later did non-formal education become noticed as a potential means of providing for the unknown millions in the informal economic sector.

The ILO had, however, already studied the sector, and in 1971 the ILO Director-General described the informal sector as:

• Unregistered and unrecorded in official statistics;

- Tending to have little or no access to organised markets, to credit institutions, to formal education and training institutions or to many public services and amenities;

- Often compelled by circumstances to operate outside the framework of the law;

- Almost invariably beyond the reach of social labour legislation and protective measures at the workplace, even when the workers were registered and respected certain areas of the law.

There appears to have been no major recommendation about education for the informal sector from the CECs until the conference held in Ghana in 1977. That meeting recommended that the Commonwealth Secretariat should:

- Carry out surveys, case studies and pilot projects in the field of non-formal education;

- Assist in the exchange of information concerning programmes designed to identify solutions to common problems in non-formal education and rural development. Inevitably non-formal education, i.e. education conducted outside formal educational institutions, became a vehicle for TVE to reach people working in the informal sector.

As a result, a Commonwealth Specialist Conference on non-formal education was held in Delhi in 1979. The conference lasted two weeks and was attended by 109 delegates from 27 countries. Observers attended from the host country, several international agencies and the UK. The conference recognised the importance of non-formal education for national development. The meeting produced no less than 61 recommendations. The following lists a selection:

- National councils or boards for the non-formal education of adults and children;

- Seminars and consultative meetings to share experiences;

- Redesigning census procedures to provide information about relevant groups of people;

- A governmental budgetary allocation for non-formal education;

- Co-operation with appropriate voluntary agencies;

- Co-operation with private enterprise where appropriate;

- Non-formal education programmes to provide 'drop-outs' and school leavers with a second chance;

- Many recommendations to involve women, both to help with, and to receive non-formal education;

- Specific training for appropriate teachers and workers with community groups;

- Provision for adult illiterate people;

- All programmes to be related to local circumstances.

Few of the 61 recommendations have been widely adopted. All remain desirable to raise the living standards of the poorest peoples in the Commonwealth.

In 1985 the *Secretary-General's Report* recorded that work in the non-formal education sector included publishing studies of non-formal education for out-of-school children and for women, and completing a survey of the involvement of Commonwealth universities in non-formal education. In 1984 a regional workshop was held in Dhaka on the evaluation of non-formal education programmes.

Professor Ashoka Chandra wrote the main working papers for a Commonwealth Workshop held in Jamaica during 1997. Professor Chandra was the Director of the Institute of Applied Manpower Research at New Delhi, India. His working paper stated that in India the organised economic sector accounted for only 8% of total employment. The bulk of employment was in the informal sector, which in manufacturing accounted for 76% of total manufacturing employment. Professor Chandra used evidence from Jamaica, India and Tanzania to analyse four broad categories of employment in the informal sector. These categories were:

- Entrepreneurs – owners of small establishments and principal workers in the enterprises;

- Establishment workers – wage earning employees, apprentices and unpaid workers;

- Independent workers – basically self-employed, street vendors, repairmen, producers of earthenware and leather products, and providers of day-to-day services of generally low market value;

- Casual workers – mainly manual labour, household workers, gardeners, sweepers, construction labourers, watchmen and others in typical casual jobs.

If we take Professor Chandra's figures of 8% of workers employed in the formal economy in India, then 92% of the working population in India, that is, say, 460 million people, are working in the categories outlined above. Manifestly, formal education cannot reach those people, and informal media of education have to be used if any level of technical and vocational education is to provide the skills to enable them to raise their standard of living.

Evidence about this desperate situation is not confined to Professor Chandra's research in Asia. The International Labour Organisation reported in November 1998 that the informal sector is a major provider of urban jobs in developing countries. In Africa as a whole, informal employment accounted for over 60% of total urban employment. Among individual countries for which statistics were available, the figures reach 57% in Bolivia and Madagascar, and 50% in the Republic of Tanzania (*ILO Governing Body Report*, November 1998).

By 1999 UNESCO published an even more worrying report. This stated that in many low-income countries, and even in medium-income level countries, employment in the formal economy was stagnant. The absorption of new entrants into the labour market takes place in the informal sector (UNEVOC Info. 3/99). Some suggestions for improving the economic position of those in the informal sector in developing countries were made in a *World Employment Report*, published by the ILO in 1998. These suggestions included:

- Upgrading traditional apprenticeship systems;
- Increasing access to new technology;
- Strengthening linkages with medium-sized and large firms;
- Increased networking to arrange cost-effective training programmes;
- Training as a crucial part of a package clearly linked to credit and institutional support.

The great virtue of non-formal education is that it is flexible in regard to timing, venue and the curriculum needs of the clientele groups. Functional NFE can range from pre-primary to adult education (*Action for Human Resource Development*, Commonwealth Secretariat, 2000). Provided NFE takes full account of the local pattern of employment of even the poorest families in the informal economy, it may be able to transfer skills which are used by families even living at subsistence level into survival skills for the future. Such families make dwellings, find food, fish, often make minor weapons, and bring up children. The potentiality is there to be used.

Issues in Education and Training (Wright, 2000: 28) summarises the important challenge in terms of access to education, namely how to ensure that those who are outside the formal system can be provided with alternative means and opportunities for acquiring the knowledge and information they need to realise their full potential for development.

9 Entrepreneurship

Entrepreneurship is the ability to combine the factors of production so as to produce saleable goods or services at prices which will enable the entrepreneur to make a sufficient profit to finance continuity of production. The factors of production in traditional economic analysis are land, labour, and capital. Entrepreneurship is sometimes regarded as the fourth factor of production. The vast expansion of knowledge over the past 100 years and its rapidly growing dissemination over the past 50 years, leads to the theory that there is now a fifth factor of production – 'specialised knowledge'. Countries with a high average level of specialised knowledge have a high standard of living. Countries with a low average level of specialised knowledge have a low standard of living. Thus, it is now the entrepreneur's task to combine land, labour, capital and specialised knowledge in order to maximise production and thus raise standards of living.

Entrepreneurship has created the vast majority of the world's wealth. When wealth became institutionalised as 'capital' in the nineteenth century the process was attacked and totally opposed by 'socialist' thinking. The capitalists supported private enterprise. The socialists believed that the state should centrally control the economy. Despite 70 years of experimentation, by the late 1980s it had become clear that total state control did not produce as rapid an increase in Gross Domestic Product as did individual enterprise in mixed economies.

Over the past 40 years, Commonwealth countries have had to adjust to the extensive changes in political philosophy and economic theory which are implied by the analysis outlined above. Many newly independent developing countries within the Commonwealth initially introduced centrally controlled economies. Even the mixed economies of the developed countries were still debating the role of the state in relation to individual enterprise through most of the twentieth century. The balance is not settled yet, but most countries of the world have 'mixed' economies, i.e. a mixture of individual enterprise and social control. The turning point came in 1989 when the Soviet Union's people changed its government's philosophy. The Soviet Union divided into its constituent parts, and several of its satellite nations in Eastern Europe dismissed their highly centralised governments and introduced partially private enterprise economies in which individual enterprise was key.

Up to 1990, relatively little was said at CECs about the need to educate for entrepreneurship. It must be noted, however, that an Entrepreneurship Development Institute had been set up in India by 1984. A keynote address to the Kenya Conference of 1987 did, however, suggest that in the then turbulent economic environment, young people should be prepared, through vocationally oriented education, for employment in small businesses and in the informal sector.

At the same meeting, education ministers noted that pressure was growing on them and the school system to prepare pupils for self-employment. More explicitly, the 1989 report of the Commonwealth Secretary-General described entrepreneurship as important in helping to create economic growth and employment. Many Commonwealth governments were keen to find ways to develop appropriate skills. Over the period 1987–89 the Commonwealth Fellowships and Training Programme allocated 600 fellowships for attendance at training courses in entrepreneurship and small industries development. Some of the courses were provided specifically for women (*Secretary-General's Report*, 1989).

With this background, it was not surprising that the Barbados Conference supported the Secretariat's activities since the previous conference in 1987, in focusing on a manageable set of activities geared to producing curriculum guidelines on entrepreneurial skills development for technical and vocational institutions. The conference report accepted a Working Party's recommendation that work on entrepreneurship should continue and should not be bound by the triennium between ministers' conferences (11CCEM, 1990). As a result of a recommendation in 1987, the Commonwealth Secretariat's Education Division initiated a three-year project focusing on entrepreneurial skills development programmes in technical and vocational training institutions. The results were published as *Designing*

Entrepreneurial Skills Development Programmes – a Resource Book for Technical and Vocational Institutions (1990). The book expressed doubts about the benefits of some technical and vocational education projects because they did not always appear to be cost effective to the national governments.

A further publication, *Entrepreneurial Skills Development Programmes in 15 Commonwealth Countries,* was produced in 1991 (Rao and Wright, 1991). That publication expressed considerable doubts about advocating an Entrepreneurial Skills Development Programmes (ESDP) for all or as part of general education. The view was expressed that changing the culture of a school to make it more conducive to promoting ESDP was an extremely difficult and long-term process. It might, therefore, be better to locate attempts to promoting ESDP within specialist institutions. The authors did, however, note that by 1991, there were already 300 agencies in India that conducted ESD programmes and promoted entrepreneurship.

By 1993, the Secretary-General's report was referring to the establishment of Youth Enterprise Development Funds. These funds were designed to assist young entrepreneurs to start small-scale enterprises and, in the example given, were organised by the Africa Centre. The same report referred to increased demand in 1991–93 for training in the area of entrepreneurship and small business development. Improving entrepreneurial skills in trade promotion and export development had been central, over the same period, to the Secretariat's export development efforts.

It soon became clear that the lack of start-up funding was a major hindrance to the expansion of entrepreneurship. As a result, in 1995 ministers responsible for youth affairs launched a Commonwealth Youth Credit Initiative. This provided small loans at low cost, and established revolving funds so that repayments could be re-utilised (*Secretary-General's Report,* 1995). As *The Commonwealth in Action – The South Pacific* pointed out in 1996, helping young people to access adequate capital is as important as nurturing youthful talents and honing business skills. The Commonwealth Youth Credit Initiative would help to finance enterprising young people, who are often ineligible for commercial credit, by providing an alternative to collateral.

A number of co-operative agencies helped to provide very limited amounts of credit in different countries of the Commonwealth, but perhaps the most famous of the approaches to providing credit to enable poor people to start up businesses is that of Bangladesh's Grameen (or village) Bank. Professor Muhammed Yunus, Managing Director of the Bank, was a major developer of micro credit. He claimed, in an article in *The Observer* (15 November 1999) that repayment of loans by people who borrow without collateral is much better than those whose borrowings are secured by enormous assets. The Grameen Bank came into existence in 1983, and by 1998 was employing 12,000 people. Similar institutions have been set up in over 50 countries.

Credit traditionally depends on the use of some asset as collateral. De Soto has stated that the most important source of funds for new businesses in America was a mortgage on the entrepreneur's home. This process is not easily available in many developing countries because there is often no clear documentary legal basis for the ownership of land, and thus no clear ownership of any property on it, such as a house which could be used as collateral for a loan from a bank.

By 1997 the Secretary-General's report was referring to the fact that women faced special problems when they wished to borrow money to start a business. In May 1996 the Secretariat had sponsored a training scheme for women entrepreneurs in Africa. Training workshops assisted would-be entrepreneurs. Of 100 people who attended such workshops, most were women. More widely, the Secretariat had been supporting the training of entrepreneurs in the establishment of appropriate legal, economic, and fiscal frameworks for the exploitation of key natural resources, and the delineation of maritime boundaries of member countries.

Professor Chandra, in his presentation to the Commonwealth workshop held in Jamaica in 1997 had suggested that each level of education could focus on developing entrepreneurial capabilities through specific content and programmes to promote a movement towards self-employment, thereby reducing excessive dependence on wage employment.

Entrepreneurship forms a fundamental part of every economy. Its influence ranges from an individual sole trader to multi-million pound multinational organisations. Many countries in the Commonwealth and elsewhere in the world are currently incorporating aspects of entrepreneurship in education for employment programmes. This is an arena in which governments are beginning to co-operate closely with the private sector of the economy and are engaging NGOs as partners. In the developed, as well as the developing, countries re-structuring of industry and commerce has caused widespread unemployment. This situation has forced many people into self-employment and entrepreneurship as a means of survival. Nevertheless, this should not be seen as a fall-back position, but as a valuable strategy for enlarging employment opportunities and thus raising standards of living.

Successful entrepreneurship combines all the factors of production into the optimal use of all resources. Entrepreneurship is thus a faculty as essential to civil servants and to local government employees as it is to buyers and sellers of goods and services.

10 The Outlook for Technical and Vocational Education and Entrepreneurship in the Commonwealth

Technical and Vocational Education in the Commonwealth has experienced continuous and productive attention over the 40-year period covered by this survey. Entrepreneurship received limited attention for the first 30 years, but has rapidly achieved recognition over the years from 1989 to 1999 and beyond.

It is possible to envisage a substantial future extension of Commonwealth activity in both TVE and entrepreneurship because both can now be seen as components in all educational processes. Those components have emerged from the past 40 years of Commonwealth educational activity and are at the following levels:

University and Postgraduate
For professional vocations such as doctors, construction engineers, veterinary experts, soil agriculturalists, and information technology specialists.

Upper Secondary School/Technical Institution
As a component, including generic studies, in all courses, and separately, as structured studies leading to preparation for employment in general, and eventually to technicians and technologists.

Lower Secondary School
As a component, including generic studies, in all courses and leading to employment as craftsmen/craftswomen, and operatives.

Primary School
As a minor component but including generic studies.
(Generic studies include literacy, numeracy, team working, problem solving, adjustment to change; and examples of the daily working lives of different peoples.)

Basic education for adults
Literacy and numeracy are pre-conditions for communication and for learning new employable skills.

In addition:
On-the-job-training
Continual upskilling will be required for everyone, whether they are employed by others or self-employed. Entrepreneurship, i.e. the capacity to manage available resources well, to respond to change and to innovate, will be required in every employment, self-, public or private. An understanding of entrepreneurship should be expected to become a component of the total curriculum at every educational level.

Given that outlook for the future, and based upon the evidence of TVE and entrepreneurship in the Commonwealth over the course of this survey, it is possible to construct an analysis of strengths, weaknesses, opportunities and threats which now face the Commonwealth in these two arenas.

a. Strengths

- The professional commitment and expertise of the Commonwealth Secretariat.
- The policy move from the giving of aid to the concept of partnership.
- Adoption of the concept that education, including TVE, is in itself development.
- Exceptional help made available to individuals in member countries at the higher levels of specialism.

- Diversity of the Commonwealth members, which offers many model solutions to human development.
- Pan-Commonwealth and regional workshops.
- A common communication language – English.

b. Weaknesses

- Insufficient resources devoted to TVE and entrepreneurship training.
- Prioritisation of resources insufficiently related to the poorest members of communities, and to the informal sector.
- Over-emphasis on academic education.
- Relative lack of provision in some developing countries of manpower planning allied to labour market analysis.
- No Commonwealth-wide TVE national network for mutual exchange of experience.
- Unequal provision of TVE and entrepreneurship training for women as compared with men.

c. Opportunities

- Use of technology to provide distance learning.
- Capacity to provide the TVE network suggested above by enabling all Commonwealth countries to establish UNEVOC centres (UNEVOC is the vocational arm of UNESCO). Twenty-five Commonwealth countries already provide UNEVOC centres. The remaining 29 could also do so, thus providing a Commonwealth subset of the global UNEVOC network.
- Engage all employers (including the state) in TVE and entrepreneurship training, by establishing the paradigm that training is the duty and social responsibility of every employer.
- Harness and co-ordinate the activities of the many Commonwealth professional associations and NGOs.
- Promote more rapid growth of National Income in developing countries as compared with developed countries. This process, if continued, could release more resources for TVE and entrepreneurship training.
- Channel aid from external sources (the World Bank and regional banks) to TVE as an investment in people.
- Initiate a common admission qualification to all institutions of higher education in the Commonwealth. This might contain a TVE component and an entrepreneurship component.

d. Threats

- Failure to provide hope via TVE for those in the informal sector. This could lead to serious social unrest.
- Information Technology and the internet could widen the gap between the standards of living in the developed countries, and those in the developing countries. This could weaken Commonwealth ties.
- Private enterprise is capable of offering distance teaching 24 hours a day, 7 days a week, 52 weeks in the year. There may need to be some control over the content of this output.
- Restructuring of industries and commerce is likely to lead to higher unemployment.
- In some developing countries, the expansion of all educational provision is insufficient to match the expanding population.

11 Conclusion

The outlook for Technical and Vocational Education and for entrepreneurship training in the Commonwealth is one of vast opportunities limited only by the resources available to finance them. Every human being must now expect a lifelong learning, training and retraining process. Skills will be required for survival at all stages in life. Inevitably, the application of TVE and entrepreneurship training will need to be related to the different cultural, social, economic and political structures in each Commonwealth country. Developed countries already have in place policies, practice, institutions and resources available to address the growing need for TVE and entrepreneurship training. Most developing countries will need all the help they can obtain, both from the global aid agencies and from Commonwealth resources. The use of resources for TVE and entrepreneurship is not a cost: it is an investment in the development of human beings.

Part Four

Higher Education:
Innovation and Argument

Chapter 6

Open and Distance Learning – Innovation in the 1990s: The Commonwealth of Learning

Gajaraj Dhanarajan

COL is very important to people like ourselves. And in its decade or so of existence it has definitely demonstrated its pivotal importance. It was one of the finer initiatives taken by the Commonwealth.

Professor Rex Nettleford, Vice-Chancellor, University of the West Indies and member of the Asa Briggs Expert Group, 1999

1 The Commonwealth of Learning: Basic Facts

The Commonwealth of Learning is helping developing nations to improve access to quality education and training. With headquarters based in Vancouver, the international organisation serves the 54-member Commonwealth with a mandate to widen opportunities for learning by promoting the development and sharing of open and distance learning knowledge, resources and communication technologies. It was created by Commonwealth Heads of Government in 1988 and became operational in 1989. The first President was Professor James A. Maraj (1930–99) and the first Chairman of the Board of Governors was the Rt. Hon. Lord Briggs of Lewes. Dr Ian Macdonald has been chairman since 1994. The author of this chapter has been its President since 1995. More of its background history is given in Chapters 1 and 4.

2 Taking Distance Education into the Mainstream

When they met in Vancouver in late 1987 Commonwealth leaders demonstrated amazing foresight in agreeing to create an agency for the promotion and development of distance education. Since It began operations in 1989, COL has grown to be a valuable asset not only to the Commonwealth but also to the wider world.

Working with associates all over the Commonwealth, the agency has been at the forefront of developing knowledge and capacity in open and distance learning around the world. By doing so it has helped change the perceptions of government leaders, policy-makers, educational managers and the lay public as to the value and importance of applying innovative techniques and technologies to take education and training to learners wherever they may be.

Today, almost all 54 countries of the Commonwealth use distance education methods for one purpose or another. COL can take pride in the role it has played in shifting distance education from being a side-stream to a mainstream provision in many of these countries. It did this by making use of the plentiful talent of the Commonwealth for the needs of the Commonwealth.

Since its inception, COL has been guided in its development by the views expressed in the two founding documents – the [Lord Asa] Briggs and [Sir John] Daniel Committee Reports – that spelt out the contribution it was expected to make to Commonwealth co-operation in education. For that co-operation to happen, COL had to be able to call upon its own critical mass of knowledge and experience from the start. Its headquarters staff comprised men and women who were experts in the specialist components of distance education. They kept in touch with national and international experts in their field. They are also well-informed about the needs of Commonwealth countries and the policy options these countries can realistically be expected to consider as they frame their approach to open learning and distance education. But COL is, and will continue to be, a small agency. It is by working alongside and through men and women in their own agencies and institutions, and by commissioning some of them to work on various projects, that COL's officers mobilise Commonwealth co-operation and perform the role of agents for change. Between 1989 and 1999, COL made use of the expertise of 400 short-term consultants from 39 Commonwealth and four non-Commonwealth countries. As important as the numbers is the fact that the exchange of expertise through these consultants was South–South as well as North–South.

COL is, therefore, a very special kind of Commonwealth agency. Its mandate is to mobilise knowledge and expertise in a field delivering education and training that is both new and undergoing rapid change in the delivery technologies used. Either of these factors by itself raises daunting policy issues for governments, education and training systems, and institutions. Taken in conjunction, as they must be, they are creating openings to the future in the way that formal educational activities are being conceptualised and put into practice.

3 Educational Technologies: Making it Happen

It is very important, therefore, to emphasise that in policy terms distance education is to be thought of in relation to the educational technologies that make it happen. Those engaged in it as students must have access to information about programmes of study as well as to the programmes themselves. They must also receive effective tutoring and other forms of personal support of one kind or another. These must be reinforced by regular feedback from the institution whose programme they are studying in the form of study materials, marked assignments and arrangements for the assessment or examination of their performance. Teachers engaged in distance teaching must have the professional expertise to know how, within the resources potentially available to them, they can devise effective programmes of distance education for their students, how these programmes can best be packaged for study purposes and how students are to be tutored and supported as they study them. Those responsible for managing distance teaching operations must administer complex activities that require infrastructural support in the form of telecommunications, the ability to produce, print, publish and distribute publications, and structures for careful forward planning and funding. And those responsible for education systems that are committed, or becoming committed, to distance education approaches must know in what ways the demands of distance education for funding, trained personnel and supporting resources differ from those of conventional, face-to-face forms of teaching – and they must have policies, funding arrangements and management systems that will enable effective distance education to take place.

To say all this is merely to spell out what is implied by the statement that distance education must be thought of in terms of the education technologies that cause it to happen. However it is organised, distance education seeks to create conditions under which effective learning can take place without the continuing presence of face-to-face teachers. To do that it must distribute, add to and recombine the elements of effective teaching – elements that good face-to-face teachers possess and express through the professional knowledge and expertise that they have at their fingertips. Whatever form they take, and however they are organised, distance education programmes are systems of teaching and learning. All the components of each system must be present and working efficiently for a distance education system to be effective.

The members of the Briggs and Daniel Committees knew from practical experience that in order for distance education to be effective in many parts of the Commonwealth, it must provide practical answers to the requirements listed above. At a time when governments and educationists were coming to grips with the policy implications of distance education, these reports gave clear advice on the objectives it could serve, its components and the importance of seeing them in system terms as sub-sets of administration, production, delivery, support and maintenance.

4 COL's Functions and Objectives

The Memorandum of Understanding (MOU) agreed by Commonwealth countries on 1 September 1988 translated that advice into COL's functions and objectives, which have monitored COL's policies and organisational responses from its beginning. They were reviewed in 1993 by the Progress Review Committee, which, in terms of the MOU, reviewed COL's performance during its first five years. The Progress Review Committee endorsed the functions and objectives as a suitable framework within which COL would be able to make any policy changes that might be needed in the future.

It will be helpful to comment on them here because they itemise both the components from which effective systems of distance education are fashioned and the functions COL was required to perform with respect to them and in the interests of human resource development in Commonwealth countries. The ten substantive functions and COL's duties encompassed:

- *Creating and developing institutional capacity:* For countries and institutions embarking on distance education, the creation and development of institutional capacity are basic policy and management requirements. COL's task was to assist member countries.

- *Programmes in distance education:* In face-to-face teaching, the basic professional requirement is suitable qualified and trained teachers who will teach students in classrooms, laboratories and workshops. In distance education, the basic professional requirement is programmes of study that have been well-conceived, planned and organised in learning modules that are user-friendly and capable of being studied independently by students who may or may not be able to call on regular tutorial assistance. Programmes incorporate all the compulsory and optional courses that are to be completed by students in line with the standards required for particular degrees, diplomas, certificates and other academic and vocational awards. The writing and production of study programmes are complex activities that combine academic knowledge and pedagogical insight with expertise in course design and appropriate use of audio and visual media, as well as print and practical knowledge of production processes. COL's task was to facilitate the channelling of resources to projects and programmes.

- *Information and consultancy:* Access to accurate, relevant information and sources of advice is essential to all effective distance education operations. COL's task was to provide information and consultancy services on any aspects of distance education, including the selection of appropriate technology.

- *Staff training and management:* Distance education has distinctive professional requirements and it is the same with its management. COL's tasks were to undertake training in the techniques and management of distance education and support the training efforts of others.

- *Communication links:* The Briggs Committee had a vision of open learning, one in which, in time, any student would be able to enrol in courses of distance learning in his or her own country or in any other Commonwealth country. Regardless of whether the vision will be realised in the bold terms in which it was expressed, communication between like-minded colleagues who are working together on common objectives is indispensable in the development and improvement of distance education. COL's task was to facilitate communication links between institutions. In our electronic age, communication links imply telecommunication in its various modes. But the links to be made are also professional links, and national, regional and Commonwealth professional associations are means to facilitate such linkages.

- *Evaluation and applied research:* Evaluation and applied research are not prominent features in education systems in most Commonwealth countries. But they are critical to the development and maintenance of effective distance education operations. COL's task was to undertake evaluation and applied research in distance education and support the efforts of others.

- *Access to teaching materials:* The writing and production of teaching materials for use in distance education programmes is time-consuming and expensive. Thousands of teaching programmes and their associated teaching materials have already been produced and are in regular use somewhere in the Commonwealth. There are always compelling reasons why, after due consideration, institutions may decide to develop their own teaching materials for use in their own study programmes. But it is not a decision that should be made without knowing what other institutions have already produced. Much can be learnt about approaches and methods from courses that may not themselves be suitable for an internal purpose. Sometimes there are parts of courses that could be used as they stand or suitably adapted. It is therefore important that people who are planning courses should have access to the already existing stock of teaching materials so that they could then make informed decisions about how they should go about achieving their intentions. COL's task was to assist in the acquisition and delivery of teaching materials and, more generally, in facilitating access to them.

- *Adapting and developing teaching materials:* Once an institution has decided what it wants to do about the teaching materials for a study programme, it then has to get them into the hands of its teachers and students. Many developing countries lack the people and resources to produce their own materials or the resources to purchase other people's teaching materials. COL's task was to commission and promote the adaptation and development of teaching materials.

- *Recognition of academic credit:* The restrictive policies of many countries and institutions on recognition of qualifications or partially completed qualifications gained in another Commonwealth country are impediments to open learning within countries, as well as between them. COL's task was to establish and maintain procedures for the recognition of academic credit.

- *Support services to students:* Typically, distance students are separated in time and place from the teachers whose courses they are studying. Too often, particularly

in developing countries, distance students have little, if any, tutorial or counselling help, whether from study centres, tutors, libraries, laboratories or workshops.
COL's task was to assist in the development of local support services to students.

5 Evolution of COL's Operations

The challenge for any new international agency is not just to do things that others
are not doing, but to take initiatives that are capable of transforming the field it is
working in. Having been assigned the mandate to respond to developments in both
distance education and telecommunications as applied to educational purposes,
COL was working at the most important educational intersection of our time.
During COL's first few years that challenge was heightened by two inherent
features of distance education itself at that time. Particularly in developing countries of the Commonwealth, it was a new field of educational endeavour that raised
important questions about models which might be relevant and technologies that
might be appropriate to their needs, circumstances and sources of funding.
Moreover – and this is the second feature – the models that might be relevant are
themselves being subjected to very considerable changes in response to innovations
in communication and information technology. In both respects, developments
worldwide, since 1988, amply confirm that COL is an international agency whose
time has come.

When COL began its work, distance education was pre-eminently a matter of
printed materials and postal and courier services, and the main contacts between
teachers and their students, as well as between teachers and colleagues working in
distance education in other institutions and countries, were by correspondence.
Printed materials remain – and will probably long continue to be – the mainstay for
most distance education programmes. But with the advent of audio-conferencing,
facsimile, desktop publishing, computerised databases, the internet, World Wide
Web, CD-ROMs and computerised multi-media, the production of printed materials, the means by which they can be accessed by students and the means by which
teachers can interact with students studying at a distance are such that distance
education, considered as a mode of education, is being rapidly transformed.

Within the Commonwealth, there is an enormous amount of innovation and
development in distance education and COL has set out to become part of it. It has
done this by identifying important questions, devising strategic approaches for
interventions and developing collaborative working relationships with key people
and relevant organisations in the pursuit of mutually agreed objectives.

When COL started work at the end of 1988, there was, understandably, no clear
perception of what it was and what its contribution to educational development
would be. At first, many people engaged in distance education, and some governments and international agencies, mistakenly thought that COL was another development assistance agency to be turned to for funding assistance for their own
projects. Ten years on, COL had established itself as the Commonwealth agency

whose funds and energies were directed towards innovation and development in distance education in the context of human resource development. In all its initiatives, there was a reciprocal relationship between action and reflection. COL reflected on what needed to be done, embarked on a course of action, reflected on the results and then decided whether further action was needed in a particular field of work and, if so, what form it should take.

This means that once COL completed an innovative project, it did not become involved in its routine operations. COL shifted the expertise of its professional staff and financial resources to other projects. Here again, it is important to underline the co-operative nature of the ventures in which COL became involved. Virtually all its innovative efforts required capital and recurrent funding if they were to outlive their initial period of trial and development and become a regular feature of distance education in institutions or education systems in developing countries of the Commonwealth. This has two important implications. First, from the outset, COL needed to keep major development assistance agencies well informed of particular projects that they should keep in mind for their own future reference. Secondly, and more importantly, it meant that COL's innovative work must be of sufficient quality with clear practical results for those for whom it is intended, such that development assistance agencies will recognise it as meriting further funding to make them permanent features of distance education programmes. Of course, in these difficult funding times, it cannot be assumed that there will always be a smooth progression from a successful innovation to its adoption as a permanent feature for ongoing funding by the institutions and countries with which COL is working.

In other respects, too, COL had to be careful not to become encumbered with routine responsibilities that would make recurring claims on its modest annual budget. One aspect of its work, to which it gave a good deal of thought, has been in the important field of acquiring sets of teaching and learning materials for distance education purposes. A number of governments proposed that COL should create a learning materials bank so that institutions and member governments could have a central point of reference. COL decided, however, that continuing to assemble and maintain such a resource would become too much of a fixed cost. COL therefore decided to carry out a more limited library role in assisting governments by creating a Materials Fund to facilitate the acquisition of materials. Helping institutions to acquire materials they can use is more important than maintaining a materials bank that merely gives access to materials for the purpose of assessing their usefulness. Another question which COL is still considering is whether it should seek a high profile on copyright matters or whether it can effectively serve distance education agencies in the Commonwealth in other ways without adding to its ongoing responsibilities.

6 Significance and Value of COL as an Institution

One further point worth making is COL's track record in making the best use of scarce resources. Simply by existing and being a point of reference, COL has performed a valuable service by enabling people in all parts of the Commonwealth to have quick access to informed answers to their questions about distance education in the context of human resource development. COL's computerised databases, specialised directories, the publications arising from round tables, meetings, symposia and workshops hosted by COL, and the reports of consultancies it commissioned are, in themselves, significant contributions to state-of-the-art distance teaching and learning. The detailed knowledge that COL's professional officers have of the latest proven developments in communications and information technology are a valued source of information and advice that has been in constant demand from people in all parts of the Commonwealth. And the various communication networks COL has developed have made these exchanges of information and advice easier to achieve. As the Commonwealth's clearing house on all aspects of distance education and its related technologies, COL is enabling administrators, teachers and users of distance education services to find informed answers to their questions much more efficiently than was the case before COL began its work.

COL could not have achieved what it has during these few years without the participation of member governments of the Commonwealth in working together towards a common goal. COL's work is a fine example of how the Commonwealth can accomplish much by pooling its limited resources and generously sharing its enormous collective experience and knowledge.

In the exciting millennium that lies ahead, everyone involved in the practice of education has an important and interesting role to play. We have the knowledge to deliver lifelong learning to users at their location of choice; we have the technology to support our endeavours; and we even have governments and their leaders urging that there should be more and more education. What remains to complete the cycle is the imagination and will of those in education to bring it all together. I think we can do it.

7 COL in Action

The best way to understand and appreciate COL's work is to describe some practical examples of ways in which it has helped Commonwealth countries build their own learning institutions and expertise. The following are just five examples of projects led by COL. Some more illustrations of its work have been given in Chapters 3 and 5 and together they provide an indication of the range of its activity and influence.

a. The Open University of Tanzania

> *While Tanzania is regarded as one of the poorest countries of the world, it has none-the-less placed a lot of faith on the role of education for development. Knowledge and skills are considered essential catalysts to the whole effort in improving not only the status of the economy of the Nation but also that of individuals at the household level. ... Sharing experiences, acquisition of knowledge and skills and commitment to succeed will see the Open University of Tanzania and similar institutions*
>
> Professor G. Mmari, Vice Chancellor, The Open University of Tanzania

In 1989, COL commissioned Alan K. Cutting of the Educational Technology Centre, City Polytechnic, Hong Kong, to serve as a consultant to the Planning Committee for the establishment of an Open University of Tanzania (OUT). His report, *The Role of Media Technology within the proposed Open University of Tanzania*, became a major planning document that fed into a subsequent joint UNESCO/COL study which drew up an implementation plan in 1993. COL further assisted with staff training programmes and materials transfer.

The Open University of Tanzania became operational in March 1993 and admitted its first intake of 766 students in January 1994. Overcoming several technological and logistical hurdles within the country, the university is using the postal system to handle printed study materials, telephone, radio, television (in a limited way), CD-ROMs, fax, computer, and audio and video cassettes.

OUT now has over 5000 registered students, including a prison inmate and the country's Minister of Science, Technology and Higher Education – both enrolled in the LL.B (law) programme. It offers seven degree programmes and a Foundation Course – a bridging course for those with inadequate preparation for university studies. The first convocation was held in 1999.

b. Restructuring University Extension at the University of the South Pacific

COL has provided continuing support to the University of the South Pacific and its extension services through various reviews, training, evaluations and international connections.

In 1991, at USP's request, COL conducted a review of distance education offered by the regional university throughout the Pacific islands. The review team comprised Bill Renwick (New Zealand), Professor St. Clair King (Trinidad and Tobago) and Dr Doug Shale (Canada). The aim was to improve the university's distance teaching procedures, and the exercise was carried out alongside a separate review of general university administrative practices commissioned by the University Council with funding from the Commonwealth Fund for Technical Co-operation. Most of the recommendations contained in the COL review were accepted by the university and formed the basis of restructuring decisions taken by the University's Council in October 1992.

In January 1993, to assist in the restructuring, COL brokered an arrangement whereby the Correspondence School (New Zealand) provided the services of its training team to university extension at USP for a short period.

University extension at USP now has four components:

- *A Secretariat*, which co-ordinates the overall operation and links the section to the rest of the university;

- *The Distance Education Unit*, which is responsible for assisting teaching departments within the university to prepare and deliver their courses in the distance mode;

- *The Continuing Education Unit,* which is responsible for preparing and running all non-credit, community outreach programmes;

- *University centres,* which operate in all 12 of the countries of the USP region, with resources that include classrooms for tutorials, seminars and workshops, a library, audio and video facilities, and computer and science laboratories.

Also at the request of the university and stemming from the review, COL conducted a review of educational communication needs in the Pacific region and a parallel review of the options available to meet these needs.

The USP Communications Network (USPNet) was established in 1974, following the creation of the USP 'Extramural Services' (now 'University Extension') to provide a basic communications system, through short-wave radio, to help bridge the vast distances between the main campus in Suva and the other USP campuses and centres. At the time, this was a pioneer venture, but by the date of the COL communications review, the university was in need of funding and technologies to provide the full telecommunications system envisaged by the reviewers.

The opportunity came in the year 2000. The 'USPNet 2000' upgrade project is now underway. The governments of Japan, New Zealand (NZODA) and Australia (AUSAID), together with the USP member countries, are funding the development of a dedicated USP satellite telecommunications network which will function independently of local telephone networks. USP's distant education students will be able to participate in audio tutorials (conducted from any campus), communicate by telephone, fax or e-mail with a lecturer/tutor or another student, watch a live video transmission of a lecture from any of the three campuses and take part in video conferences (and tutoring) with the Laucala Campus in Suva. University administration will also become more efficient with the availability of telephone; fax and e-mail communication via USPNet to all USP locations. Access to video conferencing will save time and travel in many cases.

c. Canadian Educational Technology Used to Establish Malaysian Medical Education Network

The Canadian Prime Minister, the Right Honourable Jean Chrétien, launched the expansion of the Malaysian Health Network at a signing ceremony held on 19 January 1996 in Kuala Lumpur. COL was instrumental in the development of the network and the use of Canadian technology to provide training to health professionals throughout the country.

Universiti Kebangsaan Malaysia (UKM), the National University of Malaysia, first established the Malaysian Medical Education Network in July 1993. With technical assistance from COL and support from the Malaysian Ministry of Health, the first audiographics teleconferencing systems were installed at the UKM Faculty of Medicine with remote sites at base hospitals in four regional locations. The network has since been successfully used to provide the delivery of a training programme in family medicine. This has been so successful that in late 1995 UKM moved towards expanding the network by an additional 40 sites. By enlisting COL's technical assistance and buying power, Malaysia was able to obtain the requisite equipment from a Canadian manufacturer, DETAC Corporation, of Red Deer (Innisfail), Alberta, at considerable savings. This arrangement also contributed to boosting COL's purchasing position on behalf of all Commonwealth countries.

All other UKM postgraduate medical education now employs strategies based on the successful family medicine programme. And, as a result of this effective partnership, UKM is also expanding distance education opportunities with several faculties.

In recognition of her pioneering work as project co-ordinator of the Malaysian Medical Education network, Professor Sharifah H. Shahabudin, Director of UKM's Department of Medical Education, received a COL/International Council for Distance Education Award of Excellence in June 1995 at a ceremony in Birmingham, England. In establishing the Malaysian Health Network, Professor Shahabudin was responsible for launching the first distance teaching programme at her institution and the first medical distance teaching programme in Malaysia.

As an exercise in 'model building', COL's experience in several audio-conferencing installations has demonstrated both the value and affordability of these technologies in the context of small distance education programmes. It has also provided practical lessons on the technical and functional questions surrounding the more effective deployment of this technology within the developing world.

d. Canada Caribbean Distance Scholarship Programme

Under a grant agreement with the Canadian Department of Foreign Affairs and International Trade, COL is carrying out an innovative five-year pilot programme which provides undergraduate scholarships for Caribbean students to study 'at a distance' through Canadian post-secondary institutions. The new Canada Caribbean Distance Education Scholarship Programme (CCDESP) continues to respect the academic strengths and ideals of the long-standing Commonwealth Scholarship and Fellowship Programme (CSFP), while providing an exciting new dimension by launching scholarships onto the 'information highway'. On the advice of Caribbean partners, the scholarships apply to those vocational areas in which there are identified skill shortages. The first group of students commenced studies in September 1998.

With the assistance of the University of the West Indies, the programme is being delivered in four countries by three Canadian universities. Alberta's Athabasca University is providing information technology programmes in Jamaica, Memorial University of Newfoundland is developing teacher education in Dominica and St Vincent and the Grenadines and Mount Saint Vincent University in Nova Scotia is offering tourism management in St Lucia and St Vincent and the Grenadines.

While COL is responsible for the overall programme, it works closely with

Canadian and Caribbean institutions and governments, particularly to facilitate co-operative working relationships between Canadian and Caribbean educational institutions and study centres that serve as hosts for the students. Unlike most other study-abroad schemes, this one ensures that local institutions are partners in arrangements, providing them with opportunities for further collaboration and growth. The University of the West Indies is a full and contributing partner in the CCDESP, providing it and the Canadian institutions the knowledge, experience and local infrastructure to enrich both the curriculum and learning environment.

The CCDESP is an opportunity for COL to be a leader and an architect in fashioning a new model of educational co-operation geared to today's realities. COL can thereby play a critical role in stemming the tide of weakening donor support for the present CSFP. This model also equips new generations of Commonwealth nationals to use distance learning and new communications technologies to become productive citizens equipped to lead their countries with self-assurance into the next millennium. It is an imaginative and effective means of dealing with the human dimensions of globalisation, and empowering individuals to play a confident and meaningful roles in the global knowledge-based economy.

e. Introducing Distance Education in the Training of Legislative Drafters

Good governance requires good laws, and good laws require good drafting, which in turn requires good drafters. Lawyers who need training in legislative drafting are scattered through many Commonwealth countries with widely different local conditions, but the 'common law' framework which links almost all Commonwealth jurisdictions also justifies a common base curriculum. The Commonwealth Distance Training Programme in Legislative Drafting was developed jointly by COL and the Commonwealth Secretariat to meet the needs of member jurisdictions by providing workplace training rather than having to send trainees overseas for an extended period.

The course, print materials, audio tapes and assignments were designed specifically for independent study of the principles and practices of legislative drafting and the processes of preparing government legislation. While a course co-ordinator in England guides student progress, experienced professionals within local drafting workplaces also provide support.

Thirty students, from the legal departments of 14 Commonwealth governments, were enrolled in February 1996 for a pilot delivery of the programme, administered under contract by the Royal Institute of Public Administration (International) in London and co-ordinated by Professor Keith Patchett who is also the chief course author/developer. By the time the pilot was completed in mid-1998, students from India, Malaysia, Singapore, Cyprus and the Falklands had successfully completed the course.

The distance education training course is being evaluated and revised in the light of experience and it should then again become available for individual enrolment in those jurisdictions which are willing to provide local mentor support for the trainee drafters. Meanwhile the adaptability of the training course materials is being utilised to the full with the development of regional 'hubs', through which training is offered by a mix of distance and face-to-face methods. By early 1999, regional hubs had been established in the South Pacific and in Southern Africa and it is envisaged that arrangements will subsequently be made to meet similar needs for local training in the Caribbean and in India. Several higher education institutions involved in legal education have also indicated an interest in using the course in their own programmes.

Guided independent study resources make it possible for legislative drafters to be trained in their home jurisdictions while continuing with their work and without incurring the travel and extended subsistence costs which are involved in overseas residential courses. The total cost of locally-based training, therefore, is estimated to be less that half that of overseas study.

Chapter 7

Building Bridges for Education in the Commonwealth: Issues in Student Mobility

Lalage Bown

Each has something to learn from others; each has something to give.
Report of the Commonwealth Education Conference, 1959

1 Introduction

The first task (and first action) of the first Commonwealth Education Conference in 1959 was to set up the Commonwealth Scholarship and Fellowship Plan. Exchanges of persons and of knowledge have remained at the heart of Commonwealth educational concerns ever since and have featured prominently in all the subsequent education conferences. Most of the previous chapters have alluded to aspects of such exchanges. The purpose of this chapter is to trace the main Commonwealth initiatives in student mobility, their rationales and challenges, and also other achievements.

The underlying story is one of modest success, with the main initiatives sustained over 40 years by a co-operative Commonwealth ideal, of which for some of the period Sir Shridath Ramphal, second Secretary-General, was a strong proponent. But this is counterpointed by an alternative, less altruistic, view often associated with Margaret Thatcher, British Education Minister and later Prime Minister, in which international student exchange was viewed primarily from an economic standpoint as an instrument of aid policy and more broadly as a component of international trade. These differing views were argued out especially in the Commonwealth Standing Committee on Student Mobility and Higher Education Co-operation between 1981 and 1994. That committee was the arena for a struggle for a favourable fee regime for Commonwealth students, but although it failed in that struggle, it was also (as said in Chapter 1) the progenitor of some important new Commonwealth activities relevant to higher education interchange: the Commonwealth of Learning; the Commonwealth Higher Education Programme; and the Commonwealth Universities Study Abroad Consortium.

With the collapse of the standing committee, a new policy-making climate gained ground: higher education was taken to be a commodity and the main Commonwealth host countries began to use student mobility to further regional interests, such as that of Australia in the Pacific or Britain in the European Union – to the detriment of their Commonwealth loyalties. Forty years on from the original Oxford meeting the context for international student exchange has changed not only in the policy and economic frameworks, but also because of technological advance – which has meant that the movement of *knowledge* can be an alternative to the movement of *people*, with the evolution of distance learning into borderless learning.

These are the main themes of the student mobility story. The chief constant has remained the CSFP – a continuing success story in spite of all obstacles, and an important instrument for strengthening academic institutions, reinforcing common academic standards and values across the Commonwealth, and enabling access to a wider scholarly world for poor and small countries. The Plan was mentioned and most recently endorsed in the Halifax Statement of December 2000, together with a declaration of the Commonwealth education ministers' belief in 'The value of academic interchange as well as student and knowledge mobility.'

2 The Diverse Nature of Educational Interchange in the Commonwealth

The most prominent exchange activities have been in tertiary education and have involved students from universities and other higher education institutions, so that here we will largely be studying mobility in that sector of education. It is important, however, to remember that other sectors of education also thrive on such exchanges and that there are many less formal agencies in the Commonwealth promoting them, even though their work is on a fairly small scale. The Commonwealth Youth Exchange Council, for instance, based in Britain, encourages educational visits by young people, while the Commonwealth Relations Trust, whose purpose is 'to promote understanding and communication between the countries of the Commonwealth', offers travel bursaries and fellowships to adults, particularly trade unionists, broadcasters and educators.

There are very well-established mechanisms for exchange of school teachers (this also was a subject which absorbed the attention of the first Commonwealth Education Conference). One organisation, the League for the Exchange of Commonwealth Teachers (LECT) has a history going back to 1901 and in a century of activity has arranged some 25,000 direct exchanges, with teachers swapping posts. Based in London, it is governed by a 'Declaration of Trust' and although it has close relations with the UK education ministries, it has resolutely kept its independent status. Countries in the LECT scheme in mid-2000 were: Australia, the Bahamas, Bangladesh, Barbados, Bermuda, Canada, The Gambia, Ghana, India, Jamaica, Kenya, Malawi, Malaysia, Malta, New Zealand, Pakistan, Sierra Leone, Singapore, South Africa, Tanzania, Trinidad and Tobago, United Kingdom, Zambia and Zimbabwe.

Moreover, there are several Commonwealth professional associations which are school-related, such as CASTME, described in Chapter 4, and which are instruments for interchange between teachers, educational administrators and curriculum developers through conferences and other collaborative activities. These and other organisations relevant to exchange in all sectors of education are listed in Appendix 2.

The less formal types of exchange, for short courses or research visits or for professional up-dating, have not been easily quantifiable over the years, but they represent a considerable range of educational contacts, in school education, in higher and adult education and also in the museum and library sectors. Some of the activities they generate have been noted by Commonwealth Education Conferences, but many take place almost unnoticed. There is obvious scope for a study of their scale and features. Here, however, we will be concerned with formal degree and diploma courses, mainly offered by public institutions (although it should be noted that the private sector is beginning to play a larger part in international higher education).

Intra-Commonwealth higher education mobility is partly spontaneous, and partly brought about by conscious bridge-building by members. This chapter is about that conscious bridge-building, as part of the 40-year CCEM story. There is also a story connected to the Commonwealth Fund for Technical Co-operation. The CFTC, as part of its support for member countries, builds in training in other parts of the Commonwealth and has a strong track record in South–South interchange for training. Its contribution is part of the mobility picture, but is outside the scope of this book. It is mentioned here for completeness and also because the Fund has played a role in helping to finance some of the recent initiatives in intra-Commonwealth higher education exchange.

3 Student Mobility at Tertiary Level: Its Perceived Special Significance

International educational transactions of all kinds have been seen, throughout the 40-odd years since the first Commonwealth Education Conference, in a favourable light. Student mobility has been valued for its contribution to development, its role in capacity-building and its unique part in maintaining the Commonwealth relationship. The CSFP was projected in 1959 to 'play an important part in maintaining and strengthening the common ideals on which the Commonwealth is founded' (see Appendix 3 for full quotation). In 1987, the then Secretary-General of the Commonwealth, Shridath Ramphal, saw the development of educational co-operation as marking the Commonwealth's 'further evolution towards a truly polycentric organisation'. In 1994, 'the Commonwealth Ministers of Education in Islamabad reaffirmed the centrality of educational co-operation to the Commonwealth relationship. It is the glue which binds the Commonwealth together ...'. (Some observers might see an irony in this last comment emerging from a meeting which agreed to close down the Standing Committee on Student Mobility and Higher Education Co-operation – see Section 6 below.)

The nature of the partnership in educational exchange was, however, not perceived in an identical way throughout the years or in different Commonwealth countries. Ramphal's polycentrism was not a concept current in the countries with most resources, some of whose leaders saw a project like the CSFP as an instrument of aid or technical assistance, however benevolent. At the Canberra conference of 1971, the Australian Minister of Education and Science quoted with approval from a speech made by Vincent Massey, Governor-General of Canada at the Ottawa conference of 1964: 'Aid for education is not really aid at all – it is a form of partnership. Education is a true meeting-ground for donor and receiver'. This is rather a different perspective from that quoted at the head of this chapter. It becomes questionable in any case when the pattern is one in which countries may be both donors and receivers, both hosts to international students and senders of their own students to other countries.

The case for tertiary student mobility in a Commonwealth context was fairly thoroughly thrashed out in a book published by the Secretariat in 1994, based on a workshop held, under Commonwealth auspices, in Singapore in 1992. Participants were conscious of the widening imbalance in access to knowledge between countries of high and low human development and also the greater cynicism about partnership in some of the countries of high human development.

Part of the discussion went as follows:

Within the Commonwealth, much of its partnership activity is higher education related. Almost all of the Commonwealth Professional Associations bring together professional people trained in higher education institutions and whose capacity to understand each other stems from a comparability in their training. Within universities themselves, there has been a sense of common heritage in system, standards and generally, language. It is therefore a matter of great sensitivity that higher education across the Commonwealth is seen to be genuinely open to exchange and interchange. In the eyes of many of the countries of the South, the association might stand or fall by its success in keeping up a fairer flow of people, both students and academics.

An additional point strongly relevant to a political grouping which includes many small countries was that:

The movement of students has a very high priority for the many small Commonwealth nations in any case, since they may have no university within their borders, as is the case with the Gambia, or their higher education institution may not have the resources to cater for more than a few disciplines or for any postgraduate work.

On the other hand, the climate in the 1990s led to doubts in some countries. The late Dr Elizabeth Dines of Australia noted that:

> *An initial reaction from hard-pressed policy-makers is ... likely to be:*
> * *How will increasing student mobility in general benefit my university/country?*
> * *Are there any particular advantages in a Commonwealth scheme?*
> * *Will the benefits outweigh the costs?*
>
> *These questions cannot be swept aside, for there is no point in turning to the basics of implementation ... if there is not at the outset the political will at national levels to set such a scheme in place. The extent to which the proposal captures the interest or imagination of governments and participating institutions will be directly related to their –perceived advantages from student mobility'.*

She went on to give 'a litany of potential disadvantages' and suggested that:

> *... making the case for a student mobility scheme that is restricted to participants from Commonwealth countries will be even more difficult. For many member governments the Commonwealth is no longer a 'salient category'. Australia and Canada are both actively pursuing economic ties with Asia, and the United Kingdom is increasingly looking towards an expanding and economically vibrant Europe. Singapore is extensively involved in joint ventures and development projects with countries throughout Asia and is a member, like Malaysia, of ASEAN, an economic grouping which owes nothing to Commonwealth ties ... .*

In spite of these and other negatives, Dines at the end came down with a positive case for her own country Australia to support Commonwealth student mobility programmes, based on the argument that:

1. A Commonwealth network of student exchanges provides a global network;

2. A formal framework is already established;

3. A common language is used for instruction;

4. There is a shared academic culture.

Some of these themes will be revisited later in the chapter.

4 Student Mobility in Context

During the past 40 years, international student mobility has increased substantially. There have been periods when the increase was checked (see Section 6), but the continuing trend is upwards. There is difficulty in obtaining comparable statistics, but UNESCO does provide a rough global picture annually. During the lifetime of the Commonwealth Standing Committee on Student Mobility, it commissioned a number of case studies and collected some useful statistics. Recently, the Council for Education in the Commonwealth with UKCOSA has produced a report based on substantial statistical research by Kees Maxey and the picture which emerged from its findings is described in the rest of this section.

International student mobility increased most considerably in the 1990s, with countries which stand high on the Human Development Index (HDI) of the UNDP predominating as hosts, and high and medium HDI countries being the principal senders. Low HDI countries account for only a very small proportion of international student flows and host international students on an insignificant scale. In the world as a whole, the USA is the largest individual host, receiving a third of all international students, but Australia and the UK also attract large numbers to their universities and colleges. Patterns of student flow reflect traditional national ties as well as other factors, such as language – including a very strong demand both for studying English and for courses where English is the medium of instruction.

The Commonwealth's share of all students travelling abroad for higher education has declined in relative terms, but some of its members have become more important players among the world's host countries receiving international students. Commonwealth hosts have, however, recruited a majority of their international students from countries outside the Commonwealth. In 1990, the five principal host countries within the Commonwealth took in 44% of their international students from other Commonwealth nations; but by 1996 that proportion had dropped to 36%. Notably, in 1980, the UK received half its international students from the Commonwealth and only 10% from the European Union; but by the late 1990s, the Commonwealth proportion of the UK international intake had dropped to 30%, while almost half of the intake came from the European Union.

The reason for this change was the consolidation of the European Union. The initial establishing treaty of the European Economic Community (the EU's predecessor), agreed in Rome in 1957, and the major treaty setting up the Union, agreed in Maastricht in 1992, bound members to the principle that any EU citizen, as part of their rights could study for a longer or shorter period in another EU country for the same fee as any national of that country. The principle was tested and upheld in a court in Belgium in 1980. The basic ideas on educational interchange in Europe are similar to those of the Commonwealth and are stated in the Maastricht Treaty:

Community action shall be aimed at:
- *developing the European dimension in education, particularly through the teaching and dissemination of the languages of the Member States;*
- *encouraging mobility of students and teachers, inter alia by encouraging the academic recognition of diplomas and periods of study;*
- *promoting co-operation between educational establishments;*
- *developing exchanges of information and experience on issues common to the education systems of the Member States;*

– encouraging the development of youth exchanges and of exchanges of socio – educational instructors;
– encouraging the development on distance education.

These ideas have been operationalised by a variety of exchange schemes for universities, including SOCRATES, LEONARDO and ERASMUS (as well as by youth exchange programmes). For European policy-makers, the increase in student mobility is part of a broader agenda for social cohesion in the EU, and there are signs that there will be further efforts to increase student flows across the union. An EU Green Paper on Innovation emphasises personal mobility, particularly between the research world, universities and industry and says roundly: 'This is one of Europe's most remarkable paradoxes: goods, capital and services move around more easily than people and know-how'. This all makes for obvious tensions in the UK between its obligations to Europe and its obligations to the Commonwealth, and has led to the uncomfortable situation where students from high human development countries in Europe have access to British higher education at much less cost than students from low human development countries in the Commonwealth.

In spite of all this, at the end of the twentieth century intra-Commonwealth mobility was in a reasonably healthy state. It accounted for 12% of global mobility by 1996 (a rise of 3% since 1990) and, overall, 44% of all Commonwealth inter-

Table 1. International students by country of origin (by HD level) by groups and by hosting regions (1996)

Countries of origin	Host Regions									
	Africa		North America		Asia		Europe		Oceania	All
High-HD	1,222	0%	217,075	36%	6,109	1%	342,422	56%	39,348 6%	606,176
% of total	11		43		9		50		40	44
Medium-HD	4,238	1%	225,306	39%	45,920	8%	255,593	44%	44,851 8%	575,908
% of total	37		45		65		38		46	42
Low HD	2,990	5%	18,823	30%	5,625	9%	33,408	53%	1,864 3%	62,710
% of total	26%		4		8		5		2	5
HD Unspecified	3,129	3%	43,429	37%	12,792	11%	47,336	40%	11,191 9%	117,877
% of total	27		9		18		7		12	9
Total	11,579	1%	504,633	37%	70,446	5%	678,759	50%	97,254 7%	1,362,671
Commonwealth	628	0%	149,009	50%	9,217	3%	94,081	31%	47,970 16%	300,905
% of total	5		30		13		14		49	22
Non-Commonwealth	10,951	1%	355,624	33%	61,229	6%	584,678	55%	49,284 5%	1,061,766
% of total	95		70		87		86		51	78
European Union	49	0%	41,855	15%	712	0%	217,718	83%	1,036 0%	261,370
% of total	0		8		1		32		1	19

Source: UNESCO

national students were studying in another Commonwealth country in the late 1990s. In the Commonwealth there are five main host countries: Australia, Canada, India, New Zealand and the UK. By 1996 they were taking in collectively over 350,000 students from elsewhere, of whom just over one-third were from the Commonwealth. The main Commonwealth sending countries in the 1990s were Brunei Darussalam, Hong Kong (before its change of political status), Malaysia and Singapore; their students made up 60% of all Commonwealth students going abroad. As in the world at large, so also in the Commonwealth, students from low HDI countries have recently had comparatively little access to international higher education.

Table 1 illustrates the points made above.

Against this general background of upward trends in international student mobility over the last 40 years, we will now look at specific Commonwealth initiatives. The most significant one is the Commonwealth Scholarship and Fellowship Plan, which is seen by most observers as the education flagship.

5 Commonwealth Flagship – The Commonwealth Scholarship and Fellowship Plan

a. Origins and Rationale

It might come as a surprise that the idea of the CSFP germinated in a Commonwealth Trade and Economic Conference. That meeting, in Montreal in 1958, was held at a time when membership of the Commonwealth was about to be enlarged by the arrival of a cohort of developing countries and when economists were beginning to raise awareness of development issues. Participants in the Montreal meeting were agreed that education was a basic element of social and economic development – the first time that this view was expressed in a major Commonwealth forum. The notion of an awards programme was accepted at Montreal and initially three-quarters of the awards were to be funded by the UK and Canada (one-half by UK and one-quarter by Canada).

The baton was then picked up at the Oxford conference of 1959, where, (as already said), the establishment of a Commonwealth Scholarship and Fellowship programme was that conference's first agenda. While the rationale related to development was picked up, the main vision was broadened. The text of the conference's report on the CSFP will be found at Appendix 3. In that report was the following statement of fundamental purposes:

'The Plan, based on a common effort and partnership between all the countries of the Commonwealth, will play an important part in maintaining and strengthening the common ideals on which the Commonwealth is founded. It will enrich each country of the Commonwealth by enabling an increasing number of its abler citizens to share the wide range of educational resources available throughout the Commonwealth and thus promote equality of opportunity at the highest level'.10

The vision was one of benefit to the Commonwealth as a whole through the strengthening of common ideals and of benefit to member countries through access to a pool of educational resources. The word 'enrich' seems to have been used here in a wider sense than the economic. Equality of opportunity was left undefined as to whether it was opportunity between member states or between individual students. Probably the authors meant both; the quotation at the head of this chapter seems to be about polities and individuals. The thinking about individuals certainly extended to gender equality, since the awards were to be open to men and women (although the general discourse was to be of 'men' and 'he' in the CEC reports on the programme for several years ahead).

In the euphoria of setting up what was undoubtedly an extraordinarily visionary scheme, the 1959 conference members expressed an expectation that 'within a few years of its inception the programme would cover some thousand Commonwealth scholars and fellows'. It was a period of optimism in both education and the world economy, so that the actual target of a thousand awards was seen by the founders as modest and they expressed hopes for its further expansion.

At the same time, the founders of the scheme, through a Commonwealth committee (chaired by F. G. Curtis) made very practical financial and administrative dispositions. Starting from the rationale summarised in the quotation above, they stated that educational interchange between all parts of the Commonwealth 'is essential if we are all to get the best out of the Plan and to share to the full the benefits of the special experience and facilities which our countries possess'. They wrote of 'the development of a multilateral trade in ideas'.

The Plan was to be governed by a set of straightforward principles:

1. The Plan should be additional to, and distinct from, any other plan already in operation.

2. The Plan should be based on mutual co-operation and sharing of educational experience among all the countries of the Commonwealth.

3. The Plan should be sufficiently flexible to take account of the diverse and changing needs of the countries of the Commonwealth.

4. While the Plan will be Commonwealth wide, it will have to be operated on the basis of a series of bilateral agreements to allow for the necessary flexibility.

5. The awards should be designed to recognise and promote the highest standards of intellectual achievement.

The basis of the scheme was to be for two sorts of award: scholarships, usually for graduates to proceed further, either to another first degree or to a postgraduate course; and fellowships for 'scholars of high distinction and established reputation to enable them to undertake research and perhaps teaching'. Scholarships were to be for two years and usually the awards would be 'inward' – that is to be held in the country offering the award. Sending countries were to nominate candidates, but final selection was to be the responsibility of a special agency in the receiving country. In the case of small countries with no higher education institutions of their own, students were received by the offering nation to do a full undergraduate course. There was a general responsibility on the receiving country and host universities to provide for the reception and welfare of scholars and there was a general obligation on scholars to return to their own countries at the end of their courses.

The work of the founders of CSFP has stood the test of time. The five principles which they laid down have been reiterated at subsequent Commonwealth Education Conferences and the dual framework of scholarships and fellowships has continued. Where challenges have been perceived to the working of the plan, they have been perceived largely as failures to live up to it rather than flaws in the principles themselves or the scheme itself, as we shall see in the next sub-section.

There was one omission in the 1959 expectations for the plan. New university colleges were already established in a number of Commonwealth countries on the eve of independence and there was an expansion of universities in already independent India and Pakistan. The potential of the CSFP for what later came to be called capacity-building was not fully recognised in 1959. Another task of the Oxford Conference, however, was to consider the intra-Commonwealth supply of teachers and there was a brief allusion to university teachers in that committee's report, which perhaps foreshadowed the need for the nurturing of indigenous university staff while nationals from elsewhere in the Commonwealth temporarily filled the positions.

b. Evolution of the CSFP and some Challenges Encountered

The CSFP was the subject of regular reports to CECs/CCEMs in the next 40 years and every ten years it underwent a review commissioned by the Commonwealth Secretariat for consideration by member governments. On each occasion, some technical issues came up, such as the extension of the length of awards to allow for doctoral study (New Delhi, 1962) or the demand for a register of past Commonwealth scholars (Nairobi, 1987). The flexibility of the scheme and the existence of a co-ordinating structure through the Association of Commonwealth Universities enabled such changes to be made.

New emphases were also occasionally put on the purposes of the plan. By 1968 in Lagos, awareness of the CSFP as an instrument for university staff development was articulated and energised by the British government's initiative in offering 100 new awards for postgraduate training of lecturers in medical schools. In Canberra in 1971, there was a request for more focus on rural development needs when scholars were selected – part of the general dialogue at that meeting on universities and development.

Additionally, there were several challenges encountered as the plan evolved. They were continuing issues for Commonwealth conferences and member governments.

First was the challenge of numbers of awards. The original target of 1000, adopted at Montreal, was already met by 1966. At the Accra conference in 1977, it was decided to increase numbers to 1500 and at Nicosia in 1984 the Secretary-General pleaded for member governments to reach that target. His plea was based on an appeal to the values of internationalism: 'if the principle of internationalism falters now, then nothing is safe from self-centred destructive nationalism'. It succeeded in evoking pledges increasing the total number of awards to 1650. The current goal is 2000 scholarships and fellowships for the new millennium. Achieving the numbers has proved less easy than the Oxford conference envisaged, with its euphoric 'several thousand'. One reason is probably because the cost of an award has increased, particularly in the countries which now charge full-cost fees.

Related to numbers is the challenge of the distribution of awards. The 1959 founders envisaged a sharing of educational experience between all parts of the Commonwealth and later voices also advocated the offering of scholarships by all members. There was a built-in imbalance at the start, with two countries of high human development – UK and Canada – generously pledged to subscribe three-quarters of the awards – although Canada never quite fulfilled its allotted quota. By the Accra conference in 1977, it was observed that the main providers were the developed countries, so that the student flow was from developing to developed. Since then, there have been recommendations for more South–South awards and pleas for smaller member countries of the Commonwealth to provide at least one or two awards. Meanwhile, the United Kingdom is not politically comfortable with being the largest contributor. Over 40 years, 24 member countries have from time to time offered awards and some which have dropped out are showing an interest in once more participating. The ten countries/regional institutions at present providing awards are: Brunei, Canada, India, Jamaica, New Zealand, University of the South Pacific, Sri Lanka, Trinidad, the UK and (in principle) Uganda. New or returned participants in the plan (as hosts) are: Australia, Malaysia and Mauritius; and there are positive signals too from Cameroon, Malta, Nigeria and South Africa. At the end of the 1990s the nominating/sending countries numbered 49 out of the total Common-wealth membership of 65, and there are very few countries that have not had some award-winners over the 40 years. So the distribution of beneficiaries is quite wide.

These developments show that there is continuing interest in the CSFP and that it is valued across the Commonwealth.

There are, of course, problems in applying the founding principles. While it is generally agreed that there should be some rebalancing of student flows, there is sometimes an unwillingness on the part of the students from the North to take up awards in the South. Some have doubts about real or perceived issues of security, hygiene of accommodation, food and health. On the other side of the coin, there are sometimes problems for smaller and/or poorer countries in offering scholar-ships. Some of these were described by Dr Peter Dzvimbo of Zimbabwe in his con-tribution to the Singapore workshop on Commonwealth student mobility in 1992. He explained that rapid expansion of universities and increasing demand put pressure on them to find places for Zimbabwean students and that the parallel shortage of staff had increased the pressures. In such conditions, the universities felt that they had to seek a directive from the Ministry of Higher Education before they admitted a qualified non-Zimbabwean applicant. (This was not isolationism; the universities were active in links with other institutions, but did not wish to be involved in hosting students from abroad.) Occasionally, of course, there are times when a country's political situation is fragile and it is not in a position to make foreign students welcome.

All the same, there is general support for more member countries to act as hosts to students from other Commonwealth countries, and there are moves for host countries and institutions to share experiences, problems and successes. The first meeting of host countries was held in London in July 2001. There are also several activities within the Commonwealth favouring South–South exchange. The existence in two regions of universities serving a number of countries encourages a mix of nationalities on campus; these are the University of the West Indies and the University of the South Pacific. There has also been a recent move among Commonwealth African universities each to offer at least one place for a student from another African university each year.

Another challenge is the participation of women in the plan. Fewer women than men gain access to the awards. There are reasons why fewer women come forward, to do with uneven gender access in their home countries, but there has been concern that more women should benefit from the CSFP since the Colombo conference of 1980.

With regard to scholarships, there has been a fairly steady upward trend towards a more even gender balance among award-holders and the participating countries may begin to feel that the challenge is being met, on the evidence of Figure 1.

With regard to scholarships, there has been a fairly steady upward trend towards a more even gender balance among award-holders. For the first ten years of the scheme, the proportion of women to men among them hovered between one to nine and one to seven (10–11%). The percentage of women then moved upwards to between 15% and 20% at the start of the 1990s. There followed a rapid increase in the number of women scholarship winners, so that by 1999 women made up 40% of the total. Women holding UK scholarships made up 46% of the whole cohort by the year 2001. Participating countries may therefore feel that the challenge of gender balance is being met.

The position with fellowships is less satisfactory. The average for the last decade was 22% women among fellowship holders. Clearly this remains a challenge.

There have also been requests that awards might be held at a wider range of institutions. In the early years, students applied to a small number of well-known universities in the host countries and it was felt that they should be encouraged to go to some of the less well-known (but good quality) ones as well. Further, there were requests that award-holders might go outside the university sector – to colleges of adult education (New Delhi, 1962) and to technical and professional institutions (Nicosia, 1984).

Administering such a wide-ranging programme carries burdens of miscommunication or misunderstanding which may have fundamental consequences. Some donor countries become frustrated when their scholarships and fellowships are not openly advertised in potential sending countries and suspect that the best candidates are not always put forward. This may be because bureaucrats in those countries do not understand the principles of genuinely open competition, or because communications in their countries are poor and open advertisement therefore difficult and costly, or because those bureaucrats and their political bosses see all such awards as a form of patronage. Some amelioration of this problem should come with the development of a CSFP website. When advertisements and applications are on-line, the bureaucrats and politicians may have their monopoly of information subverted.

All these points relate to improving and modifying the existing programme. There are two further issues, stemming from the South–North nature of student flows within the Plan, which pose deeper challenges. One is the challenge of alienation, of students from the South being offered in the North curricula which are not relevant to their own societies. This was strongly expressed at the conference in Kingston in 1974 and has been mentioned in Commonwealth conferences and other fora on very many occasions. One eloquent encapsulation of the curriculum problem was by Guy Hunter in a contribution to a study on British policy by the Overseas Student Trust in 1981:

> *The accusation that this was not the moment to adopt the full Western academic style sticks rather more deeply. Secondly, it is on the technical side that perhaps the most telling and still valid criticism might be raised. Have we not taught industrial technologies from the West, technologies which are labour-saving and capital-intensive in form, wholly unsuited to the factor proportion and wage-levels of a quite different economic stage? In health services have we not concentrated on fully trained doctors when what was needed above all was preventive medicine and simple services for the 70–90% rural population at village level?*

The Lagos conference in 1968 expressed the worry that Commonwealth scholars returning home might not find suitable jobs; perhaps they were not all educated suitably for the jobs available?

Full information on subjects studied by all award-holders would repay further research, but the latest CSFP report gives a picture of subject choices in the 1990s. Arts students are heavily concentrated in award-winners from countries of the 'Old Commonwealth', while there is a more even spread of subjects taken up by students from the 'New Commonwealth', i.e. the countries of low and medium human development. The nominating countries in the South have always been interested in their award-winners undertaking studies of development relevance (the subject of universities and development was already in the forefront as early as the Canberra conference of 1971); and there have been suggestions that there may be a conflict between development-related subject matter and the plan's principle of promoting 'the highest levels of intellectual achievement', since some of the highest intellectual achievers may be specialists in subjects not seen as immediately pertinent to development needs. More direct development training is funded through the CFTC, while the plan's distinctiveness lies in its encouragement of academic excellence. Without more substantial data on subjects of study and performance of CSFP award-winners it is hard to assess whether the alleged tension between relevance and intellectual distinction has been of any significance in the evolution of the plan. Anecdotal evidence does not lend credence to the allegation, although it suggests a slight shift in subjects of study from humanities to business and technology. This is a general phenomenon. The CEC/UKCOSA study in 2000 showed upturns in demand among all international students in the UK for medicine and allied fields, engineering and technology, computing science, and business and administrative studies. There was only a small upturn in agriculture, which should be highly relevant to development, but a significant increase in the number of students opting for creative arts and design – which some people might question, although others would argue that cultural studies are crucial to national development because of such diverse concerns as national identity and reliance on tourism.

Connected with alienation and the study of subjects with currency in the North (which, of course, include computing and business) is the second issue arising from South–North student flows. This is the challenge, of 'brain drain', always alluded to when international study is under scrutiny. It was foreseen as a possible problem at the outset of the plan and occasionally raised in Commonwealth meetings. There were references to 'alleged' non-return of scholars, but the scale of non-return is not known. There is however, some evidence from two tracer studies carried out to follow up the careers of former award-holders. One was done on behalf of the Commonwealth by Dr Alastair Niven and published by the Secretariat in January 1989. The other was carried out by the United Kingdom Commonwealth Scholarship Commission in 2000 and its initial findings are available. Neither study can be taken as definitive, because of the small number of respondents in each case, but they do at least provide pointers. The 1989 study showed that between 85% and 93% of award-holders from developing countries returned home immediately. The award-holders from Australia and New Zealand were the significant non-returners (42% and 43% respectively) at the end of their award period, but a further 20% and 21% of the respondents from those countries went back within five years.

The recent British research had very similar findings. Ninety-two per cent of all respondents had returned to their own countries. The main nationalities of those who relocated were Australian, Canadian and New Zealand. Some of those who reported not being in their own country were either representing their country in some forum or serving with Commonwealth or other international bodies, such as COL, WHO or the World Bank. Although the evidence is not conclusive, it is indicative and encouraging. Nevertheless, in an era of globalisation it is likely that at least some former award-holders will be found working outside their home nation. In some cases, this can be taken as positive if they are working for the Commonwealth or the UN and also if those from the South are working in other countries in the South. For instance, there is evidence that there is more inter-change of qualified academics and professionals within anglophone Africa at the present time and some of these may well be former award-holders.

All these problems relate to the CSFP as such. One further point is worth reflecting on. Prestige is attached to the awards, and beneficiaries have built valu-able careers on them, but most of them go through their programmes with little knowledge of the meaning of the Commonwealth and little opportunity to find out about it. Given that the plan is premised on a common value system, it would seem rather important that those who, through the plan, are likely to attain positions of influence in member countries, should carry forward those values and an under-standing of the Commonwealth as an institution.

c. Achievements and Impact of the Plan

The challenges posed to the CSFP should not derogate from its achievements. It was, and is, a remarkable programme based on a clear vision and well implemented – a deft combination of a multilateral scheme with a series of bilateral agreements. The numbers of beneficiaries from the scheme are large. Approximately 3000 people have taken up fellowships during the past 40 years (although at the present time the UK is the only country offering fellowships). Table 2 gives the number of scholarships.

This means that by the year 2000, over 21,000 people had participated in the CSFP. Sixty Commonwealth countries and dependent territories had sent students and academics. About 10% of students were undergraduates, while the rest were postgraduate. Both the tracer studies mentioned (1989 and 2000) picture most participants as beneficiaries. The quality of the student experience was in general appreciated – only about 1% of respondents had reservations, mostly about the applicability of their learning in their own environment (as discussed above). A member government's reaction was given by Wenike Briggs, the Nigerian Federal Commissioner for Education, at the Conference in Lagos in 1968. He said that the CSFP:

> ... has benefited our scholars immeasurably, not only because of the opportunity it has given them academically in the fields of Engineering, Technology and Medicine, but also because it has made most of them aware that knowledge is an international com-modity of exchange. On their return, we have found them enriched in knowledge and experience, eager to keep the contacts they had made abroad and more self-critical and mature in their work at home.

Table 2. Scholarships Taken up Annually under CSFP

Year	No. of scholarships	Year	No. of scholarships	Year	No. of scholarships	Year	No. of scholarships
1960/61	335	1970/71	387	1980/81	325	1990/91	502
1961/62	428	1971/72	401	1981/82	467	1991/92	620
1962/63	358	1972/73	389	1982/83	467	1992/93	614
1963/64	390	1973/74	442	1983/84	537	1993/94	608
1964/65	413	1974/75	466	1984/85	492	1994/95	618
1965/66	381	1975/76	375	1985/86	669	1995/96	608
1966/67	439	1976/77	374	1986/87	576	1996/97	488
1967/68	371	1977/78	417	1987/88	478	1997/98	400
1968/69	407	1978/79	420	1988/89	561	1998/99	412
1969/70	407	1979/80	327	1989/90	435	1999/2000	451
10-year total:	3,929	10-year total	3,998	10-year total:	5,007	10-year total:	5,321
		20-year total:	7,927	30-year total:	12,934	40-year total:	18,255

The alumni of the programme have, over the years, made their mark in a very wide variety of professions. A substantial number (the largest cluster) have become senior academics and researchers, including in their ranks directors of research institutions and several well-known vice-chancellors. This is partly the result of deliberate policy by host governments; Britain, for example, reserves 40% of its Commonwealth awards budget for Fellowships and staff development scholarships. The 2000 tracer study reports on former award-holders who have become political leaders (parliamentary Speakers and at least one Prime Minister), high court judges, senior civil servants, top bankers, journalists and publishers, the municipal engineer of one of the world's largest cities, as well as managing directors of companies. The record is impressive and it is a pity that it is only in the last dozen years that efforts have been made to define it.

There have been many voices suggesting an alumni association for Commonwealth scholars and fellows, which would, among other things, provide much more information on what does become of the award-bearers. A beginning has been made with an association of those who held British awards. Since Britain has been the largest provider, this could theoretically comprise up to 12,000 men and women (but of course not all will still be alive). The association was launched in Ghana on 19 April 2000 and is supported by a newsletter, *Omnes* (meaning 'everybody') which will include a regular feature: Where Are They Now ?

The plan has kept an aura of prestige and there is testimony that to be a Commonwealth scholar or fellow was regarded as a privilege. Through all the various reviews, the education conferences have agreed that continuing the programme is worthwhile. There was a period in the late 1980s when there was some feeling that the CSFP had become static, but since then the burgeoning of student mobility around the world has reinforced the importance of any programme which encourages mobility within the Commonwealth. There has been a renewed realisation of the vital contribution of higher education to development, spurred by the work of a recent World Bank task force on higher education and society. There have also been suggestions for some changes in the CSFP which seem likely to be put into effect – the possibility of awards for distance learning such as COL has already experimented with – see Chapter 6 – and for fellowships for senior people in the professions and business, for instance. Such modifications could be made quite easily if Commonwealth ministers of education and member countries providing awards wish it. One of the great strengths of the CSFP remains its flexibility.

The plan's other strengths include its insistence on high quality and its mode of operation. It is also virtually unique in consciously favouring countries of medium and low human development. The United Kingdom consistently targets 50% of its awards to African countries and another 30% to the Indian subcontinent, and of the 1125 scholarship holders on courses in 1996/97, 348 were from sub-Saharan Africa, 363 from south Asia and 110 from the Caribbean (these are typical proportions year on year).

6 Bone of Contention – the Work of the Standing Committee on Student Mobility

a. Brief History

Because there had been such a strong consensus on the value of the student mobility, there was an intensity to the reaction among developing countries in the Commonwealth when the main host countries raised the level of fees chargeable to students from abroad. Britain raised fees progressively from 1966, but in Commonwealth policy discussions the first mention of higher fees was made at Colombo in 1980. At that point, differential fees in the UK had become 'full-cost' fees and international higher education was beginning to be seen as an invisible export like insurance or financial services. 'Full cost' is, of course, a difficult concept. On the one hand, in market terms such fees relate to what the traffic will bear, with high-demand subjects costing more than less sought-after ones and with the most highly-reputed universities charging more than the less well-known ones. The fee data for UK universities given in Table 3 illustrates this for the academic year 2001/2002.

Clearly, laboratory subjects carry more costs than 'classroom' subjects, but the huge range of charges for, say, the MBA, must be about reputation as well as actual costs. The other side of the argument is that international students were being taught at the margin in some cases, while in others their presence was sustaining whole departments and research programmes and thus subsidising students from the home country.

In any case, the imposition of 'full-cost' fees was an immediate source of anger and bitterness in the Commonwealth. The eighth Commonwealth Education Conference Report stated:

In recent years several countries have increased the fees they charge for overseas students, causing a great deal of hardship to students from Commonwealth countries and affecting significantly the manpower needs of those countries which do not have adequate educational facilities of their own. Many of these countries sponsor their students in other Commonwealth countries at both undergraduate and postgraduate levels. Another effect of the increases will be to affect the traditional mobility of students which in the past has helped to maintain Commonwealth links and benefit not only the developing countries but developed countries as well.

Eighth Commonwealth Education Conference Report, para. 46

The conference recommended that governments for fee purposes treat as home students those receiving Commonwealth awards, national awards and recognised international agency awards, as well as an agreed number of students from developing countries in the Commonwealth which did not have adequate educational facilities of their own. This recommendation was not acted upon, but India then, and for many years after, kept fees down for all international students. Some Canadian provinces also kept fees at home levels for the international students they received. It was proposed at the Colombo conference that a 'consultative group' should be set up to look into the problem. This group, chaired by Sir Hugh Springer, at the time Secretary-General of the ACU, was the first official Commonwealth entity to tackle the subject of high fees levied on non-nationals by major host countries. The climate of opinion at the time was still one of incredulity over the charges; there was still a belief that negotiation would persuade the host nations to modify their position. In introducing their recommendations on tuition fees for

Table 3. Tuition Fees for International Students, UK Universities 2001/2002 (£ sterling)

	Median Fee	Range 5th Percentile	95th Percentile
Undergraduate:			
Classroom	6,900	5,867	8,868
Laboratory	8,375	6,353	10,608
Clinical	17,700	16,804	20,450
Taught Postgraduate:			
Classroom	7,100	6,000	8,700
Laboratory	8,755	6,498	10,333
Clinical	17,534	11,259	20,450
MBA	9,000	6,888	18,350
Research Postgraduate:			
Classroom	7,083	6,000	8,249
Laboratory	8,775	6,500	9,995
Clinical	17,660	11,334	20,450

Source: Universities UK

international students, Sir Hugh's team said: 'Until such time as fees are again fixed at considerably less than full cost, we recommend … '. This was not much more than 20 years ago, but at that stage no one fully appreciated the trend towards the commodification of higher education and the economic value to governments and academic institutions which international students represented (only a decade and a half later it was calculated that total international fee income to British universities amounted to over £700 million sterling).

The group's interest was to safeguard in the meanwhile the CSFP and similar student exchange schemes, since the fee rises hit hard at their budgets. Their recommendations (more in the nature of a plea) to member governments included (following the Colombo line) their consideration of fee exemption or support to students on approved exchange schemes or who had obtained recognised merit awards. To palliate the impact of high fees on Commonwealth student mobility, they recommended additional CSFP awards at postgraduate level, as well as short-stay and split-level programmes. They advocated a broader framework for a Commonwealth Higher Education Programme. Their thoughts on fees were bequeathed to a new body recommended by them, a standing committee of members serving in a personal capacity, with a pan-Commonwealth remit and answerable to Commonwealth education ministers.

The Standing Committee was set up and had its first meeting in July 1982, under the Chairmanship of Sir Roy Marshall, Vice-Chancellor of the University of Hull, UK and a member of the Council of the ACU; he had earlier been, among other things, Vice-Chancellor of the University of the West Indies and then Secretary-General of the British Committee of Vice-Chancellors and Principals and so brought a breadth of appropriate experience to the task. Not even he, with all his insight, could have foreseen that it was to be a task like that of Sisyphus, trying to push a boulder up-hill – against the gradient of the new Thatcherite mood in the richer countries of the Commonwealth.

The Standing Committee met annually until 1986 and then might seem to have been running out of steam (although it sponsored or commissioned various other activities in between subsequent meetings), as it only met twice afterwards, in 1989 and 1992. This was largely because there was not enough money to pay for it. It was finally put to sleep by the CCEM in Islamabad in 1994. Throughout, the Committee's main focus was on student mobility but its constructive interest from the beginning in ancillary higher education initiatives led to its title and remit being formally widened by CHOGM in 1987 – on the recommendation of the Nairobi CEC held earlier in the same year. Its title then became: Standing Committee on Student Mobility *and Higher Education Co-operation*. While its general preoccupation was still with interchange of students and scholars, its interests widened to include mobility of knowledge through distance learning and a range of means for intra-Commonwealth mutual support in higher education. Its main success was in the latter areas. A list of the Committee's reports on its meetings is given in Appendix 4.

b. The Committee in Action

In his foreword to the fifth report of the Standing Committee in 1986, the Commonwealth Secretary-General gave a useful review of what the committee had done up to that point. He said that the Commonwealth had reason to be grateful to the committee.

> *This is not just their illuminating analyses, helping us to understand the direction of the movement of students within the Commonwealth; though they have certainly produced those. But they have also challenged governments to re-examine and in some cases to modify, their policies; and they have sensitised member countries to the effect their policies may have on others within the Commonwealth. The realisation is growing – but all too slowly – that in this area a concerted approach is desirable.*

Information-gathering and analysis were important features of the committee's activity. Members made effective use of work done by other agencies; for instance, at the beginning, they were helped by data made available from the Overseas Student Trust, especially its publication, *A Policy for Overseas Students* (Williams, 1982).

Almost immediately, the committee commissioned its own data, with the energetic and dedicated help of Secretariat officials. Over the years, the committee was instrumental in producing case studies of student mobility as it affected India, Kenya, Nigeria (all 1986), Britain, Malaysia (both 1990) and Australia (1991); major policy-related studies on centres of excellence by Ian Maxwell (1983) and on international development programmes in higher education by Carol Coombe (1989); and three books – *Staff Development in Commonwealth Higher Education* (ACU, 1992), *Student Mobility from Britain to Commonwealth Developing Countries* (Callan and Steel, 1992) and *Towards a Commonwealth of Scholars* (Bown, 1994). A good deal of statistical material on Commonwealth student flows was collected, over a long enough time-scale to make trends discoverable and a model was devised to continue monitoring these flows (Tillman, 1988). Regrettably, after 1994 there was no continuation in the Commonwealth of a monitoring exercise; and this was one reason for the recent joint report by the Council for Education in the Commonwealth and UKCOSA, accompanied by detailed analyses done by Kees Maxey.

The statistics collected in the1980s showed a levelling-off of international student numbers in the Commonwealth attributed to the raising of fees by Britain, followed by other countries, or what the Committee's second report called 'the new protectionism'. From the beginning, the Standing Committee fully acknowledged that nearly all policy decisions on student mobility and on fees and awards were domestic decisions, matters for individual member governments, but efforts were continually made to make governments aware of some of the implications of their policies so that they might act both individually and collectively. Addressing individual governments, the second report said stoutly: 'it needs to be acknowledged that no country however large or sophisticated can hope to be self-sufficient in the provision of educational opportunities'. The value of co-operation both for educational purposes and for Commonwealth cohesion was stressed at every meeting – although by the second meeting the committee was already grappling with the problem of political will and commitment 'within our association' (meaning the Commonwealth). In the early 1980s it seemed that will and commitment might be shaping up, and at its fourth meeting the committee was encouraged by the 'overwhelming endorsement' of the committee's recommendations on, for example, national student exchange policies by 9CCEM at Nicosia in 1984. It was noted, though, that while the world trend in international mobility was upwards, within the Commonwealth it was at a plateau.

The levying by major host countries of the same fees on Commonwealth students as on other students continued to be a sore point until the end of the committee's life. At the same time, it sought other ways of reducing the financial burden of intra-Commonwealth higher education. The commissioned study of 1990 on Malaysia featured a number of alternative expedients, such as split-site degree programmes and off-shore campuses (much favoured by Australia).

By 1989, however, the committee painted a depressing picture of a decade in which intra-Commonwealth student exchange had dropped by 13%, which members saw as 'seriously disturbing'. They were looking by then at creative alternatives and palliatives to fee reduction, but made one more effort to crack the problem. At the seventh meeting, the Committee's most prominent agenda item was a consultation with member governments. Representatives of 32 member countries gathered to discuss a more favourable fee regime for Commonwealth students in the elegant surroundings of Lancaster House in London. Neither Australia nor New Zealand were present and the British and Canadian representatives signalled that there was no change in their governments' positions. Proposals for change:

were supported by the great majority of participants and there was acute disappointment that the industrialised host countries were neither able to change their position in any respect – nor to advance alternative proposals. The convening of the meeting appeared to most of those present to have served no useful purpose.

Not surprisingly, the Committee's report was titled *The Final Frustration* and the Committee itself was dissolved by the 1994 CCEM held in Islamabad.

The Standing Committee's success was not, however, limited to data gathering and analysis. Alongside the fee discussions there was firm adherence to wider issues of co-operation and particularly of institution-building; several of the most creative Commonwealth initiatives in higher education in the 1990s sprang from the Standing Committee's work.

c. New Approaches to Higher Education Co-operation in the 1990s: The Standing Committee as Originator

The committee's wider interests in higher education co-operation led it down new paths. Already, at its fourth meeting, it reported that in spite of the centrality of student mobility, this was only one element in higher education co-operation. Its later reports produced creative suggestions on: *open learning; capacity-building;* and *alternative forms of exchange*. First, open learning or the transmission of knowledge to people, rather than bringing people to knowledge sources, is a useful way of reducing the fee problem as well as of widening access. As communications technology improves, it becomes ever more attractive. The Standing Committee saw all this and at its fifth meeting made recommendations for the Commonwealth to develop open learning. Its urgings were a strong influence on the Secretary-General's decision to commission the Briggs Report and set up a working group to develop the Commonwealth of Learning. The history and work of COL are examined in Chapter 6. Here we should note the continuing link between the Standing Committee and COL, since three committee members were also on the COL Board and Sir Roy Marshall, the Standing Committee's Chairperson, gave various services to the Board. The vision of borderless learning continues to be an attractive one and was endorsed at the Halifax CCEM in 2000.

Secondly, schemes of capacity building evolved from the Committee's conviction that:

> ... *if developing countries are to sustain and improve the quality of higher education and to keep abreast of new developments in science and technology, their universities require additional physical and financial resources and access to international research and information networks.*

Sixth Report

At an early stage, the setting up was mooted of a Fund for Higher Education Co-operation along the lines of the CFTC. Reading it now, it seems rather utopian and the idea was scaled down to a plan for a Commonwealth Higher Education Support System (CHESS). This was the main recommendation of the Standing Committee's sixth meeting in 1989.

CHESS was to consist of three components: a programme of books, materials and library support; a higher education management programme; and a staff development programme. All of these involve some mobility of persons. The management programme evolved into CHEMS (Commonwealth Higher Education Management Service), which aimed in its mission statement 'to be ultimately recognised as the leading Commonwealth provider of specialist management consultancy help and information to higher education', and developed a register of over 90 consultants. It had five years initial funding from CFTC. CHEMS as an entity was formally wound up in January 2001, but its activities continued through the Policy and Research Unit of the Association of Commonwealth Universities and through a private sector agency known as CHEMS Consulting.

The third achievement of the Committee was to promote the institutional development of *an alternative form of student exchange*: the Commonwealth Universities Study Abroad Consortium. On several occasions, Standing Committee members considered the possibility of student exchange on a direct bilateral basis, between institutions, so that no fees are paid on either side. The idea was fleshed out at the 1992 Singapore workshop commissioned by the Standing Committee and reported finally in the book, *Towards A Commonwealth of Scholars*. The Standing Committee, at what proved to be its final meeting, pressed the idea of fee-free exchanges for institution-building and also to provide more opportunities between developing countries. It recommended that a scheme should be organised through a consortium of individual institutions.

CUSAC was planned at a meeting in Delhi in 1993 and formally inaugurated in the same year. Originally, it had 28 subscribing members. At the end of 2000, there were 74. The main transactions are the movement of undergraduates for six months or a year to study abroad for a credit towards their home university programme. The administrative costs are met partly from the subscriptions, at present £300 per institution, and partly from a grant by the CFTC. In the 1990s, there was an average of about 90 exchanges a year, though the numbers were of course lower at the beginning of the decade and higher at the end.

At first, it looked as though there would be more North–North exchanges than South–South and South–North ones, because no exchange is absolutely costless and poorer institutions found it hard to pay fares. At the end of the decade, the ACU made a grant of £300,000 sterling to provide bursaries covering air fares and part-maintenance. The pilot scheme for bursaries in 2000 was reported as successful, with 31 awards offered, involving 17 member institutions. A new round of bursaries was being advertised at the time of writing. While numbers are still small, the establishment of the consortium gives an alternative framework for exchange and students are travelling additional to those covered by CSFP. They are also probably a different category of student – undergraduates in mid-degree, travelling for only a short period. The quality of their experience can be judged from some of the testimonies in the newsletter, *CUSAC Update*. A student from the University of Cape Coast in Ghana who went to Sokoine University in Tanzania says: ' … seeing tourist regions like Arusha and Kilimanjaro was a great experience to me. In addition to that my perception has changed towards other people's views and cultures', and a student from the University of the South Pacific who went to the University of the West Indies echoes this: '[It] has opened me up to a new perception of the world'. There is no information at present on the gender balance among beneficiaries from the scheme as a whole. One third of the bursary holders in 2000 were women and two-thirds men.

The work of CUSAC was recognised by ministers at 14CCEM in Halifax.

7 The Shape of the Future

Student mobility has become steadily more important over the 40 years of Commonwealth educational activity. The growth of initiatives such as the CSFP, COL and CUSAC are to the credit of successive CECs/CCEMs – they have all been pioneering and creative. Individual countries have also made valuable contributions. The steadfast way in which India kept international fees low until quite recently has already been recognised. There has been a useful United Kingdom initiative in the Shared Scholarship Scheme (SSS), through which 200 awards a year are made and are available to Commonwealth countries only.

At the same time complacency is not in order. The story of the Standing Committee points up the deep gulf which exists between members from the South and North over access and funding and these issues, which are about politics and economics, not scholarship, remain unresolved. The basic Commonwealth values are about equality and equity and yet there is a severe imbalance in which some nations largely finance schemes of people and knowledge interchange, while there are now massive financial barriers inhibiting the access of students from the poorer Commonwealth countries to any form of international education. Much of the market in international higher education is dependent on private finance – hence the preponderance of some of the richer Commonwealth countries of south-east Asia in Commonwealth student flows. The access to international higher education, even to international knowledge through borderless learning, by poorer students from poorer countries is heavily contingent on public provision of awards. The role of the CSFP will continue to be essential for those students without private finance (or well-heeled governments) and the expansion of the programme into distance learning scholarships is a recent welcome development. Without the CSFP, COL and other schemes (such as those funded by the CFTC), the imbalance in student access between rich and poor, high and low human development would be even more marked and the 6% of students from countries of low human development would be obliterated.

Meanwhile the imbalances will continue to be a sore point in the Commonwealth. The result of recent struggles over fees has been a certain loss of camaraderie and mutual trust among member nations; but the latest CCEM in Halifax showed that there is still enough confidence to make a success of some of the alternative initiatives which have been developed.

It remains true that all members have something to learn from others and all have something to give. It is a principle of importance in an era of ever wider and faster communications. Now more than ever before it is also true that:

information is the only resource we have that is non-depletable and can be freely shared without depriving anyone of its use.

References

Chapter 2. Education for All in the Commonwealth: What are the Issues?

OECD (2001). *Knowledge and Skill for Life – First Results from PISA 2000*, Programme for International Student Assessment.

Sen, Amartya (1999). *Development as Freedom*, Oxford.

UNESCO (2000). *The Dakar Framework for Action*, 77pp.

UNESCO (2001). *Monitoring Report on Education for All*, 51pp.

World Bank (2001). Education for Dynamic Economies: Accelerating Progress Towards Education for All, Paper to the Development Committee.

Chapter 3. Gender in Education: Overview of Commonwealth Strategies

Australian Government Publishing Service (1971). *Report of the Fifth Commonwealth Education Conference: Canberra.* Canberra: Government Printer of the Commonwealth of Australia.

Commonwealth Relations Office (1959). *Report of the Commonwealth Education Conference.* London: Her Majesty's Stationery Office (reprinted 1964).

Commonwealth Secretariat (1968). *Report of the Fourth Commonwealth Education Conference*, February 26–March 9, 1968. Lagos, Nigeria: Commonwealth Secretariat.

Commonwealth Secretariat (1974). *Sixth Commonwealth Education Conference Report: Jamaica*, Jamaica: Government Printer, Jamaica.

Commonwealth Secretariat (1977). *Seventh Commonwealth Education Conference Report: Ghana*, London: Commonwealth Secretariat.

Commonwealth Secretariat (1980). *Eighth Commonwealth Education Conference Report: Colombo, Sri Lanka*, 5–13 August 1980. London: Commonwealth Secretariat.

Commonwealth Secretariat (1984). *Ninth Conference of Commonwealth Education Ministers Report: Nicosia, Cyprus*, 23–26 July 1984. London: Commonwealth Secretariat.

Commonwealth Secretariat (1987). *Commonwealth Plan of Action on Women and Development.* London: Commonwealth Secretariat.

Commonwealth Secretariat (1987). *Tenth Conference of Commonwealth Education Ministers Report: Nairobi, Kenya*, 20–24 July 1987. London: Commonwealth Secretariat.

Commonwealth Secretariat (undated Draft Document). *Engendering the Agenda: A Guide to Gender Planning.*

Commonwealth Secretariat (1991), *Eleventh Conference of Commonwealth Education Ministers Report: Barbados*, 29 October–2 November 1990. London: Commonwealth Secretariat.

Commonwealth Secretariat, Education Programme, Human Resource Development Group and Government of Botswana , Ministry of Education (1991). *Girls and Women in Science: Science and Technology Roadshow: Report and Manual.* Gaborone, Botswana: Government Printer.

Commonwealth Secretariat, Education Department, Human Resource Development Division (1993), *Commonwealth Scholarship and Fellowship Plan: Report of the Third Ten-Year Review Committee,* London, 18–21 May 1993. London: Commonwealth Secretariat.

Commonwealth Secretariat (1993). *Foundation for the Future: Human Resource Development.* Report of the Commonwealth Working Group on Human Resource Development Strategies. London: Commonwealth Secretariat.

Commonwealth Secretariat (1995), *Twelfth Conference of Commonwealth Education Ministers Report: Islamabad, Pakistan,* 27 November–1 December 1994. London: Commonwealth Secretariat.

Commonwealth Secretariat (undated). *Working Towards Gender Equality: Programme 1993–1995.* London: Commonwealth Secretariat.

Commonwealth Secretariat (1995). *A Commonwealth Vision for Women Towards the Year 2000: The 1995 Commonwealth Plan of Action on Gender and Development.* London; Commonwealth Secretariat.

'13th Conference of Commonwealth Education Ministers, Gaborone, Botswana, 28 July–1August 1997: Conclusions and Recommendations' in *Commonwealth Information.* 13CCEM(97)(CON)2.

Commonwealth Secretariat (2000). *Advancing the Commonwealth Agenda for Gender Equality into the New Millennium (2000–2005). An Update to the 1995 Commonwealth Plan of Action on Gender and Development.* London: Gender and Youth Affairs Division, Commonwealth Secretariat.

Commonwealth Secretariat (2000). *Gender Management System Handbook – A Reference Manual for Governments and other Stakeholders.* London: Commonwealth Secretariat.

Commonwealth Secretariat (2000). *Gender Mainstreaming in Development Planning.* London: Commonwealth Secretariat.

Commonwealth Secretariat (2000). *Using Gender-Sensitive Indicators – A Reference Manual for Governments and Other Stakeholders.* London: Commonwealth Secretariat.

Commonwealth Secretariat (2000). *Gender Mainstreaming in the Public Service : A Reference Manual for Governments and Other Stakeholders.* London; Commonwealth Secretariat.

Dines, Elizabeth (ed.), (1993). *Women in Higher Education Management.* Paris: UNESCO/Commonwealth Secretariat.

FAWE NEWS: Vol. 6 No4 1998 and FAWE Work Programme 1997.

FAWE NEWS. Vol. 8 No 1, Jan–Mar 2000.

Goel, Ved and Leonie Burton (1996). *Mathematics as a Barrier to the Learning of Science and Technology by Girls*. Report of a Conference, Ahmedabad, India 11–12 January 1996. London: Commonwealth Secretariat.

Harding, Jan and Emmanuel Apea (1990). *Women Too in Science and Technology*. London: Education Programme, Human Resource Development Group, Commonwealth Secretariat.

Halliday, Ian G (1995), *Turning the Tables on Teacher Management*. London: Education Department, Human Resource Development Division, Commonwealth Secretariat.

Harris, Mary (ed.) (1999). *Gender Sensitivity in Primary School Mathematics in India*. London: Education Department, Human Resource Development Division, Commonwealth Secretariat.

Jain Sharada (1994). *Education of Out-of-School Children: Case Studies from India*. London; Commonwealth Secretariat.

Leo-Rhynie, Elsa A (1996). *Report and Materials for the Mainstreaming of Gender into Commonwealth Governments' Ministries of Education*. Prepared for the Commonwealth Secretariat. University of the West Indies, Kingston, Jamaica.

Lund, Helen(1998). *A Single Sex Profession? Female Staff Numbers in Commonwealth Universities*. London: Commonwealth Higher Education Management Service.

Mohsin, Selina (1995). *Non-formal Education for Out-of-School Children: Case Studies from Bangladesh*. London: Commonwealth Secretariat.

Roberts, Audrey Ingram, *Gender Management Systems Reference Handbook*. Draft prepared for the Commonwealth Secretariat. Commonwealth Ministers Responsible for Women's Affairs Fifth Meeting, Trinidad and Tobago, 25–28 November 1996: 5.

Roy, Aruna (1984). *Education for Out-of-School Children : Case Studies of Selected Non-Formal Learning Programmes in South Asia*. London: Commonwealth Secretariat.

The Commonwealth of Learning (1900). *Report to the Meeting of Commonwealth Ministers Responsible for Women*. Ottawa.

The Commonwealth of Learning (1996). *Board of Governors Progress Report to the Meeting of Commonwealth Ministers Responsible for Women*. Trinidad.

The Commonwealth of Learning (1999). *Board of Governors Progress Report to the Sixth Meeting of Commonwealth Ministers Responsible for Women*. New Delhi, India.

The Commonwealth of Learning (2000). *Report & Recommendations to The Commonwealth of Learning On Prototype Development of the Gender Training Resources*

Database. Vancouver.

The Commonwealth of Learning (2000). *Final Report to the IACWGE on the development and implementation of the Gender Training Resources Collection.* Vancouver.

UNICEF (1994). *Education of Out-of-School Children: Case Studies from Pakistan.* London: Education Department, Human Resource Development Division, Commonwealth Secretariat.

Wamahiu, Sheila P (1996). *Gender Sensitisation and Training Programme: Synopsis.* Phase 1: 1994–1996: Botswana, Lesotho, Malawi, Swaziland, Tanzania, and Zanzibar. London: Education Department, Human Resource Development Division, Commonwealth Secretariat.

Williams, Gwendoline and Claudia Harvey (1996). *Review of ACU/CHESS Training Workshops for Women Managers in Higher Education, 1986–1996.* Unpublished Report prepared for the Association of Commonwealth Universities.

Williams, Gwendoline and Claudia Harvey (1998). *Gender Management Systems in Higher Education In the Commonwealth and other Countries.* Unpublished Report prepared for the Commonwealth Secretariat, July 1998.

Wolf, Joyce and Katherine Kainja (1999), *Changes in Girls' Lives: Malawi from 1990 to 1997.* Commonwealth Secretariat and World Bank.

Chapter 4. The Road from Oxford to Halifax: Snapshots of Science, Technology and Mathematics Education

All publications listed are those of the Commonwealth Secretariat, unless otherwise indicated.

School Science Teaching, Report of an Expert Conference held at the University of Ceylon Peradeniya, December 1963. London: HMSO, 1964.

Report of the Conference on the Education and Training of Technicians, 1966.

Trinidad Mathematics conference, 1968

Report of a Seminar on Technical Education and Industry, Hong Kong, 1976.

Interrelating Science. Mathematics and Technology Education. A Basis of General Education for All, 1985

Making Science Technology and Mathematics Education Relevant. CASTME Asia Region Workshop, 1986,

Primary Science Teacher Training for process Based Learning. Report of a workshop held in Barbados. Commonwealth Secretariat/UNESCO, 1987.

Assessment in Primary School Science. Workshop Modules for Professional Development. Commonwealth Secretariat/UNESCO, 1998.

Training of Trainers in Science and Technology Education, African edition, 1995

Training of Trainers in Science and Technology Education, Asian edition, 1996.

Training of Trainers in Science and Technology Education, Caribbean editions, 1997.

Training of Trainers in Science and Technology Education, Pacific editions, 1997.

Exemplar Modules in Mathematics for Elementary Teacher Educators, National Council for Teacher Education/Commonwealth Secretariat, New Delhi, 1999

The Production of School Science Equipment. A review of developments, 1975.

Recent Developments in the Production of School Science Equipment, 1983

Low-Cost Science Teaching Equipment, Report of a Commonwealth Regional Seminar/Workshop, Nassau, Bahamas, 1976.

Low-Cost Science Teaching Equipment: 2, Report of a Commonwealth Regional Seminar-Workshop, Dar es Salaam, Tanzania, 1977.

Low-Cost Science Teaching Equipment: 3, Report of a Commonwealth Regional Seminar-Workshop. Lae, Papua New Guinea, 1979.

A Survey of Technician Training in Commonwealth Countries of Asia, Education in the Commonwealth Series, No 12, 1976.

Project for the Training of Science Laboratory Technicians, CASTME/ UWIDITE, 1987.

Training Laboratory Technicians, Report of a workshop held at the Indira Gandhi National Open University, New Delhi. Commonwealth Secretariat/IGNOU/COL, 1996.

Training Laboratory Technicians by Distance, Workshop Report, Suva, Fiji, 1997.

Training Laboratory Technicians and the Culture of Maintenance, Workshop Report. Luanshya, Zambia, 1996.

Curriculum Development for Training Laboratory Technicians Through Distance Education, Workshop Report, Nyeri, Kenya, CAPA/COL/Commonwealth Secretariat, 1997

Training Laboratory Technicians through Open/Distance Education, Arusha, Tanzania, CAPA/COL/Commonwealth Secretariat, 1999.

Training Technicians: the Case of Nigerian Universities, 1994.

Popularisation of Science, Report of a Commonwealth Regional Workshop, Lusaka, Zambia, 1985.

Popularising Scientific and Technological Culture in the Asia/Pacific Region of the Commonwealth, Expert Group Meeting, Singapore, 1997

Popularising Scientific and Technological Culture in African Commonwealth Countries, Report of an Expert Group Meeting, Lilongwe, Malawi, 1998.

Popularising: Scientific and Technological Culture in the Caribbean. Report of an Expert Group Meeting, St Ann's Trinidad, 1998.

Popularising Science and Technology. Some Asian Case Studies, AMIC,

Commonwealth Secretariat. Singapore/London, 1999

Using Science Centres and Museums to Popularise Science and Technology Handbook for Museum Curators and Science Teachers, 2000

CASTME Awards for Innovations in Science Technology and Mathematics Education. A Selection of Award Winning Projects, CASTME.

Commonwealth Association of Polytechnics in Africa, Report of the Meeting of the Constitution Drafting Committee, Freetown, Sierra Leone, 1978.

Technical Teacher Training, Report of a Commonwealth Regional Workshop. Mombasa, Kenya, 1980.

Gender Stereotyping in Science, Technology and Mathematics Education, Report of a Commonwealth Africa Regional Workshop. Accra, Ghana, 1987.

Changes in Girls' Lives: Malawi from 1990–1997, By K. Kainja and J. Wolf. Commonwealth Secretariat with The World Bank 1999.

Women Too in Science and Technology in Africa. A resource book for counselling girls and young women, 1990.

Enhancing the Participation of Women in the Popularisation of Science Technology, Report of a Commonwealth Asia Regional Workshop, Dhaka, Bangladesh, 1987.

Girls and Women in Science: Science and Technology Road Show, Report and Manual. Commonwealth Secretariat and Government of Botswana, 1991.

Righting the Imbalance, Video film, 18 minutes.

Measures for Increasing the Participation of Girls and Women in Technical and Vocational Education and Training: A Caribbean Study, Commonwealth Secretariat/CATVET,1990.

Payne J., Cheng, Y. and Witherspoon, S. (1995). *Education and Training: for 16 to 18 year old in England and Wales: Individual paths and National Trends*, Policy Studies Institute, London.

Burton, L. and Goel, V. (eds) (1996). *Mathematics as a Barrier to the Learning: of Science and Technology by Girls*, Report of a Conference, Ahmedabad, India.

Harris, M. (1999). *Gender Sensitivity in Primary Mathematics Textbooks in India*.

CASTME Awards for Innovations in Science, Technology and Mathematics Education: Directory of Award Winners 1975–1999, CASTME and Commonwealth Secretariat, 2000

'Educational Technology for Science and Mathematics Education in the Caribbean: its social and cultural relevance for the 21st Century', CASTME Regional Conference, July 1998, *CASTME Journal*, Vol. 12, No. 2, 1998.

Anzar Uma (1999). *Education Reform in Balochistan 1990–98: Case Study in Improving Management and Gender Equity Education*, Commonwealth Secretariat/ The World Bank, 1999

Chapter 5. Skills for Survival: Technical and Vocational Education and Entrepreneurship

Alphonse (1999). *Report*, Madras Centre for Research and Development of Community Education.

Committee of Vice-Chancellors and Principals, CVCP (2000). *The Business of Borderless Education, UK Perspectives, Summary Report.*

Commonwealth Association for Local Action and Economic Development (1996). *Journal and Yearbook.*

Commonwealth Education Conferences/Conferences of Commonwealth Education Ministers (1959–present). *Reports.*

Commonwealth Foundation (1966–93). *Special Report.*

Commonwealth Foundation (1999). *Report 1996–99.*

Commonwealth Fund for Technical Co-operation, CFTC (1993). *Skills for the 1990s.*

CFTC (1995, 97, 99). *Skills for Development.*

Commonwealth Secretariat (1966–present). *Reports of Secretary-General.*

Commonwealth Secretariat (1993). *Foundation for the Future*, London, Commonwealth Secretariat.

Commonwealth Secretariat (1996). *The Commonwealth in Action: South Pacific.*

Commonwealth Secretariat (1998). *The Commonwealth in Action: South Africa.*

Commonwealth Secretariat (1999). *The Commonwealth in Action: Africa.*

Commonwealth Secretariat (1998). *Action for Human Resource Development: Partnership Between Government, the Private Sector and NGOs in Education, Training and Employment.*

Commonwealth Secretariat (2000). *Action for Human Resource Development: Empowerment of Women Through the Use of Technology, Models and guidelines for non-formal education training materials.*

Commonwealth Secretariat (2000). *Commonwealth Yearbook*, London Com Secretariat.

Council for Education in the Commonwealth/UKCOSA (2000). *Student Mobility on the Map.*

The Economist (serial).

European Centre for Work and Society (various dates). *News Sheets.*

Further Education Funding Council, UK, FEFC (various dates). *Surveys and Reports.*

HMSO (1967). *Education and Training of Technicians*, London: HMSO.

International Labour Organisation (1998). *World Employment Report, 1998–99.*

ILO (1998). *World Employment Report, Policy Implications.*

Maclennan, A. (1975). *Educating and Training Technicians,* London, Commonwealth Secretariat.

Rao, Wright and Mukherjee (1990). *Designing Entrepreneurial Skill Development Programmes,* London Commonwealth Secretariat.

Rao and Wright (1991). Entrepreneurial skill Development Programmes in Fifteen Commonwealth Countries, London, Com Secretariat.

Royal Society of Arts (Serial), *Journal.*

UNESCO/UNEVOC (1992–4). *Inventory,* Paris UNESCO.

UNESCO/UNEVOC (1997). *Directory,* Paris UNESCO.

UNESCO (1999). *Second International Congress on Technical and Vocational Education,* Paris UNESCO.

Technical and Vocational Education, *Final Report,* Paris UNESCO

Wright ed. (2000). *Issues in Education and Technology Policy: Guidelines and Strategies,* London, Commonwealth Secretariat.

Chapter 6. Open and Distance Learning – Innovation in the 1990s: The Commonwealth of Learning

General

http://www.col.org

http://www.col.org/gdhan

http://www.col.org/maraj_99.htm

Case Studies

www.col.org/10th/best/out.html

www.sidsnet.org/pacific/usp/ext

www.col.org/models/telecon.htm

www.col.org/models/skillstrain.htm

www.col.org/models/cost.htm

Chapter 7. Building Bridges for Education in the Commonwealth: Issues in Student Mobility

Cmd 841 (1959). *Report of the Commonwealth Education Conference,* 1959, London, HMSO, p.18

Foreword to *Tenth Conference of Commonwealth Ministers of Education Report,* 1987, London, Commonwealth Secretariat.

Twelfth CCEM Report (1994). London Commonwealth Secretariat, p. 6.

Fifth CEC Report, 1971, Canberra, Australian Gat Publishing Service, p. App.3.

Bown, Lalage, ed. (1994). *Towards a Commonwealth of Scholars: A new vision for the nineties*, London: Commonwealth Secretariat.

Bown, ed. (1994) op. cit. p .4.

Dines, Elizabeth (1994). Chapter 5 in Bown, op. cit.

CEC/UKOCOSA (2000). *Student Mobility on the Map*, London: CEC and UKOCOSA.

Europe (1992). Treaty on European Union, signed at Maastacht, February 1992 – *Title II*, revised Article 126 of Treaty of Rome.

Cmd 841 (1959). *Report of the CEC*, 1959, p. 5.

Ninth CCEM Report, 1984, London:Commonwealth Secretariat, p. 9.

Dzvimbo, P. (1994), Chapter 11 in Bown, ed., op. cit.

Hunter, Guy (1981) in Peter Williams, ed., *The Overseas Student Question: Studies for a Policy*, London: Heinemann for Overseas Students Trust.

Commonwealth Secretariat (1989). *Commonwealth Scholarship and Fellowship Fund Tracer Study, final report*.

World Bank (2000). *Higher Education in Developing Countries. Peril and Promise*, Washington: The World Bank.

Committee of Vice-Chancellors and Principals of the UK (1998), *International Students in UK Higher Education*, London: CVCP.

Korten, David (1998). *When Corporations Ruled the World*, London:. Earthscan

Appendix 1. Commonwealth Ministerial Conferences on Education

CEC = Commonwealth Education Conference
CCEM = Conference of Commonwealth Education Ministers

1	CEC	Oxford, United Kingdom	15–28/7/1959	
2	CEC	New Delhi, India	11–25/1/1962	
3	CEC	Ottawa, Canada	21/8–4/9/1964	
4	CEC	Lagos, Nigeria	26/2–9/3/1968	
5	CEC	Canberra, Australia	3–17/2/1971	
6	CEC	Kingston, Jamaica	10–22/6/1974	Management of education
7	CEC	Accra, Ghana	9–18/3/1977	Economics of education
8	CEC	Colombo, Sri Lanka	5–13/8/1980	Education and the development of human resources
9	CCEM	Nicosia, Cyprus	23–26/7/1984	(1) Resources for education and their cost-effective use (2) Education and youth unemployment
10	CCEM	Nairobi, Kenya	20–24/7/1987	Vocational orientation of education
11	CCEM	Bridgetown, Barbados	29/10–2/11/1990	Improving the quality of basic education
12	CCEM	Islamabad, Pakistan	27/11–1/12/1994	The changing role of the state in education
13	CCEM	Gaborone, Botswana	28/7–1/8/1997	Education and technology: meeting the challenges of the 21st century
14	CCEM	Halifax, Canada	26–30/11/2000	Education in a global era: challenges to equity; opportunities for diversity

Appendix 2. Commonwealth Organisations Relevant to Educational Exchange (with dates of foundation)

Association for Commonwealth Literature and Language Studies	1965
Association of Commonwealth Accreditation and Examination Bodies	
Association of Commonwealth Studies	2000
Association of Commonwealth Universities	1913
Commonwealth Archivists Association	1984
Commonwealth Association for the Education and Training of Adults	1988
Commonwealth Association for Education in Journalism and Communication	1985
Commonwealth Association of Museums	1974
Commonwealth Association of Polytechnics in Africa	1978
Commonwealth Association of Science Technology and Mathematics Teachers	1974
Commonwealth Association of Scientific Agricultural Societies	1978
Commonwealth Council for Educational Administration	1970
Commonwealth Higher Education Management Services Commonwealth Institute	1990
Commonwealth Legal Education Association	1971
Commonwealth Library Association	1972
Commonwealth Linking Trust (schools links)	1974
Commonwealth Relations Trust (educators, broadcasters, trade unionists travel awards)	
Commonwealth Youth Exchange Council	1970
Commonwealth Youth Programme	1973
League for the Exchange of Commonwealth Teachers	1901

Appendix 3. Commonwealth Scholarships and Fellowships Plan
(Extract from report of Commonwealth Education Conference 1959)

The Commonwealth Scholarship and Fellowship Plan

11. The idea for a scheme of Commonwealth scholarships and fellowships was conceived at the Commonwealth Trade and Economic Conference at Montreal. It was expected that within a few years of its inception the programme would cover some thousand Commonwealth scholars and fellows. Of this total the United Kingdom undertook at Montreal to be responsible for one half and Canada for one quarter. It was recognised that the contribution of other countries would be determined after they had had an opportunity to give closer consideration to their resources and to other claims on them.

12. The Plan for Commonwealth Scholarships and Fellowships, based on a common effort and partnership between all the countries of the Commonwealth, will play an important part in maintaining the strengthening the common ideals on which the Commonwealth is founded. It will enrich each country of the Commonwealth by enabling an increasing number of its abler citizens to share the wide range of educational resources available throughout the Commonwealth and thus promote equality of educational opportunity at the highest level.

13. It is clear from the promises made at the Conference by Commonwealth Delegations that the target of 1,000 scholarships and fellowships current at any one time has been attained and may soon be exceeded. Some Delegations were able to announce at the Conference the number of awards to be made by their Governments under the Plan; these are as follows:

United Kingdom	500
Canada	250
Australia	100
India	100
Pakistan	30
New Zealand	25
Federation of Malaya	12
Ghana	10
Federation of Rhodesia and Nyasaland	10
Ceylon	6
East Africa	4

These and other Governments will consider whether they can give further awards, and if so announcements will be made.

14. It is recommended that the following general principles should govern the operation of the Plan:
    (a) the Plan should be additional to, and distinct from any other plan already in operation
    (b) the Plan should be based on mutual co-operation and the sharing of educational experience among all the countries of the Commonwealth
    (c) the Plan should be sufficiently flexible to take account of the diverse and changing needs of the countries of the Commonwealth
    (d) while the Plan will be Commonwealth-wide, it should be operated on the basis of a series of bilateral arrangements to allow for the necessary flexibility,
    (e) the awards should be designed to be recognised and promote the highest standards of intellectual achievement.

15. The majority of the awards under the Plan should be to men and women of high intellectual promise who may be expected to make a significant contribution to life in their own countries on their return from study overseas. The awards should normally be available to students who have already graduated; they should be given at the undergraduate level only when university or comparable institutions do not exist in the sending country or do not offer courses in the subjects desired. It is recommended that these awards should be called Commonwealth Scholarships.

16. A limited number of awards to be called Commonwealth Visiting Fellowships – should also be made to senior scholars of established reputation and achievement.

17. The awards should normally be in the academic field, but the possibility should not be excluded of making some awards to other persons who play an important role in the life of their community.

18. It is recommended that normally all the awards should be 'inward', that is, to be made by the receiving country; but some awards might be 'outward', that is, made by the sending country. It may be desirable for some Commonwealth countries to supplement the value of some scholarships awarded by other countries to make them sufficiently attractive to their own scholars.

19. The final selection of scholars should rest with the receiving country. It is recommended that special agencies should be set up in the various Commonwealth countries to select scholars for their own awards and to nominate scholars for awards by other countries. Although these agencies would necessarily be appointed by Governments they should be so constituted as to ensure that they adequately represent academic interests.

20. Much of the success of the Plan will depend on satisfactory arrangements for the reception and welfare of scholars, and the attention of Governments and others concerned is specially drawn to this matter.

21. It is recommended that arrangements be made for recording information about awards made under the Plan and for the preparation of an annual statement on progress; this task could appropriately be undertaken by the Association of Universities of the British Commonwealth.

Appendix 4. Reports on Meetings of the Commonwealth Standing Committee on Student Mobility and Higher Education Co-operation

1st Report	Educational Interchange: A Commonwealth Imperative	July 1982
2nd Report	Towards a Commonwealth Higher Education Programme: Strategies for Action	June 1983
3rd Report	Commonwealth Student Mobility: A Time For Action	May 1984
4th Report	Commonwealth Student Mobility: A Way Forward	July 1985
5th Report	Commonwealth Student Mobility: Commitment and Resources	August 1986
6th Report	Progress Through Co-operation	June 1989
7th Report	Favourable Fees for Commonwealth Students: The Final Frustration	June 1992

Notes on Contributors

Professor Lalage Bown, Executive Committee Member, Council for Education in the Commonwealth; formerly member of the Commonwealth Standing Committee on Student Mobility and Higher Education Co-operation.

Sir John Daniel, Assistant Director-General for Education, UNESCO; previously Vice-Chancellor of the Open University, UK.

Professor Gajaraj Dhanarajan, President and Chief Executive Officer, Commonwealth of Learning; Professor Emeritus, Open University of Hong Kong.

Dr Ved Goel, Acting Deputy Director and Head, Education Section, Commonwealth Secretariat; formerly Chief Programme Officer responsible for STME in the Commonwealth; Hon. Secretary, CASTME.

Dr W. Bonney Rust, Executive Committee Member, Council for Education in the Commonwealth; Director of Research, Association for Vocational Colleges International.

Dr Jasbir Singh, formerly Programme Officer, Higher Education, Human Resource Development Division, Commonwealth Secretariat.

Dr Peter Williams, Executive Chairperson, Council for Education in the Commonwealth; Director of the Commonwealth Secretariat's Education Programme, 1984–94.